THE CATHOLIC CITIZEN

**Other Titles from the Fellowship of Catholic Scholars
Published by St. Augustine's Press**

*Voices of the New Springtime: The Life and Work of the Catholic
Church in the 21st Century*, edited by Kenneth D. Whitehead
(*Proceedings* of the 25th annual conference)

The Catholic Imagination, edited by Kenneth D. Whitehead
(*Proceedings* of the 24th annual conference)

John Paul II – Witness to Truth, edited by Kenneth D. Whitehead
(*Proceedings* of the 23rd annual conference)

Marriage and the Common Good, edited by Kenneth D. Whitehead
(*Proceedings* of the 22nd annual conference)

Science and Faith, edited by Gerard V. Bradley, J.D., and Don De
Marco (*Proceedings* of the 21st annual conference)

Is a Culture of Life Still Possible in the U.S.? edited by Anthony J.
Mastroeni, S.T.D., J.D. (*Proceedings* of the 20th conference)

*The Battle for the Catholic Mind: Catholic Faith and Catholic
Intellect in the Work of the Fellowship of Catholic Scholars,
1978–95*, edited by William E. May and Kenneth D. Whitehead

Other Titles of Note from St. Augustine's Press

The American Catholic Voter: 200 Years of Political Impact,
George J. Marlin; introduction by Michael Barone

Papal Diplomacy: John Paul II and the Culture of Peace, Bernard
J. O'Connor

The Slaughter of Cities: Urban Renewal as Ethnic Cleansing,
E. Michael Jones

*The Sacred Monster of Thomism: An Introduction to the Life and
Legacy of Reginald Garrigou-Lagrange, O.P.*, Richard
Peddicord, O.P.

Morality: The Catholic View, Servais Pinckaers, O.P.

*From Witchery to Sanctity: The Religious Vicissitudes of the
Hawthornes*, Otto Bird and Katharine Bird

Same-Sex Attraction: A Parents' Guide, edited by John F. Harvey,
OSFS, and Gerard V. Bradley

The Defamation of Pius XII, Ralph McInerny

Back to the Drawing Board: The Future of the Pro-Life Movement,
edited by Teresa R. Wagner

The Conversion of Edith Stein, Florent Gaboriau

THE CATHOLIC CITIZEN

Debating the Issues of Justice

Proceedings from the 26th Annual Conference of the
Fellowship of Catholic Scholars
September 26–28, 2003
Arlington, Virginia

Edited by Kenneth D. Whitehead

ST. AUGUSTINE'S PRESS
South Bend, Indiana
2004

Manufactured in the United States of America.

1 2 3 4 5 6   10 09 08 07 06 05 04

Library of Congress Cataloging in Publication Data
Fellowship of Catholic Scholars. Convention (26th: 2003:
Arlington, Va.)
  The Catholic citizen: debating the issues of justice / Kenneth
D. Whitehead, editor.– 1st ed.
    p. cm.
  "Proceedings from the 26th Annual Convention of the
  Fellowship of Catholic Scholars, Arlington, Virginia,
  September 26-28, 2003."
  ISBN 1-58731-173-9 (pbk.: alk. paper)
  1. Christian ethics – Catholic authors – Congresses.
  2. Christian sociology – Catholic Church – Congresses.
  3. Christianity and politics – Catholic Church – Congresses.
  4. Christian ethics – United States – Congresses. 5. Christian
  sociology – United States – Congresses. 6. Christianity and
  politics – United States – Congresses. I. Whitehead, K. D.
  II. Title.
BJ1249.F44 2004
261.8'088'282 – dc22   2004011471

∞ *The paper used in this publication meets the minimum requirements of the American National Standard for Information Sciences – Permanence of Paper for Printed Materials, ANSI Z39.48 – 1984.*

CONTENTS

INTRODUCTION

It would have been hard to pick a more pertinent subject than "the Catholic Citizen" for the 26th Annual Convention of the Fellowship of Catholic Scholars which took place in Arlington, Virginia – across the river from the nation's capital – on the weekend of September 26–28, 2003. American Society is approaching or faces a crisis situation in a number of critical areas, which cannot but pose sometimes insuperable moral problems or dilemmas for any citizen who takes Catholic teaching seriously.

The war in Iraq and its aftermath have stirred up passions not encountered since the days of the Vietnam War more than a quarter of a century ago. The question of whether the invasion of Iraq by the United States met the criteria for a just war has been hotly debated, especially in view of the very negative attitude towards the U. S. war effort exhibited by some officials of the Roman Curia, and even, to some extent, by Pope John Paul II himself. The pontiff, though, unlike many opponents of the Bush Administration's policies, quickly drew back from any further critical comments once the military victory was so quickly achieved, and began to stress the rebuilding of Iraq as now the proper focus on the issue.

Whatever the merits of anti-war or pro-war moral judgments, however – where the views of Catholic citizens might legitimately vary – the once unthinkable subject of the cloning of human embryos has meanwhile come upon our society with dismaying suddenness. There is no way that the creation of cloned human embryos could ever be considered anything but gravely evil; the same thing is true of the extraction of embryonic stem cells for experimental purposes; these procedures quite deliberately treat embryonic human life in a totally instrumental fashion; yet our society seems increasingly determined to go down the road into this "Brave New World" regardless of the evils that have already resulted from the disregard of fundamental moral principles that this road entails – evils that will surely be multiplied in manifold ways as we continue down that same road.

Of course, we started down that particular road when, more than twenty years ago, the U. S. Supreme Court, in its 1973 *Roe v. Wade* decision, legalized abortion on demand in the United States; and from that day to this, Catholic citizens, along with other Americans of good will, have perforce been in the forefront of efforts to try to restore legal rights and the equal protection of the laws to the unborn.

And as if all the anti-life manifestations represented by abortion, cloning, stem-cell research, in-vitro fertilization, and the like were not enough, the truly revolutionary idea of so-called same-sex "marriage" has also now entered dramatically upon the scene and, indeed, has made huge strides during the course of 2003, in no small measure as a result of yet another disastrous Supreme Court decision handed down in June, *Lawrence v. Texas*, legalizing sodomy, and, indeed, virtually any other sexual act between "consenting adults." Henceforth, lack of consent seems to be the *only* remaining legally penalized or socially stigmatized type of sexual behavior left in America today. Otherwise pretty much "everything goes" today. The Sexual Revolution thus truly came full circle in 2003, compounding the mounting moral wreckage of no-fault divorce, widely tolerated pre- and extra-marital intercourse, teen and out-of-wedlock pregnancies, single-parent and otherwise broken families, and sexually transmitted diseases – all of which have increasingly characterized American Society in recent years.

Such developments have naturally posed huge and increasing problems for the Catholic citizen: to what extent can Catholics who continue to take seriously the law of God and the teaching of the Church *cooperate* in such a society as ours has become? And even as all these problems beset us, there remain other more traditional moral problems such as capital punishment – which continues to be contentious in America and about which the magisterium of the Catholic Church has recently spoken in such a way that further understanding and reflection by Catholics have now become urgently necessary.

Readers of this volume will find that all of these various questions were very ably addressed by the speakers at the Fellowship's 26th Annual Convention. Their contributions came in the form of talks before an audience, of course, and hence the papers reproduced here are not always the equivalents of what might appear on the same subjects in a peer-reviewed scholarly journal. Nevertheless, readers will encounter here a very high degree of scholarly knowledge, competence, and excellence.

Oxford legal scholar and philosopher John Finnis shows how a thorough-going secular philosophy which denies all Christian criteria in public policy decisions undergirds virtually all of the negative modern developments now faced by the Catholic citizen today. A panel consisting of Notre Dame law professor (and current FCS president) Gerard V. Bradley, the Hoover Institution's Mary Eberstadt, Marquette University's Christopher Wolfe, and William E. May of the John Paul II Institute illuminate a number of the problems related to our endemic family break-ups in the United States and the resulting "non-traditional households." Franciscan University's Patrick Lee deals perceptively with significant recent developments related to the abortion question.

The important current question of possible "embryo adoption" is argued, pro and con, by the Family Research Council's William L. Saunders and Yale-trained bioethicist Father Tadeusz Pacholczyk.

Steven A. Long of the University of St. Thomas in Minnesota and E. Christian Brugger of Loyola University in New Orleans each present a somewhat different view of the significance of Pope John Paul II's "development of doctrine" on capital punishment in his 1995 encyclical *Evangelium Vitae* on the Gospel of Life – the pontiff's teaching occasioned a revision on the subject in the text of the *Catechism of the Catholic Church*.

Father John J. Coughlin, O.F.M., of the Notre Dame Law School, discusses the ways in which Catholic lawyers and judges are almost unavoidably drawn into some form of "cooperation" in a society such as ours, while Detroit's Sacred Heart Seminary Professor John P. Hittinger covers the question of how Catholics in the military must deal with some of the moral dilemmas of the day.

The University of Scranton's J. Brian Benestad clearly lays out a rather complete exposition of just war principles, while Notre Dame theologian Father Michael Baxter, C.S.C., presents what he styles a special "pacifist" perspective in seven points.

As at previous FCS conventions, where the ordinary of the diocese is customarily invited to celebrate Mass and preach to the group, the Most Reverend Paul S. Loverde, bishop of Arlington, graciously welcomed the Fellowship to Northern Virginia. His homily is included here.

All in all, the program of the 26th Annual Convention of the FCS proved to be both stimulating and informative – well worth preserving and presenting to a wider audience of the membership of the Fellowship and other readers in the present volume.

Also included in the volume are the remarks of Emory University historian Elizabeth Fox-Genovese which she made upon receiving the Fellowship's annual Cardinal Wright Award: she believes the Catholic scholar has an essential task and contribution to make in today's society for the benefit of that society.

At the convention, the Fellowship's occasional Cardinal O'Boyle Award was presented to then U. S. Housing and Urban Development Secretary Mel Martinez and his wife Kathryn – both of whom have distinguished themselves as exemplary "Catholic citizens." (Secretary Martinez subsequently resigned his post in order to run for the U. S. Senate in Florida.)

Finally, a special FCS Founder's Award was presented to the Fellowship's first president, Father Ronald Lawler, O.F.M. Cap. Very ill with advanced cancer and confined to a wheelchair, Father Lawler – who had graced with his presence virtually every previous FCS convention since the founding of the organization – delivered a moving speech accepting the award and reminding all present why the Fellowship was founded in the first place to support and defend and expound and explain the teachings of the Catholic Church through the knowledge and scholarship of FCS members working in their various scholarly disciplines. Father Lawler's appearance at the convention was a fitting capstone to a long priestly and scholarly career within and without the Fellowship. A Tribute to him is included as the last chapter in this volume.

KEYNOTE ADDRESS
SECULARISM, FAITH,
AND PUBLIC POLICY
John Finnis

"Secularism" is a word that has been used more than once by the magisterium in recent years. *Evangelium Vitae* 21 identifies it as a root of a systematized willingness to kill weak and dependent people. The Congregation of the Doctrine of the Faith's November 2002 Doctrinal Note on Participation of Catholics in Political Life says that denials of the legitimacy of using Christian criteria when making political decisions are an intolerant form of secularism. I want tonight to offer some reflections on those denials of the legitimacy of using Christian criteria when making political decisions. Some of the truth of *Evangelium Vitae* 21's observation will also emerge along the way.

Secularism is not to be confused with a healthy secularity or respect for the secular. "Secular" is *our* word, a word minted by Latin Christians. It denotes that which is not divine, sacred, or ecclesiastical. In the Vulgate it sometimes signifies, neutrally, the world of time rather than eternity, and the daily life of any society – and sometimes, pejoratively, those matters that distract us from realities and dispositions of lasting worth. In Aquinas too the term "secular" often has no negative connotations. So, for example, St Thomas will say that in matters that concern the good of the political community {*bonum civile*}, Christians should generally obey the *secular* authorities rather than the ecclesiastical: in such matters *magis obediendum potestati saeculari quam spirituali*.[1] The Doctrinal Note states the same point in different words, when it says that "the rightful *autonomy of the political or civil sphere* from that of religion and the

Church – but not from that of morality – is a value that has been attained and recognized by the Catholic Church...(cf. *Gaudium et Spes* sec. 76)."

This Christian differentiating of the secular from the sacred is one instance or aspect of wider processes often called "secularization." I am thinking especially of processes which involve the extension of human understanding and control over fields of life formerly so inaccessible to human science and technology that it seemed reasonable to try to manage them instead simply by prayer. Christian faith *encourages* secularization of this kind, by insisting on both the transcendence of God and the intelligibility of the creation, with its consequent accessibility to science and technology.

Secularism is something different. Not that it is some entirely new thing. No: In its essentials it seems to be what English philosophers and theologians, Catholic and non-Catholic, in the Shakespearean age called "atheism" – they used that word broadly. And Plato, without giving it a label, clearly identified it as a *topos* worthy of very careful analysis and critique in his *The Laws*, as a cluster of dispositions, all significantly similar as dispositions of soul and character even though shaped around one or other of three propositions each logically quite distinguishable from the others: that there is no God (in modern terms, atheism *stricto sensu*); or, that no God is concerned with human affairs (we would say, "deism"); or, that any such divine concern with the human is easily appeased by a superficial piety and requires no demanding reform of human conduct (we can say: "liberal" religiosity).[2] The urgency of Plato's concern about this cluster, like the frequent invectives of Elizabethan philosophers against atheism around them, can make us wonder whether secularism's cultural dominance today is really greater than it was in Plato's Athens.

Whatever the answer to that question, it is clear that modern secularism takes the natural world as Christian faith left it, de-sacralized and, in that sense, secularized, and proceeds to a conclusion that is against all biblical faith and understanding, the conclusion that there is no source of meaning and value save human beings. Secularism's defining unwillingness either to contemplate or take seriously creation *ex nihilo* typically draws upon materialist assumptions. But it also powerfully reinforces materialist denials or neglect of *spirit*, whether as manifested in the freedom and the intelligibility-giving character of divine creativity and providence, or as manifested in the working of human deliberation and action in and upon the material world by practical understanding, intending, reasoning, and choosing. It is no accident that the full reality of self-determining free choice is scarcely affirmed outside the ambit of influence of the Old and New Covenants. Nor is it an accident that secularized philosophers and theologians (including some Catholics) have little understanding of the significance of *intention* in the description and moral assessment of human acts, and replace that concept with some combination of causality and foresight – with devastating consequences for their ethical theories and analyses.

And with the loss of the idea of the intellectual soul, as the organizing form and *act* of the body and life and integral reality of each individual of the human species,[3] comes the loss of any account of what it is about us that makes us all equal. It is the secularist incapacity to account for that equality, and thus to affirm it rationally, that most of all makes secularism an inadequate and rationally improper basis for law and public policy.

In a given cultural context, of course, the word "secularist" may be used with any number of possible meanings along a spectrum with atheism at one end, and at the other end a refusal to declare any one religion the true religion and ratify it as such by law and public policy. So a Constitution like that of India may declare the state secular, meaning something like "there shall be no establishment of religion," with all the uncertainty that Americans are familiar with about just what that means. My focus in this paper is on the underlying position or range of positions about the existence or relevance of God, and on the relevance of that position to the foundations of political morality and life, not on the proper constitutional arrangements.

With those preliminaries, let me turn to the CDF's Doctrinal Note. I first heard of it some time after it was signed, when I was asked to write a pre-publication commentary[4] on its relation to secularism. The first thing I thought when I read it was: this is a critique of John Rawls's theory of "political liberalism," which you could also call his theory of what it is for thought or action to be properly speaking "political." And the second thing I noticed is that by the special providence that there is in the fall of a sparrow (as Hamlet says), the Doctrinal Note was signed off on the day John Rawls died, 24 November 2002. Rawls in his late writings devised and promoted a novel use of the term "political." Decisions, institutions, etc., are properly political (he says) only when made on the basis of "public reason," and public reason is not a matter of truths of theoretical or practical reason, but rather is the set of propositions accepted in an "overlapping consensus" of all "reasonable" people, with their many contradictory opinions about the true nature and point of human affairs. (This contradictoriness, or more politely, "pluralism," of *reasonable* opinions about important matters is, Rawls thinks, a wholly inevitable and proper concomitant of democratic freedom.) Having thus denatured and reoriented the concepts of the political and of reason and reasonableness itself, Rawls proposes his fundamental criterion or "moral ideal" of "democratic legitimacy." According to that criterion, citizens voting on a controverted issue involving fundamental human rights vote *illegitimately* if they try to promote the truth about who has the rights and how far the rights extend. They vote legitimately only if they set aside their opinions about the truth of the matter – of any moral or political matter – and vote in accordance with their assessment of what *opinions* about the right are within the overlapping *consensus* of "reasonable people" (including, quasi-necessarily, people whose within-consensus opinions about the right the voter judges, perhaps *correctly*, to be false). A vote cast on the basis of deliberation and judgment about the truth of the matter is illegitimate (says Rawls) because it violates the fair "reciprocity" of never imposing on other people any restriction or burden they would not, or could not, rationally be expected to accept. All that is the heart of Rawls's "political liberalism."

Rawls's writings include passages suggesting that his entire theory of "political liberalism" had in mind no target or opponent save religious believers voting in accordance with their religious beliefs, i.e., their conscience: theirs is a paradigm of illegitimate deliberation and action. To that extent, his political theory can appear to instantiate the CDF Doctrinal Note's "intolerant secularism." In Rawls's case, it is motivated not by antipathy to religion (so far as one can tell) but by fear of religious wars. In the theory's relatively recent versions, Rawls recalls rather belatedly the contribution of Christian ideas of personhood and equality to the struggle against slavery, and comes round to saying that his "public reason" must not be confused with "secular reason." Indeed, he says (stretching his point) that public reason includes "Catholic views of the common good and solidarity when they are expressed in terms of political values."[5] This proviso about "political" values uses "political" in Rawls's technical sense: it means that they must be put forward not as truths either of faith or natural law or human right, but as consensus demands and assumptions.

There is thus what one might loosely call an overlap between Rawls's final position and the Doctrinal Note when it affirms: "The fact that some of these [moral truths concerning society, justice, freedom, respect for human life and the other rights of the person] may also be taught by the Church does not lessen the political legitimacy or the rightful 'autonomy' of the contribution of those citizens who are committed to them, irrespective of the role that reasoned inquiry or confirmation by the Christian faith may have played in recognizing such truths." (sec. 6). The Doctrinal Note implicitly affirms concepts of public reason and democratic legitimacy when it affirms that voting against "policies affecting the common good which compromise or undermine fundamental ethical requirements" is not an imposition of "confessional values *per se*," *because* "such ethical requirements are rooted in human nature itself and belong to the natural moral law [and] do not require from those who defend them the profession of the Christian faith" (sec. 6). These implicit concepts of *public reason and democratic legitimacy overlap* with Rawls's.

But this Catholic understanding of public reason and democratic legitimacy is rationally far superior to the Rawlsian:

(1) It is unreasonable to propose as strongly normative a "moral ideal" of democratic politics on any ground other than that ideal's *truth*, particularly if one is proposing this "ideal" as the basis for one's exclusionary demand that, as the Note puts it, "a large number of citizens, Catholics among them...[have an obligation] not [to]...base their contribution to society and political life – through the legitimate means available to everyone in a democracy – on their particular understanding of the human person and the common good."

(2) Rawls's attempt to articulate his own theory of the political and the legitimate, as the zone in which one looks always to consensus and never to truth, certainly proves incoherent. Confronting, belatedly, the fact that there are what he calls "rationalist believers in a comprehensive religious or philosophical doctrine," who hold that their positions on fundamental rights "are open to and can be fully established by reason,"[6] Rawls sets aside his own restrictive norm of legitimacy in deliberation, by bidding us treat such a contention as

simply *mistaken*. So the views of such "believers," like others whose unreasonableness Rawls more or less covertly assumes, are not allowed to affect the "overlapping consensus."

Above all, as I suggested in my commentary on the Doctrinal Note, (3) any political doctrine like Rawls's is unreasonable because it must undermine fundamental rights by subordinating them to a sheer consensus, and thus to a *lowest common* denominator (or: to a too low highest *common* factor). Denying or neglecting the imaging of God by each human being from conception (and even under gross disablement), the practical unthinking secularism of consumerism or careerism, and the proud elitism of Nietzschean aesthetico-theoretical secularism, will converge in a consensus for ignoring the true rights of some human beings. Even when Rawlsians are not themselves secularists, they subject the freedom and equality they exalt to unjust limitation – not merely by the normal inertia of any political process, but on principle. Rawlsians, like Dworkinians, speak of the freedom and equality of "citizens," rather than of "human beings." As my commentary concluded: "This is a sign of their subjection of human rights to a political theory that would make of the prejudices of the *beati possidentes* a criterion for rejecting as illegitimate, even when democratic in method, the reasonable and legitimate political efforts of those who understand human freedom and equality in the image and likeness of the Creator and his Word."

I well remember the excitement in Oxford when Rawls's first magnum opus, *A Theory of Justice*, appeared – a large seminar room packed week after week with philosophy and politics and legal theory dons and graduate students. 1970: Escape from the decades-long wastes of meta-ethics in the linguistic mode; substantive argument and position-taking. I was commissioned by a former Catholic priest to write the review of it for the dons' fortnightly magazine, and I read the book more closely than most I've read before or since. The fallacy at its heart gradually became quite clear to me. The thought-experimental conditions under which Rawls identifies the principles of justice – the Original Position in which choosers select principles behind a Veil of Ignorance about their own beliefs and preferences, though with a carefully edited compendium of knowledge about human affairs and a bourgeois disposition to risk-aversion – these are indeed, as Rawls claims, conditions under which inter-personal bias is substantially eliminated, by the choosers' fear that, in the real world to which the selected principles will apply, they might be among the losers under any principle that (to put it broadly) benefits some at the expense of others – more precisely, that fails to maximize the position of the worst of class of people as much as possible. The thought-experimental conditions do eliminate bias, and do guarantee that the principles selected will be just in the sense of not biased by self-interest or self-preference, or, more frankly, selfishness. But it is simply fallacious to assume that because a certain principle of action, restraint or distribution would not be chosen in the Original Position, it cannot be a principle of justice in the real world in which we do know or reasonably believe much more than behind the Veil of Ignorance. This is the fallacy at the bottom of this big book.

But more. In the real world people know, or can know, that commitment and fidelity in marriage is a true good, that having children as fruit of one's marriage and honoring them by educating them towards truth are a true good, and that part of the truth towards which they should be educated is that we are all children of God. Principles of political life that ignore any or all of these will certainly be to one degree or another unjust. The fear that if one's polity were to interest itself in such matters, it might make the wrong choices, and I might be the loser, the fear that Rawls makes decisive in shaping his vision of a good and just society, is a fear which has no a priori rational claim to priority over the cautious but lively hope that the organized help of others will provide indispensable assistance in securing the milieu or social environment for bringing one's children to a maturity of virtue, and the resolution to help one's society provide such help through the assistance of law.

But the remarkable fragility of Rawls's arguments for his political principles in *A Theory of Justice* is replicated and doubled up in his second magnum opus, *Political Liberalism*, which rests on the fallacious general argument and tacitly presupposes, I think, the fallacious specification of it by an arbitrary prioritizing of risk aversion – in the case of the new book, the prioritizing of an aversion to the risk of religious war. But, as I say, the new book added its own peculiar defects in argumentation. The key concept of public reason, and the associated concept of an overlapping consensus, are each defined by reference to the concept of propositions to which "all reasonable people can be expected to agree." The phrase is repeated scores of times, from end to end of the book. Never once does Rawls attend to the radical ambiguity of the phrase, an ambiguity which I think he needs to exploit to give his position the appearance of plausibility.

"Expected" can be normative or predictive – normative when we say you're expected to show up on time and behave politely to the guests; predictively when we say that what with the air traffic problems I'm now expected at 1.00. Officially, the phrase "all reasonable people can be expected to agree to" should not be normative, in Rawls's argument. If it were normative it would presuppose that there is some standard other than consensus, a standard of truth or inherent reasonableness by which to assess the agreement and the reasonableness of the persons who are party to it, and of their willingness or unwillingness to assent to the propositions in question. And so the book would lose its point: citizens and philosophers alike would be looking to the standard, to the truth about the questions arising in public life, rather than, as the book proposes, to the overlapping consensus as a consensus. But Rawls cannot easily admit that his phrase "can reasonably be expected" is merely predictive, since then everyone – or everyone who has *some* reasonable views – would have a veto power over the content of public reason, by declining or failing to assent to widespread views, reasonably or unreasonably. When you try to interpret Rawls's text by lining up its uses of the phrase and assigning them to the predictive or the normative interpretation, by reference to the context, you finish up with two columns each equally long, with some passages where it is simply obscure.

In the end, as I have said, I think Rawls is obliged to tacitly admit that he (like everyone else!) does use his own "private" standards to assess what views are reasonable, on their merits, so that reasonable people may reasonably be *expected*, that is, *ought* – to assent. He was obliged to concede this by his eventual acknowledgement of the existence of "rationalist believers in a comprehensive philosophical or religious doctrine." Though utterly marginalized in his text, these "believers" are in fact the source of the philosophically and theologically guided western law and culture. They are people who think that the truth about human rights and basic justice is, or can in a significant number of contexts be, more important than the maintenance of social peace and stability, the values made supreme by Rawls's risk aversion and emaciated conception of human good. So rationalist believers – believers in natural law and natural rights, if not also in a revealed confirmation of the natural law – have no reason to accept any part of Rawls's conception of politics or political liberalism or public reason. They, after all, have their own conception of public reason: the classic conception of natural law and natural rights, such as you find in Aquinas, just is the proper concept of public reason, that is, of positions which are "private" because I hold them, and "public" because they can and must be argued for or defended in open discourse with anyone willing to accept the rational constraints of discourse itself. And they – that is, *we* – know that it is unreasonable, and, in the last analysis irrational, to propose, as Rawls does, a split between one's public actions and one's private judgments about the truth about what people are and are entitled to. All public action, voting, judging, legislating, enforcing or whatever, is also private action. A public realm is impossible without the allegiance of individuals and allegiance that must be given and maintained for reasons which seem to the individual truly valid. So, nothing can be sustained as part of public reason without the private reason of individuals ratifying it as, yes, reasonable – and reasonable not just in some weak sense, but in the strong sense of something that makes costly and dangerous effort and fidelity worthwhile and often mandatory in the face of every kind of temptation and resistance, inner and outer.

So the deep structure of both Rawls's books is ramshackle and, in the final analysis, negligible, despite the great ability and learning of their in many ways admirable author. But they have commanded enough cultural support to bestir, far away, the CDF itself.

Equally fragile are the arguments for liberalism advanced by my former long-time colleague and fellow-seminarian, Ronald Dworkin. I have pursued their twists and turns in a number of places,[7] and Robert George has carried on the chase even further, with rationally speaking entire success. But in some of its various forms, this family or tribe of sophistical arguments is winning in the Supreme Court. One family in this tribe of arguments says that when a democratic majority enacts a law restricting liberty, the ground and rationale for its action is precisely to subject those whose liberty is restricted to the opinions of the majority, a rationale which is obviously unacceptable because subjecting people to your opinions because they're yours is self-evidently obnoxious. Another version of the argument, the one that recently had big successes in court in this city, asserts that it is at least presumptively true that, when the majority restricts liberty, it is motivated by hostility to those whose conduct will thereby be restricted, or by a will to demean them. That is the argument that prevailed in *Romer v. Evans*, and in its more subtle version in

Lawrence v. Texas. Notice: in either version, the argument has the great advantage that it reaches its conclusion, well, "conclusorily," without one having to even enquire whether those whose decisions to cast a vote on an issue of public policy (a vote with which, as it happened, a majority of other individual voters agreed) *had any reason* for their vote, and if so what was their reason or reasons for doing so. It is very understandable that Dworkin or the court desire to be excused from investigating people's reasons for casting a vote to restrict liberty. Very often it will turn out that their reasons had nothing to do with hostility or the desire to exercise dominance over others, or to demean them, but rather a lot to do with fear of what the exercise of the liberty, if not restricted, would or will do to their own children and the children of those they love or wish to do well, or indeed will do to themselves or anyone else in times of weakness.

The Dworkinian strategy for evading having to reckon with the reasons that voters and legislators have for casting the votes which turn out to be majority votes was a strategy embraced in the notorious "Philosophers' Brief" to the Supreme Court in the assisted suicide cases in 1997, a brief in which Dworkin was joined by four other philosophers, most notably John Rawls.[8] Here they are, in the final sentence of their argument for their foundational premise:

> The Constitution insists that people must be free to make these deeply personal decisions for themselves and must not be forced to end their lives in a way that appalls them, just because that is what some majority thinks proper.

"Just because": a flagrant confusion of necessary with sufficient conditions, insinuating that the majority, the law, has no rationale, and that that supposed fact about the groundlessness of the majority's view need not be established by reasoned investigation and argument but rather is established by the fact that majority support was the necessary *procedural* requirement for the law's enactment. Never do the philosophers confront the most obvious of the available rationales: that to accept as the justifying basis for an action (assisting suicide) which cannot be private – because no community can accept without investigation the mere assertion that so and so's death just now was not sheer murder – to accept, I say, and act, upon the proposition that a person's life in such and such a kind of condition is not worth living – that they would be better off dead – is to accept into the heart of the community a ground for killing, a ground which could not be bounded by absence of consent.[9]

The Supreme Court, for one reason or another, did not openly succumb to the fallacies in the Philosophers' Brief. For some of the Justices, the reason seems to have been little more than that this would be too far in advance of public opinion. As I say, Dworkin's strategic argument about majority will had its day of triumph in the Court in *Romer v Evans*, where the Court's declarations and presuppositions about the merely hostile motives of the voters in Colorado and Texas were evidence-free, sheer a priori, in fact, I suggest, little short of impudence. When the sequence of Dworkin's arguments is considered as a whole, it is evident that, in its recent "hostility" and "demeaning" versions, it links back to his earliest version of his strategy, then advanced as a strategy for defending the proposition that a good (just) state must be neutral about competing conceptions of the good. That basic position – the state must be neutral and is unjust when it is not – was, of course, openly self-refuting, and the attempt to find independent grounding in some more limited requirement of neutrality resulted in the notion that to deny someone the liberty to do what he wants is to deny him equal concern and respect. That argument or notion in turn collapsed when it was noticed that one's motive for denying people liberty to take heroin may precisely be friendly concern for their well-being and active concern, and respect for them as human persons as entitled as anyone to a decent life of participating in true goods, not illusory and self-stultifying objects of desire. And so the sequence of arguments was set in motion – a sequence of moving targets that has traversed the decades since then.

It is the fragility of all such arguments that I want to keep in focus here. I encountered basic structural arguments of comparable fragility when asked to debate the foundations of political morality with the German social philosopher, Jurgen Habermas, someone widely read in this country. It turned out that he too uses, pervasively, an argument from the same stable. In choosing regulations of social life, he says, one must ask whether the regulation (law, declaration, and enforcement of fundamental rights) in question is "acceptable from the perspective of every other person's understanding of himself and the world."[10] Asked whether this includes the perspective and self-understanding of those for whom all ideas of justice are mere toys for fools, and all regulations a joke to be laughed at up one's sleeve, Habermas, so far as I could see, has nothing to say. (In this he resembles the preference-utilitarians, who fall silent when asked whether there is to be any sieving of preferences before they are putatively summed and netted off – whether, for example, sadistic and pedophiliac preferences get counted?) And Habermas has used analogous arguments to defend the Rawlsian conclusions that principled objections to abortion and euthanasia can and should be simply set aside because those who make them are free not have abortions and not to choose to be killed and, therefore, have no basis for not being content to coexist with – i.e., leave substantially unrestricted – those who wish to engage in these activities.[11]

I say "Rawlsian conclusion" because one of the most remarkable features of Rawls's book *Political Liberalism* was its position-taking on abortion – the position that anyone who argues that all unborn children have a right, which should also be a legal right, not to be killed at their mothers' whim, holds a cruel and oppressive opinion which it would be undemocratic to act upon by voting for restrictive legislation; and which, if supported by any comprehensive philosophical or religious doctrine, shows that comprehensive doctrine to be so far forth unreasonable. I say this was position-taking, and that is a better term than "conclusion" because Rawls felt free to say all this in his book without a shred of argument or reasoning – nothing but the assertion that "all reasonable people can be expected to agree" that healthy adult women have the right to kill their child during the first three months, if not longer. And then, under pressure of criticism of this passage in his book, he subsequently produced a few sentences of argument for the proposition that a majority decision authorizing the free killing of the unborn "is to be seen as reasonable" (and binding on all citizens) because "Catholics need not exercise the right of abortion in their own case"! He adds another argument, equally unreasonable, but let me focus on this one, which you will remember is used also, and for the same purposes, by Habermas. Here is Rawls, confronting anti-abortion citizens who claim, with good arguments, that abortion is rather like slave owning: a radical, basic injustice imposed upon people deprived of the protections of citizenship. And his response is: "*You* free citizens need not exercise the right to [own slaves] [abort your own children] in your own case, so you can and must recognize our law as legitimate as it applies to the rest of us."[12]

The fragility of these arguments by persons of powerful intellect and reflective disposition suggests that they are a device for avoiding the claim of our civilization that human beings are fundamentally equal in dignity and basic worth, and that their life – their very reality as persons in this world – is a basic and true good even when immature or smitten by disease and disability. And this evasion seems not unmotivated. The arguments, each fit only to serve as rhetoric, are in the service of conclusions of the general form: we wish to *decide who counts*, and what it is about them that makes them, for us, count (matter, have entitlements, and a life worth living and respecting).

Never so much talk of rights and equality, and so little effort to respond with frankness and energy to the challenge which all these teachers confront in almost every student in any class they hold: the challenge to show the falsity of what these students almost universally believe to be true, that all value judgments are relative, that every judgment about the good, and therefore also about the right, is no more than an appeal from the sub-rational to the sub-rational, from desire to desire, passion to passion, all crystallized in the "concepts" of a culture – concepts which rhetoricize the sub-rational appeal in a syntax of propositions in the form of truth-claims, a form which is systematically misleading a mask for desire. A welcome mask, for each of us needs to keep secret, at least on many occasions, our desire to do whatever it takes to have enough control to get what we want – a desire which, if made evident to others, would arouse their resistance.

And it is also a desire that must be kept hidden from ourselves. For, actually, the light of intelligence and the voice of conscience are not extinguished and stilled. The intelligibility of created human goods, good for and every member of the species of beings endowed from conception with the radical capacity for intelligence, remains "written on our hearts," that is, in the will, which, as St Thomas teaches, is *in* our intelligence and reason by which we are directed to those goods as to be pursued and done. That intelligibility and that directedness, like our utter dependence on the cooperation of creation and providence to achieve anything that we interest ourselves in trying to attain or be, are among the considerations which make true the biblical preaching that it is the fool who has said in his heart there is no god (Psalm 13.1),[13] and that vain or futile are those "in whom there is not the knowledge of God, who cannot conclude to him that is from these good things that are seen, and who in attending to the works fail to acknowledge the workman" (Wisdom 13.1). When we confront the claim of secularism to be the truth about the world that is, and the one common space for public discourse, we need to recall that it is a truth of faith that God as source and final point of all things can, from created things, be known with certainty by the natural light of human reason.[14] So there is an obligation, and equally a right, to employ that natural knowledge as part of public discourse, and to make plain that it is the secularists who inhabit an illusory world, falsely supposed to be closed from any transcendent origin and destiny. And it is right to draw upon the enhanced firmness and clarity which revelation – public revelation – confers upon that natural knowledge.

The fragility of the public arguments of the secularist philosophers of moral and political life is a testimony to all this, just as, taken with their talents as teachers and writers, it is also, I believe, a testimony to the truth of all three of Paul's sayings, right at this point in his meditation for the Romans: first, that "I am debtor both to the Greeks, and to the Barbarians; both to the wise, and to the unwise" (1:14); second, that "Professing themselves to be wise, they became fools, and changed the glory of the incorruptible God into an image made like to corruptible man (1:22–3); and third that, nonetheless, those "who have not the law, do by nature the things contained in the law," and "show the work of the law written in their hearts, their conscience also bearing witness" against them (2:14–15). Unaided reason itself has sufficient grounds for affirming the truth of all this, but unaided reason also can both expect and welcome a supernatural revelation which both confirms and supplements it in all the judgments it can and should make, and act on, about the dignity, obligations, and rights of each of us at every point in our earthly life.

John Finnis is Professor of Law and Legal Philosophy the University of Oxford, as well as the Biolchini Family Professor of Law at the Notre Dame Law School. He has taught law and political philosophy at Oxford for several decades, and is a Fellow of the British Academy. His books include *Natural Law and Natural Rights* (Oxford University Press, 1980; 15th impression, 2002); *Fundamentals of Ethics* (Georgetown University Press, 1983); *Nuclear Deterrence, Morality, and Realism* (with Joseph Boyle and Germain Grisez, Oxford University Press, 1987); *Moral Absolutes* (Catholic University of America Press, 1991); and *Aquinas: Moral, Political, and Legal Theory* (Oxford University Press, 1998). He has served on the Holy See's International Theological Commission and on the Pontifical Council for Justice and Peace, and is an ordinary member of the Pontifical Academy for Life. He received the Fellowship of Catholic Scholars' Cardinal Wright Award in 1989.

Notes

1 II Sent. d. 44 exp. text. ad 4.

2 See Finnis, "On the Practical Meaning of Secularism," *Notre Dame Law Review* 73 (1998) 101–126.

3 See Finnis, *Aquinas: Moral, Political and Legal Theory* (Oxford University Press, 1998), 176–180.

4 See *L'Osservatore Romano*, English Edition, 29 January 2003, p. 9.

5 John Rawls, "The Idea of Public Reason Revisited," *University of Chicago Law Review* 64 (1997) 765 at 775. He adds: "That the Catholic Church's non-public reason requires its members to follow its doctrine is perfectly consistent with their also honoring public reason." *Ibid.*, 799; Rawls, *Political Liberalism* (Columbia University Press [1993], 1996), lvii.

6 Rawls, *Political Liberalism*, 152–3.

7 See e.g., Finnis, "Legal Enforcement of Duties to Oneself: Kant v. Neo-Kantians," *Columbia Law Review* 87 (1987) 433–56.

8 John Rawls et al., "The Philosophers' Brief," *The New York Review of Books* 44 no. 5 (27 March 1997). The Brief's first words are: "These cases do not invite or require the Court to make moral, ethical, or religious judgments about how people should approach or confront their death or about when it is ethically appropriate to hasten one's own death or to ask others for help in doing so. On the contrary, they ask the Court to recognize that individuals have a constitutionally protected interest in making those grave judgments for themselves, *free from the imposition of any religious or philosophical orthodoxy by court or legislature*" (emphasis added). Do we hear talk of "imposing religious or philosophical orthodoxy" when it is a matter of slavery (including voluntary self-enslavement) or pedophilia?

9 Crucially, the Brief argues that the law and the state "*may not take one side in [the] essentially ethical or religious controversy*" about whether it is or is not a "terrible injury" and "irreversible harm" to people in certain conditions not to be allowed to choose to be deliberately killed (rather than sedated and nurtured) so as to escape those conditions, which they judge "disfigure their lives," for example, with "indignity." Focussed upon upholding a liberty of (certain) competent persons to give effect to their own side-taking in the "ethical or religious controversy" by killing themselves and to have another assist them (or do it for them?), the Brief pays no attention whatever to the fact that unless our law and

state takes sides – *and takes the right side* – in the "ethical or religious controversy" about whether people in such conditions are or are not injured by continuing to live because their condition is one of real indignity, and their life is not worth living – whether, that is, a person in that condition has a *Lebens-unwertes Leben* – we will have set off down the trail blazed by the enlightened secularist doctors and lawyers whose sophisticated urgings found a response in the German euthanasia programs for the mentally disabled of the late 1930s.

10 Jurgen Habermas, *Justification and Application: Remarks on Discourse Ethics* (Cambridge, Mass., MIT Press, 1993), 154.

11 See Finnis, "Natural Law and the Ethics of Discourse," *The American Journal of Jurisprudence* 43 (1999) 53–73; also in *Ratio Juris* 12 (1999) 354–373.

12 Finnis, "Abortion, Natural Law and Public Reason," in Robert P George and Christopher Wolfe (eds.), *Natural Law and Public Reason* (Washington DC, Georgetown University Press 2000) pp.71–105.

13 See Encyclical *Fides et Ratio* (1998), sec. 18.2.

14 Vatican Council I, *Dei Filius*, c. 2 *de Revelatione*, Denz. 1785/3005.

MEETING THE JUST DEMANDS OF NON-TRADITIONAL HOUSEHOLDS

INTRODUCTION
Gerard V. Bradley

The Fellowship of Catholic Scholars is by most measures a pretty traditional outfit. Rarely is it said that our members shrink from holding onto the good and the true and the beautiful in our heritage; many have been stalwart defenders of traditional marriage, even as it disintegrates all around us. Our panelists today are pretty traditional, too. At least we can say this about our households: each of us is married to a spouse of the opposite sex, never married to anyone else, and we have an average of 7.5 children apiece. You might wonder, then, of our qualifications to examine today's subject – just demands of *non*-traditional households. Be assured that we watch TV, read the newspapers, and listen to our kids tell us about their classmates "blended" households, single moms, and more.

Speaking now for myself, and not for the panelists or for the Fellowship over which I preside, the place to start is the severance of marital incidents from the status of marriage. This severance is a commonplace of court cases and in legislation. One notable case is *Snetsinger v. Bd. of Regents* case, currently pending in the Montana Supreme Court. There the complaining same-sex couples unequivocally stated that they did *not* challenge the legal definition of marriage as union of man and woman. They sought instead to have their relationships be a gateway to marital benefits and protections. The plaintiffs said that the state could not constitutionally limit benefits needed – or at least *enjoyable* – by people in non-marital households only to people in marital families. The claim was that where the need is the same, benefits must be the same. The state might as well say, according to the plaintiffs, that only married couples might be admitted to national parks.

This position is not incoherent. It has some appeal. But it is incomplete. I doubt whether sound principles of constitutional interpretation – or valid legal reasoning of any type – would justify a court in decreeing the extension of benefits sought by the *Snetsinger* plaintiffs. But the extension itself is worth serious legislative consideration. In my view, legislators should take account of the predominance in our society of non-marital households, and recognize that many of them include children. I believe that lawmakers have an obligation in justice to do *something* to structure and facilitate these households *as* households – but not as *families,* at least not as families in any way that implies that the sexual relationships between or among those in the home is morally licit. For neither logic nor justice requires that such relationships be called marriages because, in truth, they are not.

This legislative accommodation (if that is the right term) makes special sense now, a full generation into a revolution in marriage and family life. This continuing cultural upheaval has remade our social norms about sexual ethics and the morality of having kids. The resulting fact of the matter is that most American households are *not* marital households. A majority of our children do *not* live with their wedded mother and father, each of whom has been married only once.

Another pertinent effect of the revolution is the eclipse of *marital* incidents and protections, just as such. What I mean is this: the incidents of marriage *qua* marriage are largely *passé.* Legal aids or supports of the marital vows of permanence, sexual fidelity, and thus to have children within the marital bond, have been almost entirely abandoned in the last generation. Some of this demolition was wrought by legislators, and all of this seems to have been welcomed by elites, by the culture at large, and by many, many regular people as well. The "no-fault" divorce revolution was a legislative response to (heterosexual) persons' rebellion against the promise to stay together "until death do us part." But much was also accomplished by the courts. Eradicating legal distinctions between legitimate and illegitimate children is one example. Another is the recently decided Supreme Court case of *Lawrence v. Texas.* There the Court for the first time declared that legal prohibitions upon non- and extra-marital sexual acts could not stand. The new constitutional rule is that consent, not marriage, is the principle of any legally enforceable sexual morality.

Thus, so-called marital incidents have been reduced over the last few decades to mainly economic benefits, along with some entitlements having to do with friendship – hospital visitation and bereavement leave and the like. But these "marital" incidents do not grow out of the needs or privileges of two-in-one-flesh communion. They are ancillary to household life. And, as I said, most American households are not marital abodes.

In these circumstances, I think legislatures *ought* to extend *some* benefits hitherto reserved to the married – possibly a great many such benefits – to non-marital households, because those benefits have so much to do with what is common to marital and to non-marital *households*: an integrated economic unit involving people who care and look after each other. But this accommodation must be non-discriminatory and inclusive. The benefits and protections should run all the way to those who need them. The need goes well beyond the class of unmarried persons – homosexual or heterosexual – who are sexually involved, though such persons should be included within the umbrella of household protections. The criterion should be the existence of an enduring household or familial-type unit – not necessarily involving a sexual relationship between or among the residents.

Following these few preliminary remarks of mine on a vast subject, we have three able and stimulating discussions of various aspects of our topic of "meeting the just demands of non-traditional households."

Professor Gerard V. Bradley is a Professor Law at the University of Notre Dame Law School. He holds the J.D. degree from Cornell University. Formerly he was an assistant district attorney in New York City. He is co-editor of the *American Journal of Jurisprudence*, and has authored many articles, as well as a book, *Church- State Relationships in America* (1987). He is currently serving as president of the Fellowship of Catholic Scholars.

EMPIRICISM AND THE "ANTI-TRADITIONAL HOUSEHOLD"
Mary Eberstadt

A few months ago in the pages of *National Review*, our chairman Gerard Bradley urged us all to "stand and fight" on the issue of gay marriage. The reasons why marriage needs defending, like the related reasons why gay pseudo-marriage demands resistance, require no rehearsal here. Every name on the FCS roster has been in the forefront of this struggle and related struggles, and every soul here knows the arguments and counter-arguments by heart. I will leave to the constitutional scholars the question of the politics before us, as I will leave to the theologians among us the question of what exactly Church teaching dictates and where.

What I hope to contribute to our common purpose is something more pedestrian. For part of "standing and fighting," it seems to me, is knowing where one's allies and ammunition are. My purpose today is to report on some underutilized stockpiles for our side amassed in an admittedly unlikely place – namely, in the world of secular social science.

For many years now, and often inadvertently, secular as well as religious researchers have been amassing facts that, properly understood, independently bolster the case for the traditional family and tell against its adversaries and would-be imitators. Some of that evidence, such as the harm to children of the fatherless household, is already widely acknowledged by mainstream writers and readers. Some of it, particularly evidence pertaining to the dark side of homosexuality, remains virtually taboo. When all of it is put together, however, this evidence points to an interesting fact: empiricism, perhaps more than we realize, is on our side. This is the moral ammunition, as it were, that I would like to review here in brief.

First, a suggested clarification of terms. As William E. May points out, there are in fact a variety of non-traditional households. I will limit my remarks to that subset now posing the most immediate public challenge: the household self-consciously created in contradistinction to the natural family; the household in which, as Gerard Bradley has formulated it, the natural family can only be imitated rather than created; this household is now demanding not only recognition of some sort from society at large, but also the guarantee of moral equivalence. I suggest that we call this the "anti-traditional" household, both to distinguish it from what has gone before, and to capture something of its defiant essence. And since such households can further be divided into two variants, heterosexual and homosexual, I propose that we proceed by examining them in turn.

What this distinction immediately makes clear is something interesting and pretty much unnoticed in today's furor over gay unions: that, intellectually speaking, at least, the *heterosexual* variation of the anti-traditional household has been steadily losing ground for years now.

I do not mean that heterosexual family formation, *as practiced*, is rosy with health. Far from it. Abortion, divorce, illegitimacy, pornography, sterilization – these and other plagues on the natural family continue apace. As every scholar present also knows, underlying and sustaining all these separate attacks on the natural family is the fact that contraceptive sex, the deliberate plan to thwart participation in the natural family, is not only widespread, but is also almost universally accepted not only in the United States but elsewhere. Considered phenomenologically, the present and future of the natural family in America – and, for that matter, in much of the world – looks grim indeed.

At the same time, the bad news isn't all the news. We should recognize too one real and important achievement of late, one clear-cut victory for the traditionalist side: there has been a sea-change in the way our secular cultural elites now write and talk about non-traditional heterosexual households. Members of those elites may live in such households; they may personally feel such households to be morally equivalent, perhaps even superior, to traditional households; but they no longer, as a rule, offer full-throated public endorsements of the broken hearth.

That is a major transformation in public life. Only twenty years ago or so, as everyone here will know, not only the acceptance but the active ideological defense of such households was the intellectual norm among secular educated people. Divorce, it was commonly argued then, was not only a human right, but actually better for the child. One parent was said to be at least as good as two. Certain extreme instantiations of the anti-traditional household, such as communes and "swinging," were actively defended by mainstream voices and celebrated in the more stylish mainstream books and magazines. Just two or so decades ago, in other words, these arguments for experimental family life were all on the offensive. Today, by contrast, they are all playing defense. Whether they like it or not, whether they begrudge the fact or not, most people in the public square today have been brought around to recognizing this proposition: that the traditional family, despite its problems, is nonetheless the best arrangement yet contrived for raising children – if only by default.

How did this remarkable shift in secular opinion come about? The answer, in large part, is empiricism. This shift has been forced by the steady – and ultimately unavoidable – accumulation of empirical evidence testifying to the connections between broken homes and child problems. To cite just a few examples, this shift was due to the groundbreaking work of Daniel Patrick Moynihan in 1964 on the Negro family; to the critical research of psychologist Judith Wallerstein over several decades on the deleterious effects of divorce on children; to Barbara Defoe Whitehead's famous 1993 *Atlantic Monthly* piece (followed by a book) entitled "Dan Quayle was Right"; to David Blankenhorn's 1994 book, *Fatherless America*; to James Q. Wilson's *The Marriage Problem*, among many other related works; to Linda Waite's and Maggie Gallagher's *The Case for Marriage*; and to many other revisionist articles and books that have followed their lead. These and other writers made the case for the traditional family on largely secular grounds; and in so doing, they have re-made the way secular people think about it.

I do not mean that this view has now "won" in the public square; manifestly it has not. What I do mean is that it cannot now be ignored. To know these works is to know how intensely controversial, even shocking, they were when they first appeared; and how radically they all have shifted the ideological terrain, including even among feminists and other inveterate adversaries who have been forced by these and related literature onto the defensive. To put the matter emblematically, when Judith Wallerstein's latest book on the perils of divorce is praised by a feminist writing in the *New York Times Book Review*, you know that a small intellectual revolution has occurred.

This brings us to an apparent paradox. For even as advocates of the *heterosexual* anti-traditional household have been forced into some measure of intellectual retreat, advocates of the *homosexual* anti-traditional household have meanwhile gone from strength to cultural strength.

On inspection, of course, this is not really a paradox at all. The reasons for the success of the homosexual anti-traditionalists are plain enough. First, the more deformed heterosexual unions have become, the more they have come to resemble homosexual unions (and vice versa). It is hard to fault homosexuals for thwarting the plan of creation at a time when so many heterosexuals busy themselves with exactly that. Allow me to quote Patrick Fagan in particular (from an excellent book edited by Christopher Wolfe) for distilling the argument in a single sentence: "If one no longer considers childbearing part of the nature of the sexual act, and if married heterosexuals claim childless sex as a 'right' – they have, and the Supreme Court long ago upheld it – then it is difficult to deny this 'right' to those whose sexual acts always preclude children – that is, homosexuals."[1] This is, of course, exactly what has happened, as some gay-rights activists themselves acutely understand.

Second, homosexual anti-traditionalists have also benefited from another moral catastrophe, i.e., the continuing priest scandals. It is indeed hard to make the case for the sanctity of marriage, at least with a straight face, when a fair number of priests are caught prowling for teenage boys. The entire institution of the Church, and not only the offenders, has suffered from this dissonance. A demoralized clergy, like a demoralized laity, has little with which to fight claims of homosexual moral equivalence – or anything else.

In sum, contraception has morally disarmed the American laity, and the gay-priest-and-pedophile problem, at least in part, has simultaneously disarmed the clergy. And because of both sorts of disarmament, as James Hitchcock recently noted: "Many people who don't like the idea of homosexual 'marriage' are at a loss to say exactly why."

And here, or so it seems to me, is where empiricism enters the picture. For even as the celebrations of gay rights roar on, empirical fact, like an unwanted guest, glowers in the corner through it all. For the argument that homosexuality is "virtually normal" – the argument, that is, on which the gay-rights and gay-marriage activists have so far won – is a hypothesis that is not only wrong on theological grounds, but also wrong as a matter of established fact. By "fact" I mean the most secular sources imaginable: social science, medical science, psychological studies, and more – including sources overtly friendly to the normalization of gay rights.

None of that evidence, of course, will surprise those who actually minister to homosexual persons from a traditionalist perspective – the groundbreaking work of Fr. John Harvey comes first to mind, as do the continuing efforts by other brave counselors who do hear the pain of their clients, and who resist current therapeutic ideology. But this same evidence is almost entirely unknown, because culturally *verboten*, throughout the secular world, and particularly among our secular elites – as studiously ignored in our own time as, say, the evidence about family breakdown was in the early 1960s.

One such problem is chemical addiction – alcoholism and the related abuse of licit or illicit drugs. This propensity to addiction, while endemic to all of modern society, is ubiquitously documented to be worse among lesbians and gays. Virtually every study one can find on the subject confirms that: "The statistics do point to the *gay community*, particularly *gay* men, as being most at risk of becoming Alcoholics." This quote, incidentally, is from *Gay Community News*, one of countless gay sources to draw the attention of its members to heightened risk of alcoholism. GCN's observation is confirmed by scores of sources. As another source puts it: "The fact that alcohol, drug, and tobacco use all occur at significantly *higher* rates in the GLBT community than in the general population is one of the most widely acknowledged GLBT health concerns." This quote is from *glbthealth.org*, a gay website. Gay AA groups abound in virtually every locality – an interesting detail, given the numerically small proportion represented by the gay population. Numerous sources also report higher gay levels of use and addiction to illicit drugs. Consider as emblematic the *Journal of Gay and Lesbian Psychotherapy*, which devotes an entire recent issue to the subject of addictions in the Gay and Lesbian community.[2]

Another problem also widespread in modern society, and also

afflicting gay men and women disproportionately, is the cluster of mental disorders known generally as "depression." By longstanding documentation, these problems too appear significantly higher in the homosexual than heterosexual population. Here is a representative quote from a recent article in *Archives of Sexual Behavior* – no socially conservative rag, that – summarizing what other studies also conclude: namely, that "the levels of depression and anxiety in our homosexual subjects, whether HIV positive or HIV negative, are substantially higher than those found in representative general population samples."[3]

At the extreme of these higher rates of mental affliction is another widely-agreed upon fact: that suicide is far more likely among homosexuals than among heterosexuals. In a famous study in published in 1978, for example, researchers Bell and Weinberg found that *eighteen* percent of white homosexual males reported at least one suicide attempt (as opposed to three percent of the white heterosexual males). Remember that Bell and Weinberg, like the other sources I am quoting, were overtly sympathetic to the normalization of homosexuality. Here as elsewhere in the pro-gay literature, however, the facts about gay suicide inadvertently contradict the "virtually-normal" polemics that typically accompany them.[4]

More recently, attention to the population of underage boys self-identifying as "gay" has produced evidence of the same tragic pattern. Allow me to quote from a letter in the *Wall Street Journal* earlier this month: "Nearly one-third of gay teens drop out of school annually, three times the national average. Gay and lesbian youth are three times more likely to attempt suicide than other youth." The authors of this letter, incidentally, come not from the Family Research Council; they are founders of the Harvey Milk School for gay teenagers in New York.

Another distinguishing characteristic of homosexuality that emerges from nearly all literature on the subject, and what I believe to be the most under-examined fact of all, is this: homosexual men are significantly more likely – some researchers would say, much more likely – than heterosexual men to have been sexually abused or exploited as children and adolescents. Allow me to quote from a study in the *Journal of the American Medical Association*, 1998: "Abused adolescents, particularly those victimized by males, were up to 7 times more likely to self-identify as gay or bisexual than peers who have not been abused."[5] A pro-gay-rights book called *Lesbian & Gay Youth: Care and Counseling*, published by Columbia University Press in 1998, likewise found that: "In a survey of sexual abuse victims who attended STD clinics, for example, 37 percent of gay men had been sexually abused as children or adolescents."[6]

The gay-activist response to such problematic evidence is familiar enough: that what "drives" gay men and boys to such behaviors is: "homophobia," or the refusal of society to accept them as they are. And herein, I believe, lies the hidden weakness of gay activism today, and by extension the eventual fate of the gay anti-traditional household. For the closer society moves to the moral-equivalent view of homosexuality, the harder it becomes to blame the endemic problems of gay men on the "homophobic" rest of the world.

Sooner or later, someone is going to ask why, if being gay is cause for celebration, gay boys and men continue to kill themselves at significantly higher rates than do heterosexuals. Sooner or later, someone is going to wonder why, despite society's open arms, virtually every study of gay mental health shows higher rates of depression, alcoholism, sexual addiction, sexually transmitted diseases, and the rest. And while we are on the subject of paradox, how about this one from a new book by noted pro-gay researcher Michael Bailey that gay men in the Netherlands – surely one of the most gay-tolerant societies on earth – report *three times* the levels of depression reported by heterosexuals?[7]

This is the evidence ignored by, say, judges who place children in gay-headed households. It is also the evidence ignored by everyone who argues that homosexuality has nothing to do with sex scandals involving young boys. It is also the evidence that will not go away. The empirical reality of much of gay life contradicts the rhetoric of virtual normality; and eventually, it seems safe to predict, that the twain shall meet.

When that happens, the advocates of the homosexual anti-traditional household will be on the intellectual defensive – as, say, the advocates of the heterosexual anti-traditional household are today. This does not mean that gay men and women will wear lavender letters on their sleeves and be thrust from the public square back into the closet, any more than divorced or unwed people are ostracized today. But it does mean that today's euphoria over the anti-traditional homosexual household will someday seem as antiquated, and at least as problematic, for the children of those households, as does the hippie bliss of yesterday. And let me add one pre-emptive point here to those arguments to come. "Homophobia," that all-purpose devil, does not and cannot explain why gay men and boys in all kinds of studies report higher rates of child sexual abuse and earlier sexual experiences than do heterosexual men. This fact alone, which has the potential to topple everything built on today's view that "orientation" is fixed and inborn, is an ideological explosion waiting to happen.

But that is an argument for another time. In closing, let me briefly address the question of justice. Is it uncharitable, or unjust, to insist on seeing the world as it is, thus bringing such unwanted facts to light? Many Americans, including a great many Catholics, seem to think so. But they are wrong. And they are wrong not only on grounds of theology – there are, after all, immortal souls at stake in this argument, including our own – but also wrong as a matter of this-worldly fact. It is no service to an already conflicted adolescent to say that society is indifferent to his sexual and emotional life, when in fact the option of active homosexuality will raise his risks for sexual abuse, alcohol and drug abuse, sexually transmitted disease, depression, and all the rest. It is no service to pretend moral equivalence between homosexual and heterosexual unions, when all the available evidence points overwhelmingly to the truth that heterosexual marriages are the best place for children. It is no service to any child – it is in fact evil – to be treated like an accessory to be procured, rather than like a human being with fundamental rights independent of those who would so acquire them, including the right to be something other than an instrument of some unrelated adult's personal drama.

All of us need to be on the offensive, not the defensive, on these and other arguments, and we must also be alert to allies where we find them. Many people who do not say "yuk" to contraception do say "yuk" to polygamy, for example, which is why Stanley Kurtz's bold and influential recent essay on the subject in the *Weekly Standard* deserves mention here as a case in point. Kurtz's argument – that homosexual "marriage" will demonstrably lead to polygamous "marriage," spelled out in irrefutable detail – may not answer elemental questions of Catholic morality. At the same time, it *is* true that the gay rights boom will lead to polygamy, just as other instrumental arguments are also true – for example, that abortion *can* damage the mother's health, that single-parent families *are* statistically more likely to produce criminals than are two-parent families, or that the public practice of homosexuality is fraught with documented perils. And it is also true that, living in an increasingly dissident and post-Christian time, non-dissident Catholics especially need to think creatively, and prayerfully, about how and where to make common cause. Anyone potentially moved by reason and evidence is potentially on the traditionalist side.

All of this empirical knowledge is a mere footnote to natural law, it is true. But it helps to have the facts with us as we reach beyond the like-minded to the other-minded – including the gay-minded, whose hearts we hope also to touch. Today's struggle over gay rights *is* the struggle over modernity, because the gay condition is in critical respects the modern condition writ large: its defiance, its sterility, its atomization, its unexplained compulsions and miseries, its insistence on public recognition as substitute for private communion with God.

I would like to close with a quote by a critic who, like many of the scholars here, understood the sadness of it all very clearly: "We must face things as they are. Much of the new sensibility regarding homosexuality fails to do so, and from such a failure no one, heterosexual or homosexual, can in the long run gain." These words were written by Samuel McCracken in *Commentary* some 25 years ago, on the occasion of the publication of a massive study, *Homosexualities*, that proved a milestone in the effort to advance homosexual anti-traditionalism. Reading through that and related pro-gay literature of the time, McCracken could see plainly what I have been trying to describe: the self-destruction beneath so much of the happy talk, the problematic facts that just won't go away.

Today, just as 25 years ago, or 25 years from now, those of us on the traditionalist side of the struggle have plenty of moral ammunition in front of us. We just need to figure out how to use it.

Mary Tedeschi Eberstadt is a research fellow at the Hoover Institution and a consulting editor to *Policy Review* Magazine. Her essays and reviews have appeared in various journals and magazines, and include, recently, "The Elephant in the Sacristy" (*Weekly Standard*, June 17, 2002), "Feminism's Children" (*Weekly Standard*, November 15 2001), and "Home-Alone America" (*Policy Review*,

June-July 2001). She is currently at work on a book about the social and medical problems of American children. She is married to the writer Nicholas Nash Eberstadt and they have four children.

Notes

1 Patrick Fagan, "The Inversion of Heterosexual Sex," in *Same-Sex Matters: The Challenge of Homosexuality*, ed. Christopher Wolfe (Spence, 2000). For a particularly prophetic appearance of the same point, see also Elizabeth Anscombe's classic essay, "Contraception and Chastity," collected in Janet E. Smith, ed., *Why Humanae Vitae Was Right: A Reader* (Ignatius Press, 1993). "If contraceptive intercourse is permissible," Anscombe wrote in that essay several decades ago, then "...it becomes perfectly impossible to see anything wrong with homosexual intercourse, for example. I am not saying: if you think contraception is all right you will do these other things; not at all. The habit of respectability persists and old prejudices die hard. But I am saying: you will have no solid reason against these things. You will have no answer to someone who proclaims as many do that they are good too."

2 *Journal of Gay and Lesbian Psychotherapy*, Volume 3, Special Issue: Addictions in the Gay and Lesbian Community. 2001.

3 Weinrich, James D and Atkinson, J Hampton and McCutchan, J Allen and Grant, Igor and Group, the HNRC (1995). "Is gender dysphoria dysphoric? Elevated depression and anxiety in gender dysphoric and non-dysphoric homosexual and bisexual men in an HIV sample," *Archives of Sexual Behavior* 24 (1):55–72.

4 One reviewer who did note that contradiction at the time of Bell and Weinberg's *Homosexualities* was Samuel McCracken. See "Are Homosexuals Gay?" *Commentary*, Jan. 1979.

5 "Sexual Abuse of Boys: Definition, Prevalence, Correlates, Sequelae, and Management," William C. Holmes, Gail B. Slap, *Journal of the American Medical Association*, Dec. 2, 1998 vol. 280, No. 21.

6 Caitlin Ryan and Donna Futterman, *Lesbian & Gay Youth: Care and Counseling* (Columbia University Press, 1998).

7 Michael J. Bailey, *The Man Who Would Be Queen* (Joseph Henry Press, 2003), p. 82.

"NON-TRADITIONAL HOUSEHOLDS" AND "JUST DEMANDS"
Christopher Wolfe

Our topic today is a complicated one. I want to start by raising some questions about the title of our panel.

"Non-Traditional Households"

We are discussing "Non-Traditional Households." I take this to mean "households formed on the basis of principles incompatible with traditional moral principles," that is, households based on divorce and remarriage, illegitimacy, and cohabitation (both heterosexual and homosexual). I interpret it this way, because the focal case of a "traditional household" is a family, composed of a father and mother and their offspring – and yet I don't think the term "non-traditional households" was intended to include families based on adoption, or single-parent families based on the death of one of the spouses, although those families too could easily, in one sense, be considered "non-traditional" households.[1]

My first observation has to do with the awkwardness of the term "non-traditional" and the rhetorical problems associated with it. "Tradition" has a range of meanings, but it is usually understood to relate to something in the past. It is "backward-looking." It is easily taken to mean "the old morality," that is, the morality that has now given way to a new morality.

What this term reflects, I think, is the difficulty of coming up with a name based more on a substantive characterization of our moral views, one whose connotations involve, not its age, but its intrinsic character. "Catholic morality" is problematic, because we live in such a religiously pluralistic society, and also because what is really meant by this is often the understanding of natural law that happens to be embraced especially, but not exclusively, by Catholics. "Natural law morality" is better, but still problematic because: a) the term "natural law" has been so widely used and abused, e.g., made to apply to Locke as much as to Aquinas; b) the actual knowledge today of the classic natural law position of Aquinas is so poor; and c) insofar as natural law is understood, it too is often thought of as a morality of the past, one that is no longer widely accepted and is now simply out-dated. Perhaps the most plausible substantive characterization of our natural-law-based morality would be to call it "reasonable" or "rational" morality, but "reason" too is a term now co-opted (and abused) by so many that "reasonable morality" would not serve well.

As I cast about for alternative characterizations, however, I have come to the conclusion that nothing is very readily available.[2] John Paul II has offered an interesting alternative: what we seek to advance is "a civilization of love." This has the advantage of suggesting a very definite substantive ground to the morality, or the way of life, we seek to describe and bring about. The main objection to its use is verbal: e.g., the term, "a civilization-of-love-morality," doesn't roll right off the tongue.

But, after this semantic digression, let me move on to more substantive issues.

A Typology of Families

We might begin with a typology of families – one based on considerations of right moral principle or right reason in the establishment of families, which could be fairly complicated. It might include:

1) *"Complete families,"*[3] four examples of which are:
   a) Two-parent families with their children;
   b) Single-parent families due to the death of one of the spouses (for, in such cases, the dead parent is still, in a certain important sense, a genuine part of the family);
   c) Two-parent families based on remarriage after the death of spouse(s), which might include children from the previous marriages; and
   d) Families with adopted children.
2) *"Wounded* (but genuine) families," such as:
   a) A single-parent family that results from the absent parent's divorce or desertion (these families being deeply injured, but

there being no moral defect in the familial relation of the spouse and children that have been abandoned); and

b) A family based on single-parent adoption, which lacks one of the ordinary essential components of a family – two opposite-sex parents – and which is therefore lacking something, but which suffers from no moral defect in the fundamental familial arrangement.

3) What I will (with some hesitation) call *"incomplete"* or *"imperfectly-formed* families" – which are families based on invalid marriages, and therefore are not families in the strict sense – but which contain some genuine elements of family life that should not be disregarded by society (most obviously, a genuine parent-child relation of some sort), such as:

a) "Common law marriages" (sustained heterosexual partnership with no formal marriage) that have produced children;

b) Families based on invalid marriages after civil divorce, which produce children of their own;

c) Single-parent families based on illegitimate births with an absent biological father;

d) Lesbian motherhood, through artificial reproduction techniques or non-marital heterosexual acts; and

e) Polygamous marriages with children.

4) *"Non-families,"* such as heterosexual partnerships without children, and homosexual unions.

I think our topic today focuses on those last two categories, namely, incomplete, or imperfectly formed families, and non-families. The distinction between them is fundamental: whether or not there is a genuine relationship of parenthood. The fact of parenthood in what I call "incomplete" or "imperfectly-formed" families calls for a different stance of society toward such families.

In the balance of the paper, I will examine two issues: social recognition of partnerships (especially in relation to parenthood); and provision of social resources to what I have called incomplete families.

Just Demands: Recognition of Partnerships and Parenthood

So, what are the "just demands" of "non-traditional households," as I have described them (in categories three and four above)?

Our starting point, I think – in agreement with Bill May – is the limit to just demands: non-traditional households cannot, in strict justice, demand to be called rightly-ordered families. The law and public policy, in principle, ought not to say that these households are rightly-ordered, because they are based on various sorts of essential defects.

On the other hand, it is clear, I think, that there must be some social recognition of certain non-traditional households, since a very important demand of justice is that the offspring in various forms of non-traditional households should not be excluded from various forms of social support ordinarily owed to complete families, since they are themselves innocent of any wrongdoing.

If we are to come up with more specific guidelines for recognition of non-traditional households, however, I think we will have to make a sharp distinction between two essentially different sub-categories: those without children, and those with children.

Where No Children are Present

It is tempting to say that the partners themselves in "non-traditional households" can make no just claims on society at all, *qua partners*. More specifically, however, I would say that unmarried partnerships *without children* (category 4 in my typology) deserve no social recognition as partnerships. For example, as a matter of strict justice, should "spousal" rights to make end-of-life decisions be applied to domestic partners (heterosexual or homosexual)? I think that spousal rights *qua spousal rights* should not be conferred on them, but that effectively equivalent rights could be extended to them in some other form, e.g., there is no reason why the law cannot permit a person to confer on someone other than a spouse or relative the power to make end-of-life decisions. It might even be prudent to allow numerous permissions of this sort, if this reduces the pressure for formal recognition of improper partnerships as legitimate ones, such as gay marriage. At the same time, though, this would have to be balanced against the possibility that such permissions, rather than serving as an outlet to reduce such pressure, might be steps that encourage further movement toward such recognition. In any case, recognition of the rights of individuals as such – not the recognition of the illicit partnership – would be legitimate, in principle, and whether to grant them would be a prudential question.

Where Children are Present

Matters are much more complicated, I think, in non-traditional households that have engendered children of their own (category 3 in my typology). First, *children* of not-really-married partners (domestic partners, remarried divorced Catholics) may have just claims on society, and their best interests may include social recognition of their parents as parents. These just claims might be viewed as deriving not from the improper partnership per se, but from the best interests of the children.

But, secondly, do parents, as parents – even if they are in objectively immoral partnerships or living arrangements – have any rights of their own in regard to their children (i.e., rights that are not simply implications of the best interests of the children, even if we think the children's interests are the predominant consideration)?

We could start by recognizing that, as parents, they at least would still have strong natural duties to their children in such situations that derive simply from the fact of parenthood. Such duties normally involve not only physical or financial resources, but also personal commitment and affection and the direction of the children's education. This would suggest that these parents might have the ordinary parental rights that are essential to facilitate those duties.

And yet I think there are circumstances in which the state might legitimately prevent all contact between a biological father and his child. I am thinking of the sort of situation involved in the Supreme Court case of *Michael H. v. Gerald D.* (1989), which involved a constitutional challenge to a California statute providing that a child born to a woman residing with her husband is presumed to be the child of that husband.[4] California (and the Supreme Court) upheld the law, vindicating the husband's rights in this case and refusing to grant a demand for visitation rights by the man who, through an adulterous affair with the mother, was the actual father of the child (according to a 98% certain paternity test), and with whom the mother had lived off and on for several years after the birth of the child, before she moved back in with her husband. (And the courts rejected the demand, in spite of the fact that the daughter herself supported it.)

It seems to me that the California law was a quite legitimate one. The granting of legal rights based on biological fatherhood in this kind of case would significantly undermine or disrupt the unity and stability of the home based on the valid marriage. I don't say that California could not have provided differently. A case could have been made for visitation rights in the circumstances of this case, based on the fact that the child had lived with the mother and actual father for at least three years, and presumably this had created a bond between father and daughter (confirmed by the daughter's support of the father's demand for visitation rights) that might legitimately bear on what the actual best interests of the child were.[5] But, in any event, I don't think there was a legitimate demand for paternal rights in the case *as a matter of strict justice.* Considerations of family unity and stability could plausibly be considered to trump biological paternity, as a matter of general state policy.

Other strange combinations of circumstances might contribute to complexity here. What if the child in *Michael H.* had been conceived and born *before* the mother's marriage to Gerald D.? It might be said that his paternal rights could still be extinguished by the subsequent marriage of the mother, because he had not formalized his paternity by marrying the mother of the child (and perhaps a flat refusal to marry the mother might sometimes justify that loss of rights – though one could imagine sound as well as unsound reasons for the refusal). But what if he had been willing to marry, but the mother had refused (and especially if she had refused on grounds that might raise questions about her superior fitness to raise the child)?

Given these complexities, I cannot imagine how these issues can typically be resolved by recourse to arguments about what strict justice demands. Justice might rule out some considerations, but within those limits I suspect that a wide range of legitimate prudential judgments could – and would have to – be made.

Just Demands:
Provision of Social Resources to "Incomplete Families"

One form of just demand of traditional households that should, it might be argued, be extended to non-traditional households is access to basic necessities of life (food, clothing, shelter, medical care, education).[6] But I do think this raises some complicated issues. Is it a matter of strict justice, for example, that government provide subsidies for such resources to mothers of illegitimate children? Without such resources, it might be said, the well-being of the children in those families – who are innocent of any wrongdoing themselves –

may be seriously jeopardized, and the obligation of the political community to foster the well-being of such children would make the failure to guarantee such resources unjust.

On the other side, it might be said that the common good is harmed if the political community, in effect – even if unintentionally – provides an incentive to have illegitimate children. Moreover, one might have doubts about a policy which makes it possible for unmarried women to "extort" resources from the political community by having illegitimate children.

Concerns such as these help to explain state refusal to provide additional welfare for more than a certain number of illegitimate children, a policy upheld by the U.S. Supreme Court in *Dandridge v. Williams* (1970). But, someone might ask, is this not simply the reverse case of the state threatening to harm (by its failure to act) future innocent children – unjustly – as a way of deterring actions by their parents? Would it be legitimate, or even more just, to consider that an unmarried woman who persisted in having child after child without the means to support them might have demonstrated sufficient irresponsibility to justify the state taking away her children and placing them in the custody of someone more responsible (if such a family or person is available) – even given the importance parental rights should have?

But termination of parental rights is itself fraught with serious difficulties, first, because such determinations are often very difficult to make,[7] and second, because alternative child custody arrangements often have their own very serious drawbacks.

The question of appropriate social support for incomplete families is further complicated by factors such as the relative merits of spending limited public funds in different ways: the tensions among different public obligations and priorities.

Having discussed these complications, however, we still must come back to the important obligation of those who have charge of the common good to foster the well-being of children in these incomplete families. This will perhaps lead us to focus our efforts on evaluating the various strengths and weaknesses, benefits and costs, of different ways of providing social supports. In particular, I think it should induce us to think of ways that tie the provision of services to various forms of education and training, especially moral education, that try to deal with the roots of these problems and not just the symptoms. One way to accomplish this would be to encourage and promote faith-based programs of social services and moral uplift, which can often attack the roots of social problems much more effectively than direct government programs.

There are, then, in this area genuine "just demands" of "non-traditional households." But decisions about the best ways to meet these demands will be difficult and complex.

Conclusion

Both of the previous discussions – relative to recognition of parental rights and legitimate demands on socially-provided resources – seem to me to be good examples of the fact that, according to natural law theory, the more distant conclusions derived from natural law principles are not always so well known and are subject to more exceptions.

Moreover, as a practical matter, it is overwhelmingly likely that we will have to face these questions, not in a society that generally adheres to natural law principles regarding family life (that is, one that has swung back from the current, degenerating state of our mores), but in one that steadfastly rejects them (as in the cases of divorce and remarriage, contraception, *in-vitro* fertilization, and legal toleration or protection of extra-marital sex).

In such circumstances, I think that decisions about what the just demands of non-traditional households are, and how they are to be met, will receive only a rather general guidance from moral principles, and will typically involve highly contingent and complex judgments. For sound approaches to deciding these questions, the musings of moral theologians and political theorists will provide only a very general framework, within which the real concrete decisions will be made, based on the knowledge, experience, familiarity with particular circumstances, and sound judgment of practitioners – themselves well-formed in moral principles – in various aspects of social and family life.

Christopher Wolfe is a professor political science at Marquette University. His areas of research and teaching include constitutional law (in which he authored the notable book *The Rise of Modern Judicial Review* (Basic Books, 1986) and religion, morality, and politics (including edited books on the family and homosexuality). Dr. Wolfe is the founder and president of the American Public Philosophy Institute, composed of a group of scholars from various disciplines who seek to bring natural law theory to bear on contemporary scholarly and public issues. He is currently working on a project entitled "natural law liberalism." Dr. Wolfe is married to Ann McGowan Wolfe, and they have been blessed with ten children and three grandchildren.

Notes

1   Bill May has surveyed various types of such households: single-parent households formed due to divorce or desertion; single-parent households due to illegitimate births; unmarried heterosexual partners, with or without children; same-sex partnerships, sometimes with children. The main omission in this list is two-parent households in which at least one of the spouses had a previous valid marriage (which technically could be part of the "unmarried heterosexual partners," if "unmarried" is understood as "not married to each other."

As Bill indicated, the first category (single-parent families due especially to divorce) is the largest, though I would add that, due to the dramatic expansion of births to unmarried women, the difference between the first two categories has narrowed significantly. In 1960, there were over ten times as many single-female-headed households due to divorce and separation as those due to illegitimacy (50.2%, compared to 4.4%), while in 1992 there were about twice as many (60.4%, as opposed to 30.6%). Other interesting data on change during the same period include the following: 1) the percentage of single-female-parent families headed by widows plunged from 32% to 5.8%; and 2) the total number of such families went from 1.89 million to 7.04 million. And by 1992, one-fifth of single-parent families were father-child families (although these families accounted for only 3% of children living in single-parent households). See Suzanne M. Bianchi, "The Changing Demographic and Socioeconomic Characteristics of Single Parent Families," in *Single-Parent Families: Diversity, Myths, and Realities*, eds. S. Hanson, M. Heims, D. Julian, and M. Sussman (New York: Haworth Press, 1995).

2   I experienced similar difficulties in my attempts to characterize the purpose of the American Public Philosophy Institute in the discussions that led to its establishment in 1989. At that time, I settled on a description that focuses on advancing natural law views, but experience has indicated some of the limitations of that approach.

3   These families are complete with respect to the essential basic requirements to form a true family. No human family is ever "complete" or "perfect" in the full sense of that term, of course.

4   There were some limited ways of overcoming this presumption, but the California courts held that those circumstances did not exist in this case.

5   It would certainly differentiate the case from a case of purely biological paternity, such as that involved in artificial insemination – a situation that may become more common with the desire of lesbians to have children, in what are already sometimes legally ratified partnerships, and may soon be legally treated as marriages.

6   In this section, I will take as given the Church's teaching on the rights of people to food, clothing, shelter, medical care, education, and other necessities, and the duty of those who have charge of the common good to ensure that such rights are vindicated to the extent possible. I want to emphasize, however (along with Bill May), that these rights and this duty do not necessarily require "government programs" providing such necessities. There are various ways in which they can be provided, and the fundamental principle of subsidiarity dictates a preference for provision by families, voluntary associations, and lower levels of community, where they are able to fulfill this function adequately.

7   The difficulties of divorced and deserted mothers are well-known. See Lenore Weitzman. But the shortcomings of family court determinations can also be seen in mounting anecdotal evidence that sometimes fathers can be the unfairly treated party. For example, the laudable desire of society to ensure that fathers who engender children provide support for them, and the preference often given to mothers in family courts, sometimes results in women being able to manipulate the system very effectively and unjustly against the fathers of their children, obtaining court orders that cut off their rights to see their children and impose draconian child support obligations. Judges are not always in a position to ascertain the truth of competing allegations in such cases.

MAGISTERIAL TEACHING CONCERNING "JUST DEMANDS" AND "NON-TRADITIONAL HOUSEHOLDS"

William E. May

I believe that, as a moral theologian, I can contribute to this panel by calling attention to some important teachings of the magisterium relevant to this issue and showing how they might be of help. Before looking at these teachings, however, I want first to *exclude* an "*unjust* demand" and second to *identify* different kinds of "non-traditional households."

1. AN UNJUST DEMAND

The demand to recognize "domestic partnership" relationships, whether heterosexual or homosexual, as "marriages," or equal in dignity to marriage, is *not* a just demand; and, indeed, justice requires the firm rejection of this claim.[1]

2. KINDS OF "NON-TRADITIONAL" HOUSEHOLDS

There is a wide variety of such households. Without attempting to be exhaustive, I identify the following as the more significant for our consideration: (1) "single parent" households with children, usually headed by a woman, caused when a husband/father (or less frequently wife/mother) abandons spouse and children;[2] (2) "single parent" households with children, usually headed by a woman who has never been married and may at times not even know who the father(s) of her children may be; (3) "domestic partners" or "live-in" heterosexual lovers, some with children, others without; (4) "same-sex" couples, more frequently women than men, rarely with children but some with children either begotten in former heterosexual unions or generated through new reproductive techniques; (5) "households" formed by persons of the same sex, but not for the purpose of sexual congress but rather for economic reasons and mutual friendship, e.g., a household formed by two widows or widowers who are friends and have no desire for sexual union, but who wish to share a common life and help one another economically, or by a daughter and her widowed mother or spinster aunt.[3] Type (1) is statistically the most predominant in our culture today; type (2), although found among various ethnic groups, is more commonly found in the black community.[4]

3. RELEVANT MAGISTERIAL TEACHING
   A) Pope John Paul II, *Familiaris Consortio* (November 22, 1982).

In numbers 79–84 John Paul II considers the following "irregular situations": (a) trial marriages, (b) *de facto* free unions; (c) Catholics in civil marriages; (d) separated or divorced persons who have not remarried; and (e) Catholics who have remarried after divorce. Although Catholics in civil marriages (c) and Catholics who have remarried after divorce (e) pose serious pastoral challenges, I do not consider them among the "non-traditional" households with which we are concerned here, insofar as these are families or households rooted in persons who are recognized by civil law as husbands and wives. However, those involved in trial marriages (a) and in *de facto* free unions (b) are equivalent to the heterosexual "domestic partners" and "live-in lovers" identified as (3) above. The separated and divorced Catholics who have not remarried (d) can be included in the "single parent" households with children which I identified as (1) above, although, as noted already, Wolfe would *not* call these "non-traditional *households*" but rather "wounded *families*."

With respect to those involved in trial marriages (a) and in *de facto* free unions (b), the pope has two principal concerns. The first is to refuse any recognition of them as valid marriages (=my excluding the unjust demand above). The second is to discover ways of preventing such unions. Here, in speaking of *de facto* free unions, John Paul II proposes that we can help *prevent them by educating people to the truth of marriage, and also by removing difficult economic and/or cultural obstacles that at times almost force some people into such unions rather than marriage.* I consider this aspect of his teaching in *Familiaris Consortio* quite relevant to our problem.

B) *Congregation for the Doctrine of the Faith,* Considerations regarding Proposals to Give Legal Recognition to Unions between Homosexual Persons *(June 3, 2003).*

This document is chiefly concerned with giving reasons why persons of the same sex cannot marry. It likewise insists that civil authorities must not allow children to be adopted by persons in such unions, declaring that to do so "would actually mean doing violence to these children." In a passage quite relevant to meeting the *just demands* of same-sex couples, which I identified as (4) above, the Congregation had this to say:

> Nor is the argument valid according to which legal recognition of homosexual unions is necessary to avoid situations in which cohabiting homosexual persons, simply because they live together, might be deprived of real recognition of their rights as persons and citizens. *In reality, they can always make use of the provisions of law…to protect their rights in matters of common interest.* It would be gravely unjust to sacrifice the common good and just laws on the family *in order to protect personal goods that can and must be guaranteed in ways that do not harm the body of society* (n. 9).

C) *Charter for the Rights of the Family* (October 22, 1983).

In my opinion, the following teachings set forth in this document are most relevant for our problem: (1) "All children, *whether born in or out of wedlock,* enjoy the same right to social protection, with a view to their integral personal development" (Article 4e); (2) "Since they have conferred life on them, parents have the original, primary and inalienable right to educate them," and to do so in conformity with their moral and religious convictions, along with the right to choose schools and other means necessary to do so, and this requires public authorities to ensure that public subsidies are so allocated that "parents are fully free to exercise this right without incurring unjust burdens" (Article 5); (3) "Divorce attacks the very institution of marriage and of the family" (Article 6b); (4) "Families have the right to measures in the social domain which take into account their needs, especially in the event of the premature death of one or both of the parents, of the abandonment of one of the spouses, of accident, or sickness or invalidity, in the case of unemployment, or whenever the family has to bear extra burdens on behalf of its members…" (*Ibid*);

(5) "The work of the mother in the home must be recognized and respected because of its value for the family and for society" (Article 10b; see also *Familiaris Consortio,* no. 23).

4. HOW MIGHT THESE TEACHINGS BE OF HELP IN MEETING THE "JUST DEMANDS" OF "NON-TRADITIONAL HOUSEHOLDS"?

These teachings are most helpful, in my opinion, in the following ways. First of all, if civil society were to take seriously its obligation to promote the dignity of marriage and to recognize it as the rock on which the family is built, it must take steps to discourage divorce and in this way help prevent the formation of "single parent" households with children (=Wolfe's "wounded families"), statistically the most numerous of "non-traditional households," and also to prevent the formation of households formed by "domestic partners" and "live-in" lovers, some of which arise simply because, as John Paul II noted, some persons are *almost forced* into *de facto* free unions because marriage is made so onerous, economically or culturally.

Second, if society recognized, as it ought, the inestimable contribution that mothers make to society by caring for their small children at home, it would meet many of the demands justly made by "single parent" households, whether caused by abandonment of a spouse or by so-called free-love unions.

Third, if society adequately recognized parental rights and obligations regarding the education of their children, whether born in or out of wedlock, this would help meet many of the other just demands of both "single parent" households and of households formed by heterosexual "domestic partners."

Fourth, if civil society provided adequate means whereby persons who are homosexually oriented could secure recognition of their rights *as persons and citizens*, this would meet the just demands of same-sex couples and, at the same time, justly protect the dignity of marriage and the family by refusing to legalize such unions or recognize them as marriages, or as equal in dignity to marriage. As Wolfe (see his contribution to this discussion) rightly says, such households, along with non-traditional households formed by heterosexual "free unions" without children, should *not* have spousal rights, *qua spousal*; they should not be given them, but, rather, "effectively equivalent rights could be extended to them in some other form; e.g., there is no reason why the law cannot permit a person to confer on someone other than a spouse or relative the power to make end-of-life decisions" – or, I would add, to confer on someone other than a spouse or relative rights of inheritance, etc.

This issue was greatly clarified during the final meeting of the members of the Fellowship on Sunday, September 28, 2003. Our president, Gerard V. Bradley, noted in some final remarks (after a discussion of current movements to prevent recognition of same-sex unions as marriages, or as morally equivalent to marriage) that it would be morally upright to concede to households formed by individuals who are indeed of the same sex (male or female) various civil rights *not* because of any *sexual relationship* but rather on the basis that they form a valid kind of economic/social household built on friendship, e.g., two widows or widowers, a son and his elderly widowed mother, a daughter and her elderly I widowed mother, etc., who choose to live together for purposes of friendship and of economy.[5] In the discussion, I myself noted that an arrangement of this kind to meet the *just* demands of non-traditional, i.e., non-familial, households, had been arranged in 1997 in San Francisco, at a time when some sought to coerce the archdiocese of San Francisco into granting such civil rights to households rooted in the *sexual orientation and sexual relationship* of its members, i.e., same sex couples united in their desire to engage in acts of sodomy. This effort was successfully thwarted by recognizing the *just* civil demands of households formed by persons of the same sex for purposes of economic stability and common friendship and *not* for the purpose of engaging in non-marital sexual acts.[6]

It is, finally, most important to recognize the principle of subsidiarity. This means that the responsibility to meet the *just demands* of non-traditional households does *not fall* exclusively on the central government, e.g., in the U.S., the federal government, but also on state and local governments *and on* other social units, e.g., "faith-based" communities, the local church (diocese or archdiocese), neighborhood parish, etc. These various human communities can in many ways be of tremendous help in meeting the just demands of non-traditional households. The welfare state, in my opinion, is definitely not the answer.

William E. May has been, since 1991, the Michael J. McGivney Professor of Moral Theology at the John Paul II Institute for studies on Marriage and the Family located at the Catholic University of America in Washington, D.C. From 1971 through 1991, he taught moral theology at CUA itself. He is the author of more than a dozen books, the translator and/or editor of several, and the author of more than 200 articles and essays. His books include such notable titles as *An Introduction to Moral Theology* and *Marriage: The Rock on which the Family Is Built.*

By appointment of Pope John Paul II, Professor May served on the Church's International Theological Commission from 1986 through 1997. He received the *Pro Ecclesia et Pontifice* Medal in 1991. In September, 2003, the Holy Father appointed Professor May a consultor to the Congregation for the Clergy. A past president of the Fellowship of Catholic Scholars, he received the Fellowship's Cardinal Wright Award in 1980.

Professor May is married to Patricia Keck May. They are the parents of seven children and the grandparents of twelve.

Notes

1   On this see. John Finnis, "Law, Morality, and 'Sexual Orientation,'" *Notre Dame Law Review* 69.5 (1994) 1049–1076; Robert George and Gerard Bradley, "Marriage and the Liberal Imagination," *Georgetown Law Journal* 84 (1995) 301–320.

2   In his excellent contribution to this discussion, Christopher Wolfe uses the expression "wounded but genuine families" to designate households of this kind, which I here identify as one kind of a "non-traditional" household. Unfortunately, Wolfe's paper was not available prior to the meeting at which the panel discussion took place; hence, I had no opportunity until after the meeting to refer to his helpful presentation.

3   I had not included this type of "non-traditional" household in the draft of this paper written and presented at the Fellowship meeting in September, 2003. However, discussions during the convention and particularly in the final session chaired by Gerard V. Bradley and William Saunders, specifically remarks made by Bradley in response to questions, made it very evident that this is one kind of "non-traditional household" with just demands, and that it can even include gays and lesbians, *not as persons living together for the purposes of congress, but for economic reasons and friendship.*

4   Wolfe notes in his paper that non-traditional households headed by a single parent, usually a woman, resulting from divorce or separation, is indeed still the largest category. However, he goes on to point out that the second kind of non-traditional household that I identify, i.e., households headed by a single parent, usually a woman, whose children were

born out of wedlock, dramatically increased in the final decades of the 20th century. On fatherlessness in black American families, see the fine STD study of Emmanuel Afunogo: *Fatherlessness in African-American Families* (Washington, D.C.: Pope John Paul II Institute for Studies on Marriage and Family, 1997).

5   See above, the 5th kind of "non-traditional" household identified, and footnote no. 3.

6   On this, see http://www.cwnews.com/news/viewstory.cfm?rec-num=4248.

LEGALIZED ABORTION

RECENT DEVELOPMENTS IN THE ABORTION DEBATE
Patrick Lee

The abortion debate has raged in earnest for the last thirty or thirty-five years. In any debate, there are twists and turns and sometimes unforeseen shifts. I believe the philosophical debate on abortion has undergone some significant shifts in the last seven or eight years. As I view the terrain, it seems to me that there have been six significant developments in the debate in the last 7 or 8 years. I will just briefly mention the first four developments, but I would like to discuss in some detail the last two, since these consist of new arguments or new emphases in arguments.

I. DEVELOPMENTS 1–4

First, there have been significant improvements in sonograms in the last five to seven years. This has clearly helped people to see more clearly the reality of pre-natal human life.

Secondly, there has been a series of significant advances made in embryology in the last five to seven years. I will not go into those in detail here, but suffice it to say that recent embryology has shown clearly that the human embryo from day one on, from the two-cell stage onward, is not a mere clump of cells, but is a distinct, whole human organism, actively developing himself or herself toward full maturity. From day one on, recent embryology has shown, there is complex, internally coordinated self-development.[1]

The third development in the abortion argument was the political debate about partial-birth abortion. This event made it clear to many Americans that many on the pro-abortion side are quite willing to condone what is obviously morally indistinguishable from infanticide. Partly due to this event, no doubt, in the last few years the percentage of Americans who say they think abortion should be legal in all circumstances has significantly decreased.

The fourth recent development in abortion argument emerged because of the political debate concerning stem cell research and cloning. In the last three years the debates about stem cell research and then cloning have become hot political issues. Because of this, the abortion debate has focused, in some quarters, on the strictly biological or embryological question: Is the human embryo a whole human being? I think that even six or seven years ago most pro-abortion academics shied away from the embryology and concentrated their arguments on other points. But this new development is very interesting. As I mentioned, on the political scene before stem cell research and cloning became the central life issues, the heated topic was partial-birth abortion. The pro-abortion people, I think, were made intensely uncomfortable by that issue. It was an issue on which it was difficult, logically and politically, for them to back down on, and yet it was an issue on which they were defending what is clearly a grisly, brutal, and murderous act. So, when the debate about using human embryos for stem cell research emerged, they thought they saw their opening, a way to move off of the ropes, so to speak, where they had found themselves in the partial-birth abortion debate.

But I think this has actually been a tactical error on their part. For the first time in thirty or more years, proponents of the morality of abortion have become willing to discuss in some detail the basic facts of genetics and embryology. But this is a very big mistake on their part. For the more that people look at the real facts, the more likely they are to come around to the pro-life position.[2] And it seems to me – though I may not be totally unbiased about this – that the pro-abortion side has been clobbered in debates about these issues.

II. DEVELOPMENT 5

The fifth development in the abortion debate is a new boldness in claiming that personhood, or whatever it is that makes us valuable as subjects of rights, is *an acquired characteristic*. Pro-abortionists used to argue very frequently that what is killed in abortion is not a person because he or she does not yet have self-consciousness, but they would usually deny that you and I once were human embryos and human fetuses. In effect, they were taking the position that you and I are different entities than the human organism or the human animal. That position, however, has been difficult to maintain. In effect, they were identifying the self with a consciousness that *has* or *inhabits* a body, and it is difficult to maintain that human beings are not identical with living, moving, sensing, and, when mature, rational bodily entities. So, recently pro-abortionists will often admit that you and I were once human embryos, but will now openly argue that what makes someone valuable as a subject of rights is some characteristic, some ability, that is *acquired after birth*.

To clarify this point, let me summarize the basic pro-life argument in just four steps:

1. What is intrinsically valuable is what we are (that is, we are intrinsically valuable in virtue of what we are).

2. What we are are human physical organisms.

3. Human physical organisms come to be at conception.

4. Therefore, what is intrinsically valuable comes to be at conception.

Thirty years ago pro-abortionists, I think, more frequently denied #2 here. However, in the last seven or eight years they have begun more frequently to deny step #1. That is, they used to deny (most frequently) that you and I ever were embryos or fetuses. But now more often they admit that you and I once were embryos and then fetuses, but these writers now say that what makes someone valuable as a subject of rights is an acquired characteristic.

Those who advance this argument concede that you and I once were human embryos, and so proponents of this view do not identify the self or the person with a non-physical consciousness. What they say is that being a person is an accidental attribute. That is, it is similar to being a basketball player or being a musician. Just as you come to be at one time, but become a basketball player or a musician only much later, so, they say, you and I came to be when these physical organisms came to be, but we became persons only at some time later.[3] So, they admit that the thing referred to by "I" or "you" is a physical organism. What they deny is that this entity was intrinsically valuable at every stage of its duration. Thus they openly claim – unlike most defenders of abortion ten or fifteen years ago – that what makes someone intrinsically valuable, in the sense of being a subject of rights, is an acquired characteristic.

Judith Thomson argues for this position by comparing the right to life with the right to vote. Thomson argues: "If children are allowed to develop normally they will have a right to vote; that does not show that they now have a right to vote." So, according to this position, it is true that we once were embryos and fetuses, but they argue that we came to be at one point, but then acquired the right to life only much later during our life.[4]

We can begin to see what is wrong with this position by considering Thomson's comparison of the right to life with the right to vote. Thomson fails to advert to the fact that some rights vary with respect to place, circumstances, talents and other factors, while other rights do not. We recognize that one's right to life does not vary with place, as does one's right to vote. One may have the right to vote in Switzerland, but not in Mexico. Moreover, some rights and entitlements accrue to individuals only at certain times, or in certain places or situations, and others do not. But to have the right to life is to have *moral status*; to have the right to life, in other words, is to be the sort of entity that can have rights or entitlements to begin with. And so it is to be expected that *this* right would differ in some fundamental ways from other rights, such as a right to vote.

In particular, it is reasonable to suppose (and I will give reasons for this in a moment) that having moral status at all, as opposed to having a right to perform a specific action in a specific situation, should be based on the *type of thing* (or substantial entity) something is. And so, just as one's right to life does not come and go with one's location or situation, so it does not accrue to someone in virtue of an acquired (i.e., accidental) property, capacity, skill, or disposition. Rather, this right belongs to a person, a substantial entity, at all times that he or she exists, not just during certain stages of his or her existence, or in certain circumstances, or in virtue of additional, accidental attributes.

The pro-life position is that human beings are intrinsically valuable, as subjects of rights, in virtue of *what* we are, not in virtue of some attribute that we acquire some time after we have come to be. Obviously, defenders of abortion cannot maintain that the accidental attribute required to make one a person (in addition to being a human individual) is an *actual* behavior. They, of course, do not wish to exclude from personhood people who are asleep or in reversible comas. So, the additional attribute will have to be a capacity or potentiality of some sort. Thus, they will have to say that sleeping or reversibly comatose human beings will be persons because they have the potentiality or capacity for higher mental functions.

But human embryos and fetuses also possess, albeit in radical form, a capacity or potentiality for such mental functions; human beings possess this radical capacity in virtue of the kind of entity they are, and possess it by coming into being as that kind of entity (viz., a being with a rational nature). Human embryos and fetuses cannot of course *immediately* exercise these capacities. Still, they are related to these capacities differently than, say, a canine or feline embryo is. They are the kind of being – a natural kind, members of a biological species – which, if not prevented by extrinsic causes, in due course develop the immediately exercisable capacity for mental functions. (Of course, the capacities in question become immediately exercisable only some months or years after the child's birth.) Each human being comes into existence possessing the internal resources and active disposition to develop the immediately exercisable capacity for higher mental functions. Only the adverse effects on them of other causes will prevent this development.

So, we must distinguish two sorts of capacity or potentiality for higher mental functions that a substantial entity might possess: first, an immediately (or nearly immediately) exercisable capacity to engage in higher mental functions; second, a basic, natural capacity to develop oneself to the point where one does perform such actions. But on what basis can one require, as do proponents of the position we are now considering, the first sort of potentiality – which is an accidental attribute – and not the second? There are three decisive reasons against supposing that the first sort of potentiality is required to qualify an entity as a bearer of the right to life.

First, the developing human being does not reach a level of maturity at which he or she performs a type of mental act that other animals do not perform – even animals such as dogs and cats – until at least several months after birth. A six-week old baby lacks the *immediately (or nearly immediately) exercisable* capacity to perform characteristically human mental functions. So, if full moral respect were due only to those who possess a nearly immediately exercisable capacity for characteristically human mental functions, it would follow that six-week old infants do not deserve full moral respect. If abortion were morally acceptable on the grounds that the human embryo or fetus lacks such a capacity for characteristically human mental functions, then one would be logically committed to the view that, subject to parental approval, human infants could be disposed of as well.

Secondly, the difference between these two types of capacity is merely a difference between stages along a continuum. The proximate, or nearly immediately exercisable, capacity for mental functions is only the development of an underlying potentiality that the human being possesses all along simply by virtue of the kind of entity it is. The capacities for reasoning, deliberating, and making choices are gradually developed, or brought towards maturation, through gestation, childhood, adolescence, and so on. But the difference between a being that deserves full moral respect and a being that does not (and can therefore legitimately be disposed of as a means of benefiting others) cannot consist only in the fact that, while both have some particular feature, one has more of it than the other. A mere *quantitative* difference (having more or less of the same feature, such as *the development* of a basic natural capacity) cannot by itself be a justificatory basis for treating different entities in *radically* different ways. Between the ovum and the approaching thousands of sperm, on the one hand, and the embryonic human being, on the other hand, there is a clear difference in kind. But between the embryonic human being and that same human being at any later stage of its maturation, there is only a difference in degree.

Note that there *is* a fundamental difference (as shown above) between the gametes (the sperm and the ovum) on the one hand, and the human embryo and fetus, on the other. When a human being comes to be, then a substantial entity that is identical with the entity that will later reason, make free choices, and so on, begins to exist. So, those who propose an accidental characteristic as qualifying an entity as a bearer of the right to life (or as a "person" or being with "moral worth") are *ignoring* a radical difference among groups of beings, and instead fastening onto a mere quantitative difference as the basis for treating different groups in radically different ways. In other words, there are beings a, b, c, d, e, etc. And between a's and b's on the one hand and c's, d's and e's on the other hand, there is a *fundamental difference*, a difference in kind not just in degree. But proponents of the position that being a person is an accidental characteristic ignore that difference and pick out a mere difference in degree between, say, d's and e's, and make that the basis for radically different types of treatment. That violates the most basic canon of justice: similars should be treated similarly.

Thirdly, being a whole human being (whether immature or not) is an either/or matter – a thing either is or is not a whole human being. But the acquired qualities that could be proposed as criteria for personhood come in varying and continuous degrees: there is an infinite number of degrees of the *development of* the basic natural capacities for self-consciousness, intelligence, or rationality. So, if human beings were worthy of full moral respect (as subjects of rights) only because of such qualities, and not in virtue of the kind of being they are, then, since such qualities come in varying degrees, no account could be given of why basic rights are not possessed by human beings in varying degrees. The proposition that all human beings are created equal would be relegated to the status of a superstition. For example, if developed self-consciousness bestowed rights, then, since some people are more self-conscious than others (that is, have developed that capacity to a greater extent than others), some people would be greater in dignity than others, and the rights of the superiors would trump those of the inferiors where the interests of the superiors could be advanced at the cost of the inferiors. This conclusion would follow no matter which of the acquired qualities generally proposed as qualifying some human beings (or human beings at some stages) for full respect were selected. Clearly, developed self-consciousness, or desires, or so on, are arbitrarily selected degrees of development of capacities that all human beings possess in (at least) radical form from the coming into existence of the human being until his or her death. So, it cannot be the case that *some* human beings, *and not others*, possess the special kind of value that qualifies an entity as having a basic right to life, by virtue of a certain degree of development. Rather, human beings possess that kind of value, and therefore that basic right, *in virtue of what they are* (i.e., in virtue of *the kind of being* they are); and *all* human beings possess intrinsic value as a subject of rights – not just some, and certainly not just those who have advanced sufficiently along the developmental path as to be able immediately (or almost immediately) to exercise their capacities for characteristically human mental functions.[5]

Since human beings are intrinsically valuable as subjects of rights in virtue of what they are, it follows that they have are intrinsically valuable, and have the rights that that entails, from the point at which they come into being – and that (as embryology has shown) is at conception.

In sum, human beings are valuable (as subjects of rights) in virtue of what they are. But what they are are human physical organisms. Human physical organisms come to be at conception. Therefore, what is intrinsically valuable (as a subject of rights) comes to be at conception.

DEVELOPMENT 6:
REFINEMENTS OF JUDITH THOMSON'S EARLY ARGUMENT IN DEFENSE OF ABORTION

The sixth development in the abortion debate (and the second one that I wish to discuss in detail) has emerged from refinements of an argument first presented by Judith Jarvis Thomson in 1971. Following Thomson, some philosophers have attempted to justify abortion by denying (in effect) that all abortions are intentional killing. They have granted (at least for the sake of argument) that an unborn human being has a right to life, but have then argued that this right does not entail that the child *in the womb* is morally entitled to the use of the mother's body for life support. In effect, their argument is that, at least in many cases, abortion is not a case of intentionally killing the child, but is rather a choice not to provide the child with assistance – that is, that abortion is a choice to expel (or "evict") the child from the womb, despite the likelihood or certainty that expulsion (or "eviction") will result in the child's death (Thomson, 1971; McDonagh, 1996, Little, 1999).

Various analogies have been proposed by people making this argument. The mother's gestating a child has been compared to allowing someone the use of one's kidneys or even to donating an organ. We are not *required* (morally, or as a matter of law) to allow someone to use our kidneys, or to donate organs to others, even when they would die without this assistance (and we could survive in good health despite rendering it). Analogously, the argument continues, a woman is not morally required to allow the fetus the use of her body. I will call this "the bodily rights argument."

It may objected that a woman has a special responsibility to the child she is carrying, whereas in the cases of withholding assistance to which abortion is compared there is no such special responsibility. Proponents of the bodily rights argument have replied, however, that the mother has not voluntarily assumed responsibility for the child, nor has she consented to a personal relationship with the child, and we have strong responsibilities to others only if we have voluntarily assumed such responsibilities (Thomson, 1971); or only if one has consented to a personal relationship which generates such responsibilities (Little, 1999). True – say proponents of this argument – the mother may have voluntarily performed an act which she knew may result in a child's conception, but that is distinct from consenting to gestate the child if a child is conceived. And so (according to this position) it is not until the woman consents to pregnancy, or perhaps not until the parents consent to care for the child by taking the baby home from the hospital or birthing center, that the full duties of parenthood accrue to the mother (and perhaps the father).

In replying to this argument I wish to make several points. It seems to me true that in some few cases abortion is not intentional killing, but a choice to expel the child, the child's death being an unintended, albeit foreseen and (rightly or wrongly) accepted, side effect. However, these constitute a small minority of abortions. In the vast majority of cases, the death of the child *in the womb* is precisely the object of the abortion. In most cases the end sought is to avoid being a parent; but abortion brings that about only by bringing about the death of the child. Indeed, the attempted abortion would be considered by the woman requesting it and the abortionist performing it to have been *unsuccessful* if the child survives. So, in most cases abortion *is* intentional killing. And so, even if the bodily rights argument succeeded, it would justify only a small percentage of abortions.

Still, in some few cases abortion is chosen as a means precisely toward ending the condition of pregnancy, and the means to bring that about is the removal of the child. A pregnant woman may have less or more serious reasons for seeking the termination of this condition, but if that is her objective, then the child's death resulting from his or her expulsion will be a side effect rather than the means chosen. For example, an actress may wish not to be pregnant because the pregnancy will change her figure during a time in which she is filming scenes in which having a slim figure is important; or a woman may dread the discomforts, pains, and difficulties involved in pregnancy. (Of course, in many abortions there may be mixed motives: the parties making the choice may intend both ending the condition of pregnancy and the death of the child.)

Nevertheless, while it is true that in some cases abortion is not intentional killing, it is misleading to describe it simply as choosing not to provide bodily life support. Rather, it is actively expelling the human embryo or fetus from the womb. There is a significant moral difference between *not doing* something that would assist someone, and *doing* something that causes someone harm, even if that harm is an unintended (but foreseen) side effect. It is more difficult morally to justify the latter than it is the former. Abortion is the *act* of extracting the unborn human being from the womb – an extraction that usually rips him or her to pieces or does him or her violence in some other way.

It is true that in some cases causing death as a side effect is morally permissible. For example, in some cases it is morally right to use force to stop a potentially lethal attack on one's family or country, even if one foresees that the force used will also result in the assailant's death. Similarly, there are instances in which it is permissible to perform an act that one knows or believes will, as a side effect, cause the death of a child *in the womb*. For example, if a pregnant woman is discovered to have a cancerous uterus, and this is a proximate danger to the mother's life, it can be morally right to remove the cancerous uterus with the baby in it, even if the child will die as a result. A similar situation can occur in ectopic pregnancies. But in such cases, not only is the child's death a side effect, but the mother's life is in proximate danger. It is worth noting also that in these cases *what is done* (the means) is the correction of a pathology (such as a cancerous uterus, or a ruptured uterine tube). Thus, in such cases, not only the child's death, but also the ending of the pregnancy, are side effects. So, such acts are what traditional casuistry referred to as *indirect or non-intentional*, abortions.

But it also is clear that not every case of causing death as a side effect is morally right. For example, suppose a man's daughter has a serious respiratory disease and the father is told that his continued smoking in her presence will cause her death. It would obviously be immoral for him to continue the smoking. Similarly, if a man works for a steel company in a city with significant levels of air pollution, and his child has a serious respiratory problem making the air pollution a danger to her life, certainly it would be wrong for him to continue living (along with his family) in that city. He should move, we would say, even if that meant he had to resign a prestigious position or make a significant career change.

In both examples, (a.) the parent has a special responsibility to his child, but (b.) the act that would cause the child's death would avoid a harm to the parent but cause a significantly worse harm to his child. And so, although the harm done would be a side effect, in both cases the act that caused the death would be an *unjust* act, and morally wrongful *as such*. The special responsibility of parents to their children requires that they *at least* refrain from performing acts that cause terrible harms to their children in order to avoid significantly lesser harms to themselves.

But (a.) and (b.) also obtain in intentional abortions (that is, those in which the removal of the child is directly sought, rather than the correction of a life-threatening pathology) even those few which are not, strictly speaking, intentional killing. First, the mother has a special responsibility to her child, in virtue of being her biological mother (as does the father in virtue of his paternal relationship). The parental relationship itself – not just the voluntary acceptance of that relationship – gives rise to a special responsibility to a child.

Proponents of the bodily rights argument deny this point. Many claim that one has full parental responsibilities only if one has voluntarily assumed them. And so the child, on this view, has a right to care from his or her mother (including gestation) only if the mother has accepted her pregnancy, or perhaps only if the mother (and/or the father?) has in some way voluntarily begun a deep personal relationship with the child (Little, 1999).

But suppose a mother takes her baby home after giving birth, but the only reason she did not get an abortion was that she could not afford one. Or suppose she lives in a society where abortion is not available (perhaps very few physicians are willing to do the grisly deed). She and her husband take the child home only because they had no alternative. Moreover, suppose that in their society people are not waiting in line to adopt a newborn baby. And so the baby is several days old before anything can be done. If they abandon the baby and the baby is found, she will simply be returned to them. In such a case the parents have not voluntarily assumed responsibility; nor have they consented to a personal relationship with the child. But it would surely be wrong for these parents to abandon their baby in the woods (perhaps the only feasible way of ensuring she is not returned), even though the baby's death would be only a side effect. Clearly, we recognize that parents do have a responsibility to make sacrifices for their children, even if they have not voluntary assumed such responsibilities, or given their consent to the personal relationship with the child.

Moreover, the bodily rights argument implicitly supposes that we have a primordial right to construct a life simply as we please, and that others have claims on us only very minimally or through our consent (either directly or indirectly through our consent to a relationship). On the contrary, we are by nature members of communities. Our moral goodness or character consists to a large extent (though not solely) in contributing to the communities of which we are members. We ought to act for our genuine good or flourishing (I take that as a basic ethical principle), but our flourishing involves being in communion with others. And communion with others of itself entails duties or responsibilities – this is true even if we find ourselves united with others because of a physical or social relationship which precedes our consent. Moreover, the contribution we are morally required to make to others will likely bring each of us some discomfort and pain. This is not to say that we should simply ignore our own good, for the sake of others. Rather, since what I am, who I am, is in part constituted by various relationships with others, not all of which are initiated by my will, my genuine good includes the contributions I make to the relationships in which I participate. Thus, the life we constitute by our free choices should be in large part a life of mutual reciprocity with others.

For example, I may wish to cultivate my talent to write and so I may want to spend hours each day reading and writing. Or I may wish to develop my athletic abilities and so I may want to spend hours every day on the baseball field. But if I am a father of minor children, and have an adequate paying job working (say) in a coal mine, then my clear duty is to keep that job. Similarly, if one's girlfriend finds she is pregnant and one is the father, then one might also be morally required to continue one's work in the mine (or mill, factory, warehouse, etc.).

In other words, I have a duty to do something with my life that contributes to the good of the human community, but that general duty becomes specified by my particular situation. It becomes specified by the connection or closeness to me of those who are in need. We acquire special responsibilities toward people, not only by *consenting* to contracts or relationships with them, but also by having various types of unions with them. So, we have special responsibilities to those people with whom we are closely united. For example, we have special responsibilities to our parents, and brothers and sisters, even though we did not choose them.

The physical unity or continuity of children to their parents is unique. The child is brought into being out of the bodily unity and bodies of the mother and the father. The mother and the father are in a certain sense prolonged or continued in their offspring. So, there is a natural unity of the mother with her child, and a natural unity of the father with his child. Since we have special responsibilities to those with whom we are closely united, it follows that we in fact do have a special responsibility to our children anterior to our having voluntarily assumed such responsibility or consented to the relationship.[6]

The second point is this: in the types of cases we are considering, the harm caused (death) is much worse than the harm avoided (the difficulties in pregnancy). Pregnancy can involve severe impositions, but it is not nearly as bad as death – which is total and irreversible. One need not make light of the burdens of pregnancy to acknowledge that the harm that is death is in a different category altogether.

The burdens of pregnancy include physical difficulties and the pain of labor, and can include significant financial costs, psychological burdens, and interference with autonomy and the pursuit of other important goals (McDonagh, 1996, Ch. 5). These costs are not inconsiderable. Partly for that reason we owe our mothers gratitude for carrying and giving birth to us. However, where pregnancy does not place a woman's life in jeopardy or threaten grave and lasting damage to her physical health, the harm done to other goods is not total. Moreover, most of the harms involved in pregnancy are not irreversible: pregnancy is a nine month task – if the woman and man are not in a good position to raise the child, adoption is a possibility. So the difficulties of pregnancy, considered together, are in a different and lesser category than death. Death is not just worse in degree than the difficulties involved in pregnancy; it is worse in kind.

It has recently been argued, however – by David Boonin and Margaret Little, for example – that pregnancy can involve a unique type of burden. It has been argued that the *intimacy* involved in pregnancy is such that if the woman must remain pregnant without her consent then there is inflicted on her a unique and serious harm. Just

as sex with consent can be a desired experience but sex without consent is a violation of bodily integrity, so (the argument continues)
pregnancy involves such a close physical intertwinement with the
fetus that not to allow abortion is analogous to rape – it involves an
enforced intimacy (see Boonin, 2003, p. 84; Little, 1999, pp.
300–303).

However, this argument is based on a false analogy. Where the
pregnancy is unwanted, the baby's "occupying" the mother's womb
may involve a harm; but the child is committing no injustice against
her. The baby is not forcing himself or herself on the woman, but is
simply growing and developing in a way quite natural to him or her.
The baby is not performing any action that could in any way be construed as aimed at violating the mother.[7] So the comparison with sex
without consent is a false analogy.

Let me mention, also, that some have recently claimed that, by
prohibiting abortion, the state is forcing women to undergo pregnancy, and so that in such circumstances the state would be inflicting this
harm, namely, gestation without consent. However, while it is true
that in some sense being bodily "occupied" when one does not wish
to be *is* a harm, it certainly is *not* true to say that the state – or as I
just explained the child – inflicts such a harm on the mother, in circumstances in which the state prohibits abortion. By prohibiting
abortion the state would only prevent the woman from performing an
act (forcibly detaching the child from her) which would unjustly kill
this developing child, who is an innocent party.

It is true that the fulfillment of the duty of a mother to her child
(during gestation) is unique and in many cases does involve a great
sacrifice. The argument I have presented, however, is that being a
mother *does* generate a special responsibility, and that the sacrifice
morally required of the mother is significantly less burdensome than
the harm that would be done to the child by expelling the child, causing his or her death, to escape that responsibility. The argument I
have presented equally entails responsibilities for the father of the
child. His duty does not involve as direct a bodily relationship with
the child as the mother's, but it may be equally or even more burdensome. In certain circumstances, his obligation to care for the
child (and for the child's mother), and especially his obligation to
provide financial support, may severely limit his freedom and even
require months or, indeed, years, of extremely burdensome physical

labor. Historically many men have rightly seen that their basic responsibility to their family (and country) has entailed risking, and in many cases, losing, their lives. Different people in different circumstances, with different talents, will have different responsibilities. It is no argument against any of these responsibilities to point out their distinctness.

Thus, I have shown, I hope, that the two most recent parries by defenders of abortion are not sound arguments in defense of abortion. First, it is not true to say that only some human beings are intrinsically valuables as subjects of rights in virtue of (an arbitrarily selected) degree of development of a basic capacity which all human beings already possess from their beginning. And second, the burden of carrying the baby, for all its distinctness, is significantly less than the harm the baby would suffer by being killed; the mother and father have a special responsibility to the child; and so intentional abortion (even in the few cases where the baby's death is an unintended but foreseen side effect) is unjust and therefore objectively immoral.

Patrick Lee is a professor of philosophy at the Franciscan University of Steubenville in Steubenville, Ohio. He received his Ph.D. at Marquette University in 1980. Dr. Lee's book, *Abortion and Unborn Human Life* was published in 1996, and he has written frequently for various scholarly journals, including the *American Philosophical Quarterly, Faith and Philosophy, Philosophy, and Bioethics*. He is currently working on a book tentatively entitled *Dualism and Contemporary Ethical Issues*.

Bibliography

Bailey, Ronald, Lee, Patrick, and George, Robert P. (2001) a debate on the Moral Status of Human Embryos in the context of obtaining stem cells for research: on the internet at: http://reason.com/rb/rb080601.shtml.

Beckwith, Francis (2000) *Abortion and the Sanctity of Human Life* (Joplin, MO: College Press).

_____ (1993) *Politically Correct Death: Answering the Arguments for Abortion Rights* (Grand Rapids, MI: Baker).

Boonin, David (2002) *A Defense of Abortion* (New York: Cambridge University Press).

Carlson, Bruce (1994) *Human Embryology and Developmental Biology* (St. Louis: Mosby).

Chappell, T.D.J. (1998) *Understanding Human Goods: A Theory of Ethics* (Edinburgh: Edinburgh University Press).

Dworkin, Ronald (1993) *Life's Dominion: An Argument about Abortion, Euthanasia, and Individual Freedom* (New York: Random House).

Finnis, John (2001) "Abortion and Cloning: Some New Evasions," on the internet at: http://lifeissues.net/writers/fin/fin_01abor-cloneevasions.html.

_____ (1999) "Abortion and Health Care Ethics," in Helga Kuhse and Peter Singer, eds., *Bioethics: An Anthology* (London: Blackwell Publishers), 13–20.

George, Robert (2001) *The Clash of Orthodoxies: Law, Religion, and Morality in Crisis* (Wilmington, DE: ISI Books), especially the Afterword, "We Should Not Kill Human Embryos – For Any Reason."

Gilbert, Scott (2003) *Developmental Biology* 7th edition (Sunderland, MA.: Sinnauer Associates).

Grisez, Germain, "When Do People Begin?" *Proceedings of the American Catholic Philosophical Quarterly*, 63, 1990, 27–47.

Lee, Patrick, *Abortion and Unborn Human Life* (Washington, DC: Catholic University of America Press, 1996).

_____ "The Pro-Life Argument from Substantial Identity: A Defense," *Bioethics*, forthcoming in 2004.

Little, Margaret Olivia, "Abortion, Intimacy, and the Duty to Gestate," *Ethical Theory and Moral Practice* 2 (1999), 295–312.

Marquis, Don, "Why Abortion Is Immoral," *Journal of Philosophy* 86 (1989), 183–202.

McDonagh, Eileen, *Breaking the Abortion Deadlock: From Choice to Consent* (New York: Oxford University Press, 1996).

Moore, Keith, and Persaud, T.V.N. (2003) *The Developing Human, Clinically Oriented Embryology, 7th ed.* (New York: W.B. Saunders).

Muller, Werner A. (1997) *Developmental Biology* (New York: Springer Verlag).

Oderberg, David (2000) *Applied Ethics: a Non-Consequentialist Approach* (New York: Oxford University Press).

O'Rahilly, Ronan, and Mueller, Fabiola (2000) *Human Embryology and Teratology*, 3rd edition (New York: John Wiley & Sons).

Pavlischek, Keith (1993) "Abortion Logic and Paternal Responsibilities: One More Look at Judith Thomson's 'Defense of Abortion'," *Public Affairs Quarterly* 7, pp. 341–361.

The President's Council on Bioethics (2002) *Human Cloning and Human Dignity, The Report of the President's Council on Bioethics* (New York: Public Affairs).

Schwarz, Stephen (1990) *The Moral Question of Abortion* Chicago: Loyola University Press).

Singer, Peter (1993) *Practical Ethics, 2nd ed.* (Cambridge, UK: Cambridge University Press).

Stone, Jim (1987) "Why Potentiality Matters," *Journal of Social Philosophy* 26, pp. 815–830.

Stretton, Dean (2000) "The Argument from Intrinsic Value: A Critique," *Bioethics* 14, pp. 228–239.

_____ (2004) "Essential Properties and the Right to Life: A Response to Lee," *Bioethics*, forthcoming.

Thomson, Judith Jarvis (1971) "A Defense of Abortion," *Philosophy and Public Affairs* 1, pp. 47–66; reprinted, among other places, in Joel Feinberg, ed., *The Problem of Abortion*, 2nd ed. (Belmont, CA: Wadsworth, 1984).

_____ (1998) "Abortion," *Boston Review*, on the internet at: bostonreview.mit.edu/BR20.3/thomson.html.

Tooley, Michael (1983) *Abortion and Infanticide* (New York: Oxford University Press).

Warren, Mary Ann (1984) "On the Moral and Legal Status of Abortion," in Feinberg, *The Problem of Abortion*. 2nd ed. (Belmont, CA: Wadsworth, 1984).

Notes

1   This is treated more fully in Patrick Lee and Robert George, "The Wrong of Abortion," in *A Companion to Applied Ethics* (Cambridge University Press), eds. Christopher Wellman and Rey Frey, forthcoming.

2   On some of the embryological data, see: See, for example: O"Rahilly and Mueller (2000), chapters 3–4;. Muller (1997), Ch. 1–2; Gilbert, (2003), pp. 183–220, 363–390; Moore and Persaud (2003), chapters 1–1–6; Larson (2001), chapters 1–2; Carlson (1994), chapters 2–4.

3   Judith Thomson, "Abortion," *Boston Review*, 1995, which can be obtained on the internet at bostonreview.mit.edu/BR20.3/thomson.html.

See also Ronald Dworkin, *Life's Dominion: An Argument About Abortion, Euthanasia, and Individual Freedom* (Random House: New York, 1993), 22ff.

4   Judith Thomson, *op.cit., n.7, p.194*. The use of the term "fertilized egg" is inaccurate. Once fertilization has occurred, what exists is simply not an egg any longer, but a distinct, actively developing, whole (though new and immature) human organism.

5   In arguing against my article, forthcoming in *Bioethics* (2004), Dean Stretton claims that the basic natural capacity of rationality also comes in degrees, and that therefore the argument we are presenting against the position that moral worth is based on having some accidental character-istic would apply to our position also (Stretton, 2004). But this is to miss the important distinction between having a basic natural capacity (of which there are no degrees, since one either has it or one doesn't), and the *development of that capacity* (of which there are infinite degrees).

6   David Boonin claims, in reply to this argument (in an earlier and less developed form, presented in my 1996 book, p. 122), that it is not clear that it is impermissible for a woman to destroy what is a part of, or a con-tinuation of herself. He then says that to the extent the unborn human being is united to her in that way, "it would if anything seem that her act is *easier* to justify than if this claim were not true" (Boonin, 2003, p. 230). But Boonin fails to grasp the point of the argument (perhaps under-standably since it was not expressed very clearly in the earlier work he is discussing). The unity of the child to the mother is the basis for this child being related to the woman differently than other children. We ought to pursue our own good *and the good of others with whom we are united in various ways*. If that is so, then the closer someone is united to us, the deeper and more extensive our responsibility to the person will be.

7   In some sense being bodily "occupied" when one does not wish to be *is* a harm; however, just as the child does not (as explained in the text), nei-ther does the state, inflict this harm on the woman, in circumstances in which the state prohibits abortion. By prohibiting abortion the state would only prevent the woman from performing an act (forcibly detach-ing the child from her) which would unjustly kill this developing child, who is an innocent party.

AN EXCHANGE ON THE ETHICS OF EMBRYO ADOPTION

EMBRYO ADOPTION APPEARS TO BE MORALLY LICIT
William L. Saunders

Let me begin by quoting G. K. Chesterton – "Beyond stating what he proposes to prove, [a speaker] should always state what he does *not* propose to prove."[1]

Per Chesterton, I do *not*, most emphatically, seek to prove that embryos should be frozen, or that they may be created by *in vitro* fertilization (IVF) in the first place. I assume we are all united in accepting the teaching of the Congregation for the Doctrine of the Faith in *Donum Vitae* that IVF, as well as embryo freezing, is not morally licit.[2] That teaching is not at issue in this debate, and I certainly do not dispute it.

What I propose to prove, or at least to argue, is that it is morally licit, laudable though not mandatory, to "adopt" frozen embryos. What I intend to signify by the term "adopt" is precisely what is ordinarily meant by the term "adoption," viz., to take a child into one's family and to raise that child as one's own. (Be advised that different participants in the debate use different terms to describe what is taking place, as we will see shortly.)

Please note that what we are considering is an act *separate from* an act creating the embryo in the first place. It is a second act *in response* to the reality – the injustice – created by the first. We must keep this distinction in mind or our moral analysis will be confused.

It was in *Donum Vitae* that the first commentator on this issue, Msgr. William Smith, found language which he believed suggested that embryo adoption was impermissible, and for this and other reasons, he concluded that embryo adoption was not licit.[3] This prompted a response by Geoffrey Surtees, who was then a student at the John Paul II Institute, and his teacher, William May. The debate was thus joined, and has been pursued by, among others, Mary Geach and Helen Watt in the *Linacre Quarterly*, and William May, Germain Grisez, Nicholas Tonti-Filipini, John Berkman, Robert George and myself.[4]

DONUM VITAE

Most participants in this debate, including those I have just identified, do not believe the language of *Donum Vitae* has conclusively resolved this matter, and so they make moral arguments either for or against embryo adoption, awaiting an authoritative teaching by the Holy See. However, for those unfamiliar with the details of this debate, I will review the argument based on *Donum Vitae*.

Donum Vitae says: "In consequence of the fact that they have been produced in vitro, those embryos which are not transferred into the body of the mother, and are called 'spare,' are exposed to an absurd fate, with no possibility of their being offered safe means of survival which can be licitly pursued."[5]

This sentence, it is argued, prohibits embryo adoption. Let me note several points in response.

First, the sentence itself seems to permit the transfer of the IVF embryo into the genetic mother's womb, which, in turn, seems to preclude the argument that IVF embryos may *never* be transferred to a womb.

Second, it should be noted that the immediately preceding sentence in *Donum Vitae* says: "It is...not in conformity with the moral law deliberately to expose to death human embryos obtained *in vitro*." This would seem to preclude the course often preferred by those who oppose embryo adoption – thaw them, baptize them, and permit them to die. If the genetic mother (the woman who supplied the ovum or egg that was fertilized during IVF) were unable, for whatever reason, to gestate the frozen embryo, and if, under *Donum Vitae*, one were morally precluded both (a) from transferring that embryo to an adopting mother and (b) from "deliberately exposing" the embryo to death (i.e., permitting it to die after it had been "thawed"), we would have a truly absurd situation – frozen embryos must be kept forever frozen but alive in storage, and, thus, forever denied any chance of the beatific vision.

Third, such truly absurd results can be avoided if we understand the sentences from *Donum Vitae* in their context. The burden of the section in which the quoted sentences appear[6] is concerned with answering this question: "How is one morally to evaluate the use for research purposes of embryos obtained by fertilization in vitro?" Thus, the focus was on the question of the moral permissibility of using IVF embryos in research. It was not directly concerned with the question before us, i.e., whether embryos may be licitly transferred to, or adopted by, other(s). *Donum Vitae*'s statement about embryo transfer is similar to what lawyers call "dicta" – statements made by the court in the course of rendering a decision but which are not strictly necessary to the resolution of the case. Such statements are entitled to some deference in future cases, but they are not "controlling" because they do not concern the matter upon which the court ruled.

For these reasons, it seems clear to me that the language of *Donum Vitae* does not *settle* the issue, but, rather, *raises* it. It is surely the case that a matter involving something as important as the life of an embryonic human being deserves a thorough briefing and more than a one-sentence treatment by the CDF. In order to help the Church in the consideration of this difficult but important moral question, it behooves us, as scholars faithful to the magisterium, to explore the issue. Let us turn to that now.

THE MORAL ARGUMENT

As you are probably aware, there are thousands of embryonic human beings created yearly by IVF in the United States. During the IVF procedure, eggs are harvested from a woman, then fertilized, and, finally, implanted.[7] The process results in the creation of many more embryonic human beings than can be implanted. These non-implanted embryos are sometimes called, as *Donum Vitae* also calls them, "spare." These embryonic human beings are then "stored" at the clinic, i.e., they are placed, and kept indefinitely, in liquid nitrogen at very low temperatures in cryogenic tanks. Sometimes the original couple will, following the success or failure of the first procedure, return to the clinic to have one or more of the frozen embryos implanted. Often, however, the couple does not return, and the embryos remain in frozen storage. A recent estimate is that there are upwards of 400,000 frozen embryos in the United States.[8] A small number of these frozen embryos have been "thawed" and implanted in the womb of a woman who wishes to adopt them, and have resulted in healthy live births. [9]

The question I am considering – the problem placed before us by the existence of these hundreds of thousands of frozen embryonic human beings – is this: may a faithful Catholic "adopt" one or more of these embryonic human beings from the eternal deep freeze by having it "thawed" and implanted in her womb? Of course, the mere fact, however troubling, that frozen embryos exist does not, of itself, decide this question one way or the other. The end does not justify the means. The question is, are there licit means to help embryos escape cryo-preservation?

I believe embryo adoption is morally permissible, at least under the following conditions: 1) it is restricted to married couples; 2) the adoptive couple intends to rear the child as their own; 3) the couple made no arrangement with the IVF clinic or the genetic parents to adopt a "surplus" embryo before the embryo was, in fact, determined to be "surplus"; and 4) adoption is permitted only if the genetic mother a) were incapable of gestating the embryo herself or b) had abandoned it. With these conditions, which I intend to respond to concerns of justice and fairness, I think the practice might be not only permitted but encouraged.

As is implied by these conditions, I am inclined to think that adoption by an unmarried woman – what I will call, to avoid confusion, "rescue" – is not normally morally licit, though my conclusion on this point is tentative. Some of the reasons will become clear in the following discussion. In addition, I will note the following: some commentators have pointed to the case of a woman who becomes pregnant through rape, and who can licitly give up the child at birth to be adopted, as demonstrating that it would be morally licit for an unmarried woman who adopted an embryo to do the same. While a single woman might, through rape or otherwise, "find" herself to be pregnant without ever having intended to be, she must still act morally in the circumstances in which she finds herself. Such moral action might include, or even require, giving up the child for adoption. However, the case of embryo rescue where the unmarried woman *plans from the first* to give up the child for adoption is, I believe, different. There while the woman *intends* to become the *mother* of the child, her intention is *limited* – she intends to become mother to the child *temporarily*. Such an intention seems contrary to the meaning of motherhood. I think a woman in this case is very close to being a surrogate since she has intended from the first to give up the child to others, and surrogacy is expressly prohibited by *Donum Vitae*.[10] Of course, an unmarried woman might intend to raise the child herself. In that case, the act of rescue would still be morally troubling, however, because unmarried women are unable to provide what justice requires for the child, namely, that the child be raised in a family characterized by the married love of husband and wife. Thus, in intending to be its mother without being married, she is willing contrary to the good of the child.[11]

Returning to embryo adoption, let me spend a moment on each condition I proposed.

1. Restricting embryo adoption to married couples.

This condition would ensure the best situation for the child. Children prosper best in a household with a married father and mother. Also, such a restriction would reinforce, and would do nothing to undermine, society's traditional commitment to marriage.

2. Requiring that the adoptive couple intend to rear the child as their own.

This requirement rebuts any suggestion of surrogacy.[12] The woman is not carrying the child for someone else. There is no risk that her body (womb) will be instrumentalized. Nor is the child treated in a manner inconsistent with human dignity. The commitment to the child made by the adopting couple is complete and all-embracing.

3. Precluding prior arrangements between the adoptive parents and the IVF clinic or the genetic parents.

This insures that the adoptive parents would not risk complicity in the original immoral decision to conceive the child by IVF. They would, instead, be responding, in compassion and justice, to a situation created, outside their control, by others. They would be doing nothing that endorsed or encouraged the practice of IVF. Neither the clinic nor the genetic parents would be able to assuage either guilty consciences or public scrutiny by arguing that, due to prior arrangement, no "surplus" embryos were being created. If the adoptive parents stated publicly their opposition to IVF, the risk of scandal should be avoided, i.e., no one would be reasonably mislead into believing the couple was disregarding the teaching of *Donum Vitae*. They would be acting in a manner analogous to the politician considered in *Evangelium Vitae*, who is permitted to support restrictions on evil practices (abortion) so long as he makes known his opposition to the practice.[13] Furthermore, the mere fact of a married woman being pregnant would not, unlike the case of a single woman, suggest that there was anything morally irregular in the initiation of the pregnancy, leading to scandal.

4. Permitting adoption only after it is certain that the genetic mother will not implant the child in her own womb.

By restricting adoption until the genetic mother could no longer bear children or has abandoned her frozen embryonic children, the possibility for the natural and best-case scenario (genetic mother and gestational mother are the same) is preserved. Once that is no longer possible, adoption would be permitted. Furthermore, since the child gestates within the woman who will be his birth mother and who will rear him, the mother-child bond established in embryo adoption has a physiological dimension and duration not present in traditional adoption. Of course, because the life of a human being is at stake, the delay in adoption – while we wait to see if the genetic mother will implant the embryo – must not exceed the time during which the embryo may safely be kept alive and "healthy" in storage.

Some have objected that embryo adoption severs the links between conception and motherhood. However that link has already been severed by the IVF conception of the embryo. If the embryonic child is placed within a married woman, it seems little different from so placing the born-child. In either case, the child is separated from its biological/genetic parents; the links of conception, gestation, birth, and child-rearing are severed. With embryo adoption, the link is broken after conception. With traditional adoption, the link is broken after birth. This difference seems to be of no moral significance.

Others suggest that embryo adoption is in certain decisive respects like adultery. They argue that in each case, the woman's giving of her reproductive system – her womb – to one who is not her husband violates the integrity of the marriage. The difference in intention, however, is critical. In the case of adultery, the woman intends to violate her marital commitment to her husband: she intends to give herself to a man other than her husband; she intends to engage in sexual acts outside the marital bond. With embryo adoption, however, the wife's intent is qualitatively different. Unlike cases of adultery, a child already exists; the woman intends to help that child. She intends that the child be placed inside her womb, but she has no intent to engage in sexual acts with a man who is not her husband, or to violate her marital vows. She intends, along with her husband, to welcome a new member into the family. The intention with both traditional adoption and embryo adoption is the same. Additionally, and crucially, the act is objectively different in each case. Adultery involves a sexual act; embryo adoption/implantation does not. Embryo implantation is like a surgical procedure during which a doctor must enter into a woman's womb. Though that entry is by a man (assuming the doctor is a man) who is not the woman's husband, there is no sexual act, and, hence, no violation of the marital relationship.

As a variation on this point, some argue that pregnancy is never morally licit unless it comes about as the result of conjugal relations between husband and wife. However, in my view, pregnancy is properly understood as the result of an act. The question is whether *the act* (the transfer of the embryo to the woman's womb) is morally illicit, and, for the reasons discussed, I do not believe that it is. It is not the implantation of the embryo that dissociates pregnancy from the conjugal act; that link has already been broken by the IVF procedure that created the embryo in the first place. Finally, it cannot be objected that the pregnancy is illicit because it was artificially caused for *Donum Vitae* itself states that "these [artificial] interventions [regarding procreation and the origin of human life] are not to be rejected on the grounds that they are artificial."[14]

Finally, some argue that embryo adoption should not be permitted because doing so would create a "market" for embryos. The view of those making this argument is that the existence of couples willing to adopt embryonic children would cause clinics to create embryos to fill this demand. It seems sufficient to meet this objection to refer to what I said previously – there are already over 400,000 frozen embryos in existence. The IVF "industry" is already well-established and operating beyond the bounds of reason and justice. Embryos are already being created and frozen, in large numbers, and this has not been in response the willingness of couples, a few of whom have only come forward in the last couple of years, to adopt those who are frozen. Indeed, when one considers that there were approximately 120,000 adoptions in 1996 (the last year for which there are complete statistics),[15] one realizes it would take many years and much effort to convince 400,000 couples to adopt the children who are currently frozen.[16]

In conclusion, I am of the view that embryo adoption is morally licit. The end – providing a home and family to an abandoned child – is good. The means – unfreezing the embryo and implanting it in the woman's womb – does not violate a moral norm. There are no significant negative side effects. The intention is morally upright.

In its essence, therefore, embryo adoption is not different from the adoption of an already-born child.

William L. Saunders, J.D., a graduate of Harvard Law School, is the Senior Fellow and Director of the Center for Human Life and Bioethics at the Family Research Council in Washington, D.C. He was the principal drafter of the Council's *Building a Culture of Life: A Call to Respect Human Dignity in American Life*. His principal focus is on bioethics and biotechnology. He has spoken and written frequently on topics such as stem cell research and cloning. He has also often appeared in the media, including on BBC World News, Fox News, and National Public Radio, on these topics. His articles and book chapters on issues of bioethics, the family, and Catholic social teaching have appeared in a variety of publications.

Notes

1   Chesterton, G.K.: *Orthodoxy*. Doubleday, New York 1990, p. 10.

2   CDF, *Donum Vitae* I,6.

3   Smith, W.: "Rescue the Frozen?" *Homiletic and Pastoral Review*. October 1995.

4   Berkman, J.: "Gestating the Embryos of Others," in *The National Catholic Bioethics Quarterly*, Summer, 2003; Geach, M. , and Watt, H.: "Are there any circumstances in which it would be morally admirable for a woman to seek to have an orphan embryo implanted in her womb?" In *Issues for a Catholic Bioethic*, The Linacre Centre, London 1999; Grisez, G: *The Way of the Lord Jesus Christ. Christian Moral Principles*. Volume 3, Franciscan Herald Press, Chicago, 1983; May, W.: *Catholic Bioethics and the Gift of Human Life* .Our Sunday Visitor Publishing Division, Huntington, Indiana, 2000; Saunders, W.: *The Whole Truth about Stem Cell Research*, Family Research Council, Washington D.C. 2001; Tonti-Filippini, N.: *The Embryo Rescue Debate*, in *The National Catholic Bioethics Quarterly*, Spring, 2003.

5   CDF, *Donum Vitae* I,5.

6   *Ibid.* I,5.

7   There are many variations on the parties involved. For instance, a woman other than the one supplying the ovum might carry the child to term once it has been implanted. A man other than the husband of the first woman might supply the sperm with which to fertilize the egg. Whatever the variation, the CDF has held, in *Donum Vitae*, that the procedure is illicit.

8   Weiss, R.: "400,000 Human Embryos Frozen in U.S. Number at Fertility Clinics Is Far Greater Than Previous Estimates, Survey Finds," *Washington Post,* May 8, 2003.

9   See, e.g., "Embryo Adoption, on the rise, is still a moral question mark," April 7, 2003, Zenit.: No state in America has granted legal recognition to the concept of embryo adoption; however, five states offer legal protections for the parents of adopted embryos."

10 CDF, *Donum Vitae* II,A,3.

11 While the intention of the unmarried woman might not make the act of "adoption" intrinsically immoral, it would still, I think, be an immoral act *in most cases* because its side-effects would violate norms of fairness and justice.

12 *Donum Vitae* defines "surrogacy" as carrying an embryo to term "with the pledge to surrender the child once it is born to the party who commissioned or made the agreement for the pregnancy" (DV II,A,3 FN).

13 *Evangelium Vitae* 73: "…when it is not possible to overturn or completely abrogate a pro-abortion law, an elected official, whose absolute personal opposition to procured abortion was well known, could licitly support proposals aimed at limiting the harm done by such a law…"

14 CDF, *Donum Vitae,* Introduction, 3.

15 For domestic adoptions, see, Connaught Marshner and William L. Pierce, *The Adoption Fact Book*, 1999, Park Press Quality Printing, Waite Park, Minnesota, page 26; for foreign adoptions, see, www.adoptioninstitute.org.

16 As noted in the discussion above, one condition for morally upright adoption would be to require that the couple not cooperate with the clinic in the creation of the embryos or in any plan to have them adopted. Also, as noted, the adopting couple should make public their opposition to the practice of IVF in the first place. With these two conditions, it seems far-fetched to suggest the IVF industry would be aided and abetted by adopting couples.

FROZEN EMBRYO ADOPTIONS ARE MORALLY OBJECTIONABLE
Rev. Tadeusz Pacholczyk

A great deal of debate and controversy exists over the question of frozen embryo adoption. My aim is to offer several reasons why I believe that it is very unlikely, nearly impossible to imagine, in fact, that the Catholic Church will one day grant her stamp of approval to embryo adoption and rescue.

In order to do so, it is helpful to review the series of steps involved in *in vitro* fertilization (IVF), and to explore how, as of 2003, clinics in the United States have managed to reach the point of cryo-preserving nearly 400,000 human embryos. The initial step in IVF involves treating the woman with hyper-ovulatory drugs so that she releases a large number of ova, which can then be collected and used in the laboratory. The next step involves the collection of a sperm sample, generally through masturbation, and the addition of those sperm into a petri dish containing the ova, which results in extra-corporeal fertilization *in vitro* (meaning, literally, "in glass").

Quality control is then carried out, so that embryos appearing to be defective in their growth and development may be frozen, excluded from subsequent use, or discarded. Several of the embryos that pass muster are then implanted into the woman's uterus by using a long catheter which passes through the cervix. Other embryos, so called "spares," are frozen in liquid nitrogen and cryo-preserved for long-term storage. The assumption is that initial implantation attempts may not succeed in producing a pregnancy, and by freezing extra embryos it will be possible to use them in subsequent cycles of implantation without having to re-harvest and re-fertilize extra-corporeally.

The core question for our purposes here involves the final step of the IVF process, and whether the transferring of an embryo into a woman's uterus is licit from the moral point of view. Undoubtedly, thinking about these matters and coming to moral conclusions can be difficult. At the point in which the embryos are transferred to the womb, we are dealing with a small grouping of usually no more than a few hundred cells that comprise the blastocyst, or the early embryo. In order to better understand this issue and its context, it is helpful to reflect on the nature of the extra-corporeal embryo, the embryo outside the body. Eric Cohen, who often writes about issues of technology and society, remarks about the peculiarity of extra-corporeal embryonic life when he observes:

> The first problem that we encounter when trying to understand the early stage human embryo is the strangeness of reasoning about this being at all. We are reasoning about something that is, by nature, mysterious. Something conceived naturally in darkness. Something whose presence in cases of natural conception cannot be known until after the fact. Before in vitro fertilization allowed us to create human embryos outside a woman's womb, we never encountered the earliest stage human embryo when it actually existed. We never knew it was there when it was actually there. We only traced its shrouded presence looking back once we came to know that a pregnancy had begun and once the developing life was more fully formed."[1]

This drives home the strikingly unnatural situation we find ourselves in at the present time as we routinely deal with human embryos in a sterile laboratory setting outside of a woman's womb. Today, one can readily open a publication and find a picture, a scanning electron micrograph, of an early human embryo positioned on the point of a needle. Fifty years ago such a picture would have been unthinkable. Today we cannot avoid confronting the radically abnormal circumstances in which the human embryo has become inextricably lodged due to the IVF process. As Eric Cohen, again, asks:

> How are we to reason rightly about the human embryo, especially the early stage embryo outside the human body, so severed as it is from its natural human contacts? Yuval Levin in an essay in the first issue of the *New Atlantis* describes the dilemma as follows: 'We look at this creature

that has been manufactured, molded, examined, and up to a certain point developed under the lights of the laboratory. It is growing but can only grow so far without further biotechnical intervention. It is living but only because the scientists have created it artificially. It is human to the extent that our humanity is in our genes and our potential. It is useful as a resource for medical research but would develop into a mature human adult if implanted into the body of a woman and permitted to grow. What in the world are we supposed to do with this thing? How is ethics supposed to serve us in this circumstance?[2]

We find ourselves faced with this unusual situation of having to ask moral questions that deal with a human embryo in a setting in which it doesn't really belong. We must recognize how there have been enormous boundary transgressions which precede many of these questions and necessarily condition them. That is to say, when the embryo is entirely out of its proper context, the challenge of resolving these ethical questions invariably becomes even more acute and complex. Again from Eric Cohen:

With *in vitro* fertilization, we created human embryos outside the body by uniting sperm and egg in the laboratory bringing the very earliest stages of embryonic development to new light. The significance of doing so is something that we have barely begun to fathom. It is a boundary that we crossed with little forethought and little reflection. It may turn out to be a profound turning point in the history of human life and culture. All the absurdity, all our dilemmas stem from this new reality.[3]

Hence we are faced with difficult and, at times, seemingly intractable questions, questions like the licitness of embryo adoption, which devolve from these enormous boundary transgressions. By dissociating the gametic generative powers of man and woman from the setting of marital intimacy, and transposing them into the setting of the laboratory, we find ourselves in unfamiliar new terrain.

To begin to approach the manifold questions about frozen embryo adoption we first need to ask: What principles should guide us? Some initial hints of guiding principles can perhaps be found by turning to *Gaudium et Spes*, the Second Vatican Council's Pastoral

Constitution on the Church in the Modern World. There we are reminded that:

> When it is a question of harmonizing married love with the responsible transmission of life, it is not enough to take only the good intention and the evaluation of motives into account; the objective criteria must be used, criteria drawn from the nature of the human person and human action, criteria which respect the total meaning of mutual self-giving and human procreation in the context of true love.[4]

While this passage was not written with the question of embryo adoption in mind, two phrases seem to recommend themselves to the issue under consideration. First, there is the phrase "harmonizing married love with the responsible transmission of life." Married love must be harmonized with the responsible transmission of life because the two manifest an intrinsic interconnectedness. The responsible transmission of life in the Christian tradition has always presupposed married love, and more specifically, *conjugal* married love. Second, there is the phrase, "respect the total meaning of mutual self-giving and human procreation." This seems to suggest a general formulation pertaining to human sexuality, along these lines: those actions which are compatible with married love and responsible procreation will always fully respect the "total meaning of mutual self-giving." Actions which might "transmit" life, but which prescind from or otherwise attempt to circumvent the total meaning of the conjugal act, are likely to be morally suspect. Yet as we begin to stress the importance of respecting "the total meaning of human procreation," we are faced with the need to clarify what the Church really understands by "procreation."

Some authors have ventured to claim that embryo adoption has practically nothing to do with procreation. The procreative act, they maintain, has been completed in IVF, and what exists now is a post-procreative reality, namely an early human being whose life can be saved only if he or she is transferred into someone's womb. I would like to suggest, however, that this notion of the procreative act as automatically completed *in vitro* is not correct. On the contrary, it would be more accurate to conclude that the procreative act has not really even begun when referring to the case of fertilization *in vitro*. In the final analysis, when speaking of IVF, one is referring to an alternative to the procreative act. IVF may be a creative act in the sense of creating something new, but it is not genuinely procreative because procreation uniquely derives from conjugal acts.

The conjugal act thus achieves its procreative finality in a much broader context than what happens in a petri dish when an embryo is mechanically produced. A proper understanding of the term "procreation" must extend well beyond the biological events of fertilization, and take into consideration the entire process of *pro*-creation, or that which is done "on behalf of" the creation of a new person inside the woman's body, through conjugal acts of self-giving love. In other words, a more expansive grasp of the reality of procreation is called for if we are going to properly appreciate its "total meaning," as *Gaudium et Spes* urges. To delineate this point further, it is helpful to refer to discussions that have occurred over the centuries concerning the purposes of marriage.

In various documents and teachings of the Church regarding the purposes of marriage and the marital act, one finds statements affirming that the principal *finis operis* of marriage is the procreation and education of children. This phrase, "the procreation and education of children," can be found, for example, in the encyclical *Casti Connubii*, when in 1930, Pius XI stated:

> ...let Us sum it all up by quoting once more the words of St. Augustine: 'As regards the offspring it is provided that they should be begotten lovingly and educated religiously' – and this is also expressed succinctly in the Code of Canon Law – "The primary end of marriage is the procreation and the education of children."[5]

We encounter the inherent duality of the phrase, *the procreation and education of children,* as the primary end of marriage. Other sources, such as *Familiaris Consortio,*[6] and *Gaudium et Spes,*[7] phrase the matter similarly: "By their very nature, the institution of matrimony itself and conjugal love are ordained for the procreation and education of children, and find in them their ultimate crown." Clearly, this notion of "the procreation and the education of children" is the key to any discussion of conjugal love and the meaning of marriage itself. More contemporary treatments of this theme in Church documents shift the emphasis away from identifying the *primary* end of marriage, and instead stress a two-fold end, namely, *mutual help* (sanctification), and the *procreation and education of children*. These nuances complement and broaden the Church's longstanding appreciation of the importance of the *procreation and education of children* in marriage. Implicit in the basic formulation is the idea that whatever precedes the education of children (formally beginning at birth) would be "procreative" in character. *Birth seems to be the significant threshold where procreation ends and education begins.* This understanding of procreation as the expression and fruit of conjugal love, reaching through the various stages of early human life until birth, is thus distinct, but complementary, to its counterpart, education, which we generally envision as commencing at birth and extending a number of years thereafter.

St. Augustine, when mentioned in *Casti Connubii* above, captures the same theme by referring to how children must be *begotten and educated.* The idea of begetting children seems to be essentially coterminous with the notion of procreation during much of the history of the discussion. Thus in speaking of *begetting* children or *procreating* children, we are clearly referring to something that extends well beyond the physical act of intercourse of husband and wife, well beyond the mere generation of an embryonic human. We refer to begetting or procreating children in the inclusive sense of the entire act of marital self-giving with its attendant pregnancy, leading up to and culminating in the birth of a child.

To explicate these notions further, it may be helpful to consider a simplified human timeline which extends from the conjugal act to

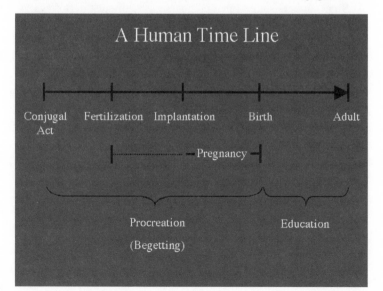

A Human Time Line

| Conjugal Act | Fertilization | Implantation | Birth | Adult |

├─────────── Pregnancy ─┤

Procreation
(Begetting)

Education

adulthood. Anywhere from zero to two days after the conjugal act, and perhaps as late as five days, fertilization occurs, which is the union of sperm and egg. This is followed within the space of six days by implantation of that embryo in the uterus. Approximately nine months later the baby is born, and many years later he or she enters adulthood.

Pregnancy is sometimes characterized as beginning at implantation, though it more properly begins with fertilization, continues through implantation, and concludes with the birth of the baby. Pregnancy begins at fertilization because with the genesis of an embryo, the woman is now carrying and caring for a new human individual within her body. Even if implantation were to ultimately fail to occur, she would still be gravid, pregnant with the new reality of a living human being within her person, at least until such time as that embryo were to die or be lost from her body. On the timeline, procreation is presented in the broad sense described earlier, as extending from and including the conjugal act, through fertilization, implantation, pregnancy, and up to birth. This is the way we beget children; this is the traditional concept of procreation. Procreation, in this ample context, encompasses the inscribed intentionality and "readout" of the conjugal act, up to its implied finality at birth, and includes all the stages of pregnancy. Pregnancy is thus an essential and integral dimension of procreation.

Some authors suggest that pregnancy is really just nurturing, not procreation. If we can nurture a child that is not our own through breast-feeding, they argue, shouldn't it be licit to nurture an embryo that is not our own through pregnancy? But pregnancy and breast feeding are two very different kinds of nurturing. Pregnancy signals and embodies a unique relational exclusivity between mother and child. Nursing a baby does not signal or embody that same unique relational exclusivity, since the procreative threshold of birth has now been crossed, and the baby's being out and away from his mother signals a new stage of availability for other relational encounters, including the encounter with other women who may serve as wet-nurses. So pregnancy is procreative and exclusive in its essential nature, while breastfeeding is not. In other words, pregnancy bespeaks the exclusivistic relational language of human sexuality in a way that nursing does not.

Another principle which can be brought to bear on the question of the licitness of embryo adoption is the famous Principle of

Inseparability, elucidated with remarkable clarity in *Humanae Vitae.* Pope Paul VI states:

> That teaching, often set forth by the Magisterium, is founded upon the indissoluble connection, willed by God and unable to be broken by man on his own initiative, between the two meanings of the conjugal act: the unitive meaning and the procreative meaning. Indeed, by its intimate structure, the conjugal act, while most closely uniting husband and wife, capacitates them for the generation of new lives, according to laws inscribed in the very being of man and woman. By safeguarding both these essential aspects, the unitive and procreative, the conjugal act preserves in its fullness the sense of true mutual love and its ordination towards man's most high calling to parenthood.[8]

This passage unambiguously describes the conjugal act as that which capacitates a husband and wife to become parents to new human life. Great stress is laid on the fact that these dimensions, the unitive and the procreative, are intimately connected to each other, and it is never acceptable to intentionally fluster or break this connection. In the case of embryo adoption, what the couple is ultimately choosing to do is to invoke some of the procreative powers of the woman in the absence of this unitive aspect, in the absence of the conjugal act between the couple. Separating the two aspects represents a fundamental violation of the nature of marital sexuality between the spouses and of the covenant they share in their marriage, whereby they belong exclusively to each other in their procreative capacities, precisely in and through the shared conjugal act.

Pope Pius XII recognized this connection between conjugal love and procreation in 1956 when he condemned the pursuit of either of these two realities in isolation from each other. He said: "Never is it permissible to separate these different aspects so as to exclude positively either the aim of procreation or the conjugal relation."[9] In the case of embryo adoption, one is systematically obviating the conjugal relation while pursuing a procreative aim by the approach of initiating a pregnancy by embryo transfer. Embryo adoption thus represents the pursuit of a procreative aim in strict separation from its required conjugal relation. We can begin to discern another potential objection pertaining to the aim or the goal of what we are doing in embryo adoption. Often advocates of embryo adoption stress that this activity represents a form of rescue, and that what is being pursued is the saving of a child's life. This can certainly be a key part of the total dynamics of the decision to implant an abandoned embryo. But it may also be worthwhile to pursue the question of whether another disordered dynamic may not also be operative in the scenario of embryo adoption. Is there some sense in which we are attempting to "secure a child" through embryo adoption, either as a means or as an end? We must inquire whether it is fully proper for us to be intentionally involving ourselves in this kind of "objectifying" tendency which disturbs the inner order of human procreation. The basic structure of human sexuality embodies a very different "aim" or "goal." What one is willing or choosing to do is not to go after the child as an end, but rather to give oneself in totality to one's spouse, to give oneself in an act of complete openness and donation of body and spirit. The inner meaning and language of sexuality is primarily one of total self-gift, and only secondarily one of seeking or pursuing a baby. If it happens that through the mutual and total donation of self in the conjugal act, that the great blessing of a child results, the couple rejoices. If no child is forthcoming, the couple still remains in a radical openness and acceptance to the fact that God has not yet chosen to send them a child. The overarching aim in conjugal activity is to be open to this vertical collaboration with Almighty God, rather than to set out on the path of securing a child as a project.

Embryo adoption raises other difficulties, including the fundamental problem of causing a "fissure in parenthood." This fissure is introduced into both motherhood and fatherhood in virtue of the fact that embryo adoption fails to fully respect the exclusive nature of the couple's marital covenant and the exclusive nature of their conjugal union. A passage from the Congregation for the Doctrine of the Faith's 1987 document, *Donum Vitae*, reminds us that "the bond existing between husband and wife, accords the spouses, in an objective and inalienable manner, the exclusive right to become mother and father solely through each other."[10] In other words, it is only in and through marriage, and specifically through conjugal acts, that a man and a woman are each capacitated to become true father and true mother. In the case of the woman, she is capacitated to conceive and give birth to a child, that is to say, to enter into the pregnant state, through conjugal acts with her husband. In his Apostolic Letter, *Mulieris Dignitatem*, the Holy Father notes how pregnancy is properly linked to the marital union and to the mutual self-giving of spouses: "In this openness, in conceiving and giving birth to a child, the woman 'discovers herself through a sincere gift of self.' The gift of interior readiness to accept the child and bring it into the world is linked to the marriage union, which should constitute a special moment in the mutual self-giving both by the woman and the man."[11] This passage conveys how pregnancy has a special link to its proper marital and conjugal context, as do motherhood and fatherhood.

To understand the fissure in parenthood that embryo adoption causes, it can be helpful to dissociate motherhood into distinct subgroups or subsections. Generally we identify three categories: *genetic*, *gestational*, and *social* motherhood. We refer to a mother as the genetic mother when she is genetically related to her offspring, speaking about the interval from the conjugal act up to and including fertilization. Second, we recognize gestational motherhood as extending from fertilization, including implantation and pregnancy, until the birth of the child. A woman becomes a gestational mother after becoming a genetic mother in the normal course of events. Of course, a genetic mother is, in most cases, the woman who is also the "sexual mother," the one who had relations with the father and was responsible for setting into motion this entire timeline. The third category is the social mother, extending from the time following birth and into adulthood.

These distinctions of motherhood are useful when we discuss, for example, traditional adoption. Traditional adoption involves becoming, at birth or sometime after birth, an adoptive or a social mother for the child. Meanwhile, if a woman adopts a frozen embryo we would refer to her as a gestational mother. She is the gestational mother and assuming that she raises that child born from the embryo, she would also become the social mother. So we can say that in the standard situation, motherhood is consequent to the conjugal act and it includes genetic, gestational, and social motherhood (as well as the initial "sexual motherhood"). In other words, this is the full and unmitigated sense of "being a mother." This is what it means to be fully and properly a mother. The mother is the person who engages in a conjugal act with her husband and then has the genetic, gestational, and social relationship of motherhood with the developing child.

In the case of post-natal adoption, as mentioned earlier, one is assuming the role of social motherhood. However, it should be pointed out that we always stress how a mother who adopts an infant is called "his adoptive mother," as opposed to his real mother. The integrality of motherhood is not properly achieved in adoption. By presenting oneself to the adoption agency and going through the steps of adopting an infant, one becomes an *adoptive mother*, which is something rather distinct from a mother in the full and proper sense. Clearly, though, one is not violating any of the goods of procreation by adopting an already born child because at that point, one is educating, rather than procreating. Ideally, the same parents who procreate should also educate, but if someone else educates, no *intrinsic wrong* is committed by the one who does the educating. Procreation has essentially ceased and there is no violation of the procreative goods entrusted by God to us in our sexuality, nor of the ways that he intends us to realize those goods. We might say that there is no "procreative hijacking" which occurs in the case of normal adoption, while such hijacking invariably occurs in the case of embryo adoption. Hence, there is no intrinsic moral objectionability in the case of traditional adoption of an already-born baby.

In embryo adoption, though, one is trying to assume the role of gestational mother without having conceived that same embryo through a conjugal act with one's husband. This is in actuality the essence of surrogacy, understood broadly, which violates, instead of respecting, the goods of motherhood and procreation by implanting an extra-corporeally-generated embryo into one's uterus. Embryo adoption thus raises this problematic aspect of the woman's attempting to commandeer a particular procreative good, namely the fecundity of the pregnant state, as she pursues the status of a gestational mother.

In other words, a surrogate mother becomes such through an improper agent or means, for example, through a technician or through the powers of reproductive medicine. One ought not become a parent through any means other than through one's spouse. One ought not attempt to become a "mother" in any other semi- or pseudo-procreative manner. One should not make use of this special part of marriage outside of its proper and reserved context. In other words, we have to respect the integrity of marriage and the way in which we are intended to invoke the procreative powers of our bodies. This is meant to occur only in and through exclusive acts of conjugal self-giving between husband and wife, which have pregnancy and birth as their natural sequelae and finality.

The procreative expression on the part of the husband is much more limited than that which is available to the wife. This becomes especially apparent when considering embryo adoption and fatherhood. In the general scheme of marriage, the procreative expression that is open to the man is made available only in and through the conjugal act since this is the unique manner in which he becomes a proper participant and partner in the pregnancy and gestation of the child. However, in the case of embryo implantation, the man's participation in the conjugal act is systematically obviated (as it is for the woman). Normally, prior to birth of a newborn, the father is incidental to practically everything except for the conjugal act itself, but in the case of embryo adoption, he now becomes truly incidental to the entire prenatal enterprise. In this foundational sense, both fatherhood and "husbandhood" are gravely and intrinsically violated by the decision to adopt and implant a frozen embryo into the wife's uterus.

It can be instructive to consider how motherhood is violated twice, so to speak, in the case of a husband and wife who decide to use *in vitro* fertilization with their own gametes (sometimes referred to as *homologous IVF*). I would like to suggest that IVF really involves a kind of double evil on the part of the mother who undertakes it. The first violation flows from allowing one's gametes to be used generatively outside of the conjugal act itself, by allowing conception outside the body. The second way that motherhood is violated is at the point of embryo transfer, by attempting to become a gestational mother without being capacitated for that role by its proper prior conjugal act. The woman, on some level, is becoming a surrogate mother to her own genetically related offspring. In other words, her own children who were conceived outside of her body, do not stand in a normal *maternal* relationship to her, but rather in a *surrogate* relationship to her.

Surrogacy, in the final analysis, is represented by the instance when a woman makes the decision to receive an embryo into her uterus in a way other than as a consequence of conjugal relations with her husband or with another man. If a woman commits adultery and becomes pregnant, this would not an example of surrogacy, because the embryo conceived in the adulterous act came into being through an act of sexual intimacy rather than being created extrinsically and imported into her body. If a woman is raped and becomes pregnant, this also would not be an example of surrogacy, since the embryo again came into being through an act of (forced) sexual intimacy. Both adultery and rape partake of a grave violation of the meaning of motherhood and fatherhood, but not because of the evil of surrogacy.

Surrogacy is sometimes considered intrinsically wrong because it can involve payment: a woman consents to gestate an embryo for a fee. It has been suggested that this kind of payment would comprise the essential illicitness of surrogacy. It has also been suggested that the idea of gestating an embryo on behalf of another person rather than for oneself constitutes the illicitness of surrogacy. In other words, the decision to gestate an embryo that one does not intend to raise as one's own child, but rather to hand off to others, would be morally problematic. Still others have suggested that surrogacy is the gestating of any non-genetically related embryo, which would be illicit, while gestating an embryo that is genetically related to oneself (e.g. derived from IVF) would not partake of the evil of surrogacy. Perhaps surrogacy can be most amply categorized and analyzed by recognizing that its fundamental illicitness lies in choosing intentionally to receive an embryo *ab extra* into one's uterus, an embryo which is not the consequent and direct fruit of a particular act of sexual self-giving between man and woman. This is perhaps the most fundamental expression of what surrogacy entails.

In this respect, it is interesting to consider the case of a husband and wife who decide to advert to IVF. They show up at the infertility clinic and they donate their gametes, their egg and sperm, and the technicians join the egg and sperm and grow them for a few days. The wife then comes back to the clinic, she gets up on the table and is ready to have some embryos implanted. If she suddenly were to repent of ever having generated these embryos in the first place, what should she do now? Should she simply remain there and allow the technician to implant the embryos into her, or not? I would suggest that the morally proper step for her to take would be to immediately get off the table and walk out of the clinic, even though these embryos, of which she is the genetic mother, are truly her own children. By this bold step, she would put the brakes on the intrinsically disordered chain of events she had initiated, and avoid involving herself in a second evil act of becoming a surrogate mother to the embryos that she and her husband had generated at the clinic. The overall argument, with respect to motherhood, is that there is really a double violation of what it means to be a mother whenever one engages in IVF.

The designs over motherhood and fatherhood as given to us by God always imply an act of total, mutual, and exclusive self-giving. This is written right into the structure of the conjugal act between husband and wife, which is that special and unique kind of human act that affords the necessary condition to capacitate a woman and a man each to become parents through the other. Any attempt to become a parent by invoking the procreative powers of their bodies outside the specific setting of committed marital intimacy represents a violation of the gift of their mutually committed sexuality and a violation of its intrinsic meaning as established by God in the beginning. Because embryo adoption would always involve the husband and wife in a transgression of this nature, we conclude that it cannot be morally licit.

So what are we to say about the fate of the hundreds of thousands of frozen embryos now in storage? What should be done with them if they cannot be adopted? We are faced with the urgent and mounting problem of the disposition of these embryos. Had our society (and even rank-and-file Catholics) heeded the Church's urgent pleas over the years not to do IVF and not to produce extra-corporeal human embryos, we would doubtless not be in the position of having to ask this perplexing question. In a sense, the question is one that unfairly backs the Church into a corner, asking her to resolve a problem that she forewarned would arise if we chose to ignore the basic demands of the moral law.

At this juncture, we can only strive to offer an approximate "best answer" to this question, recognizing that the existence of frozen embryos really situates us "between a rock and a hard place." Perhaps the first and most essential point to be made in attempting to resolve this question is to insist that strong and decisive steps be taken to preclude the continuation of practices that result in the creation of extra-corporeal human embryos. If we are serious about resolving the awkward situation of frozen human embryos, we cannot allow IVF to continue unabated in its present form. In some countries laws exist which require that all the embryos made during IVF procedures be implanted. That is to say, so-called "spares" may not be produced to be frozen and stored. Such a requirement might serve in some measure to mitigate the unconscionable rate at which newly created human embryos are being frozen in this country and elsewhere. However, this would likely bring its own set of objections.

For example, the clinics where these procedures are carried out are frightfully concerned about their own success rates, which are published on the internet, and which can be consulted by potential customers. In an attempt to beat the success rates of the clinic down the street, and assure a fortuitous revenue future for themselves, clinics are pressured to prepare and inject multiple embryos, four or five or more at a time, in the hopes of successfully inducing a pregnancy. In a fair number of instances, as borne out by the statistics available to date regarding these procedures, the outcome would be "multiplets": twins, triplets, quadruplets, or even higher order pregnancies. These pregnancies are highly risky for both the children and the mother. Sadly, there are already procedures in place in certain clinical settings to encourage a mother of "multiplets" to undergo a "selective reduction" in order to improve the prognosis for the remaining two or three of her children at the expense of the others who are "reduced." At the end of the day, of course, the core problem in terms of "spare" embryos is not with the particular details of *how* IVF is being carried out. The core problem inheres in the fact that it is allowed to be done at all, precisely because this results in a willingness and a readiness to objectify and instrumentalize early human life at the hands of clinic operators.

So again we ask: what should be done with all the cryo-preserved human embryos that now exist, so as to carefully avoid further violation of their human dignity? Clearly, one choice we cannot make with respect to these frozen embryos is to donate them for research and stem cell extraction. This always violates their intrinsic dignity by harvesting their cellular components and causing their immediate death. Moreover, we have concluded that they cannot be adopted in a morally licit fashion and implanted into a woman's uterus to be gestated and raised. What other alternatives present themselves? What about the scenario of baptizing them and then allowing them to thaw and die? Recognizing that they are completely out of their proper context, residing in this orphan state in a completely unnatural setting, frozen in liquid nitrogen, some have argued that their situation is analogous to a case where extraordinary, or disproportionate, means are used to preserve a dying person's life. For example, if we imagine a person who is being sustained by numerous tubes, ventilatory supports, and other systems which are merely extending a very imminent and unavoidable dying process, we are not obliged, from a moral point of view, to keep that person on life support. Likewise, the argument has been proffered that we may not be obligated to extend the embryos' dying process by maintaining them in this suspended state of animation in liquid nitrogen. It may be morally licit, therefore, to remove these extraordinary and disproportionate means of support, allowing the frozen embryos thaw and die a natural and imminent death.

Again, because of the unusual extra-corporeal embryonic context in which we find ourselves, it is particularly difficult to define our moral obligations and actions. Are the parallels between an end-of-life case and the case of a frozen embryo really morally instructive? In this case, moreover, there does seem to be the implication that by removing the embryo from its frozen orphanage, our very act is the direct and primary cause of death. The embryos achieve their demise through human agency. It might reasonably be argued that we should therefore not thaw them but maintain them in a frozen state.

Some evidence exists which suggests that the longer an embryo is stored in this suspended cryogenic state, the less the likelihood of thawing it successfully. If this is the case, with the passage of time the viability of cryo-preserved embryos declines even in the liquid nitrogen. One could argue then, that what we need to do is to carry out studies on the decay rates of frozen embryos when stored in liquid nitrogen (using, for example, other primate embryos). Based on the decay rates, one could identify a point in the future, perhaps several hundred years from now, when there would be a 99% probability that all the embryos in storage would already be dead, and then at that point, let them thaw. In this way, the thawing would not be the cause of their demise. However, all these proposed solutions present their own awkwardness, and none are really compelling, especially considering that the creation of embryos continues unabated in society at large.

We have attempted to outline certain conclusions which identify the intrinsic evil of frozen embryo adoption because of its instrumentalization of the goods proper to procreation and marriage. These goods, and the goods of parenthood itself, are intended to be accessed only and exclusively through means of the conjugal act between husband and wife. Recently, I was discussing the topic of embryo adoption with a friend of mine who is married and is the father of six children. At one point in our conversation I asked him, "How would you feel if Janet were to be implanted with an adopted frozen embryo?" He promptly responded, "The only way that my wife should get pregnant is with me." His answer reflects a fundamental grasp of the exclusivity that stands at the core of marriage. His response bespeaks the importance of safeguarding marital exclusivity in all of its richness and depth, by respecting the intentionality and integrity of the procreative gifts which are intrinsic to the marital state through conjugal acts.

To conclude, I'd like to highlight the well known passage from *Donum Vitae* which states: "In consequence of the fact that they have been produced *in vitro*, those embryos which are not transferred into the body of the mother and are called "spare" are exposed to an absurd fate, with no possibility of their being offered safe means of survival which can be licitly pursued."[12] Notwithstanding the contextual particulars of this passage – that it was not written to address the question of frozen embryo adoption – I would nevertheless conclude that we are caught on the horns of a dilemma of precisely the sort described by the passage. Extra-corporeal human embryos are exposed to a genuinely absurd fate, one which seems to offer little in the way of a morally licit path to resolution.

The Rev. Tadeusz Pacholczyk is a bioethicist, neuroscientist, and Catholic priest. He currently serves on the Ethics Committee at St. Anne's Hospital in Fall River, Massachusetts, and is in residence at St. Patrick's Church in Falmouth, Massachusetts. He has lectured widely and testified before the Massachusetts Senate on stem cell research and cloning. He holds a Ph.D. in neuroscience from Yale University and has carried out post-doctoral work at Harvard University and at the Massachusetts General Hospital in Boston. He is the co-author of some seven scientific articles and four abstracts. Fr. Pacholczyk was ordained a priest in 1999.

Notes

1   Cohen, Eric, "Of Embryos and Empire," *The New Atlantis* 2, Summer 2003, 10.

2   Cohen, 12.

3   Cohen, 11.

4   Flannery, Austin, O.P. ed., *Vatican Council II: the Conciliar and Post Conciliar Documents* (Northport, NY: Costello Publishing Company, 1992), s.v., Pastoral Constitution of the Church in the Modern World, *Gaudium et Spes,* §51.

5   Pope Pius XI, On Christian Marriage *(Casti Connubii),* (1932), §17.

6   Pope John Paul II, On the Role of the Christian Family in the Modern World *(Familiaris Consortio),* (1981), §14.

7   *Gaudium et Spes,* §48.

8   Pope Paul VI, On the Regulation of Birth *(Humanae Vitae),* (1968), §12.

9   Pope Pius XII, Address to the Second World Congress and Fertility and Sterility, May 19, 1956, *Acta Apostolicae Sedis* 48 (1956): 470.

10 Congregation for the Doctrine of the Faith, Instruction on Respect for Human Life in its Origin and on the Dignity of Procreation *(Donum Vitae),* (1987), §5.

11 Pope John Paul II, On the Dignity and Vocation of Women on the Occasion of the Marian Year *(Mulieris Dignitatem),* (1988), §18.

12 *Donum Vitae,* §5.

CAPITAL PUNISHMENT

EVANGELIUM VITAE AND THE DEATH PENALTY
Steven A. Long

INTRODUCTION

I'm grateful for the opportunity to be with you today to discuss the Church's teaching about the death penalty. As Dr. Brugger will shortly remind us, *Evangelim Vitae* and the revised *Catechism of the Catholic Church* often are thought of as preludes to a doctrinal abolition of the death penalty.

Yet, because the essential validity of capital punishment has been taught by several prior popes and catechisms, and is the traditional understanding of the Church, the issue arises how we should understand the remarks in *Evangelium Vitae*. Are they prudential in nature, or do they propound a doctrinal shift away from tradition and toward a principled abolition of the death penalty?

While there exists an understandable tendency to mix considerations drawn from the personal reflections and local utterances of Pope John Paul II with the formal teaching instruments of his pontificate, it is fitting that our attention should rest upon *Evangelium Vitae*. This encyclical – in conjunction with the *Catechim of the Catholic Church* – constitutes the most formal contemporary articulation of the magisterium on the question of the death penalty. Granted their manifest importance, nonetheless, neither the topical utterances of the Holy Father, nor his personal theology, most formally communicate the teaching of the ordinary magisterium, as do encyclicals or the *Catechism of the Catholic Church*.

According to *Evangelium Vitae*, cases in which the death penalty is justified today "are very rare, if not practically non-existent" (section 56). Nonetheless, the implication that there are conditions, howsoever rare, in which the penalty may be justified indicates that the encyclical does not consider the death penalty to be a *malum in se*. Clearly, no encyclical would speak of an intrinsic evil as something which one may even "only rarely" perform. The very idea of a papal encyclical counseling that murder, rape, or genocide are *rarely permissible* is preposterous. In the list of intrinsically evil acts provided in *Evangelium Vitae,* the death penalty does not occur. Nor does the *Catechism* condemn or totally suppress the penalty. Even after revision, the *Catechism* reminds us (#2266) that "legitimate public authority has the right and the duty to inflict punishment proportionate to the gravity of the offense"; and that "assuming that the guilty party's identity and responsibility have been fully determined, the traditional teaching of the Church does not exclude recourse to the death penalty, if this is the only possible way of effectively defending human lives against the unjust aggressor"(#2267).

Hence the problem is not that the encyclical teaches capital punishment to be intrinsically evil or denies its essential justice. Rather, the problem is that in the common, *prima facie*, or what I call the "reductionist" interpretation of the encyclical, the understanding of the nature and purpose of the death penalty appears to be inconsistent with prior Catholic tradition.

Today I will emphasize five strategic points pertinent to the encyclical. First, I will highlight the apparent difficulty with the common reading of the encyclical. Secondly, I will point out what it is in the text of *Evangelium Vitae* that renders this surface interpretation deeply problematic. Along the way I will quote authors who seem to imply that the magisterium's current teaching is incompatible with tradition, whether this claim is made with approval or disapproval. Thirdly, I will present five principles from Catholic tradition that are essential for grasping the continuity of *Evangelium Vitae* with the Catholic tradition. Fourthly, I will offer a positive account of *why* and *how* it is true that the deepest reasons within Catholic tradition – reasons that *favor* the doctrinal validity of capital punishment as a form of just penalty – become, in the pervasive circumstance of the culture of death, *reasons generally not to impose the death penalty*. Fifthly, and by way of postscript, if time avails I will indicate certain of the philosophic sources for the misjudgment of *Evangelium Vitae*.

I. THE *PRIMA FACIE* READING

According to the common reading, the encyclical is said to restrict use of the death penalty to cases where it is absolutely necessary for the protection of society in a sense comparable to justification of the use of lethal force in self-defense. Since the death penalty is supposed to be needed only for protection of minimal public order, in advanced societies which can otherwise maintain such order, and which have access to an extensive and well-developed penal system, use of the penalty is thought to be rarely if ever needed. But this doesn't seem quite right. In the Catholic tradition, the imposition of judicial penalties is clearly distinct from the nature of defense. Further, the primary purpose of the death penalty according to Catholic tradition is not simply maintaining minimal public order, but it also entails manifesting and vindicating a transcendent norm of justice.

Let us consider the comparison of judicial penalty and the use of force in defense. The common interpretation of the encyclical founds this comparison in the following lines of the encyclical (section 55):

> Moreover, "legitimate defense can be not only a right but a grave duty for someone responsible for another's life, the common good of the family or of the State." Unfortunately, it happens that the need to render the aggressor incapable of causing harm sometimes involves taking his life. In this case, the fatal outcome is attributable to the aggressor whose action brought it about, even though he may not be morally responsible because of a lack of the use of reason.

Now here the encyclical cites St. Thomas Aquinas (*STh*.II-II.64.7). But in the passage cited, St. Thomas is not referring to any application of judicial penalty, nor even to state-authorized and directed killing in time of war. Rather, in the cited text, St. Thomas is referring to the anomalous case of the use of lethal force in self-defense by a private individual – something quite different from the application of judicial penalties by the state.

Likewise, the following lines from *Evangelium Vitae* (section 56) may seem to generate unnecessary tension with Catholic tradition:

> ....the nature and extent of the punishment must be carefully evaluated and decided upon, and ought not go to the extreme of executing the offender except in cases of

absolute necessity: in other words, when it would not be possible otherwise to defend society. Today however, as a result of steady improvements in the organization of the penal system, such cases are very rare, if not practically non-existent.

In any event, the principle set forth in the new *Catechism of the Catholic Church* remains valid: "If bloodless means are sufficient to defend human lives against an aggressor and to protect public order and the safety of persons, public authority must limit itself to such means, because they better correspond to the concrete conditions of the common good and are more in conformity to the dignity of the human person."

On the reductionist reading, "absolute necessity" and the "defense of society" are given a markedly minimalist sense that in other contexts might be called positivist or naturalist. But one may reasonably ask whether, in traditional Catholic doctrine, judicial penalty truly is viewed as merely an expedient for the physical protection of minimal public order – as the equivalent of a riot cannon or "crowd control writ large." A careful survey of the sources of traditional Catholic doctrine suggests that judicial penalty is also ordered to manifest a transcendent norm of justice, whose vindication by the state is a far higher and nobler end of penalty. In the Catholic tradition, the exaction of retributive penalty is not only a matter of minimal public order, but of preserving the moral integrity and purity of society.

The Catholic tradition in general, and *Evangelium Vitae* in particular, then, acknowledge that there are circumstances in which one may justly in defense kill someone who is guilty of no deliberate evil act – for example, a person acting under the influence of a lesion on the brain who unintentionally endangers others. If such a person is shot while threatening the life of another, it is not because this person has been judged guilty of deliberate evil and held worthy of death. It is merely because he constitutes a threat to the safety of others that is reasonably stoppable in no other way. But by contrast, the imposition of judicial penalty is understood within the Catholic tradition as following upon a judgment of *guilt*, and as involving a *direct intent* on the part of the state to chastise the guilty party.

II. *EVANGELIUM VITAE'S* TEXT RULES OUT THE SURFACE READING

This brings us to the second strategic point. If we read *Evangelim Vitae* apart from the tradition we are in danger of understanding the encyclical as confusing and confounding the nature of public and private authority. *Yet a careful reading of the document itself shows that the encyclical cannot intend to declare that the formal doctrinal reason for capital punishment is some species of mere defense.* For a judicial *sentence* of death, followed by a legal *imposition* of the death penalty pursuant to such a sentence, would *never* be just in the case of one *who was not morally responsible.* In defense, there *is* no judicial sentence, *no simple intent to kill,* but only *action proportionate to the end of defense.* The *governing idea or ratio* of defense is one of stopping an assault with no necessary reference to a judgment of guilt. An act is denominated "defensive" by reason of its proportion to stopping such an assault. And as the text of the encyclical explicitly reminds us, just defense may be undertaken *even when the assailant is not morally responsible for his action.*

If the death penalty truly were meant to be included within the category of defense, *then* this *ratio or idea of* defense – according to which a person who is not morally responsible may at times justly be killed – would necessarily apply also to the death penalty. *Recall the words of the encyclical about defense:* "The fatal outcome is attributable to the aggressor whose action brought it about, *even though he may not be morally responsible because of a lack of the use of reason*" (my emphasis – SL). These words by their very nature cannot be used regarding either the death penalty or criminal penalty as such, because such penalty formally presupposes a *prior judgment of guilt* whereas, as the encyclical makes clear, defense requires no such judgment of moral guilt. For this reason it is utterly implausible to suggest that the pope intends to identify the *doctrinal* justification for the death penalty with that of defense. Criminal penalty – especially the death penalty – is not a mere act of defense, but a deliberate chastisement that formally presupposes a judgment of guilt. Accordingly there must be a different reason for the stress on defense – a point I will address in due course.

Notwithstanding this analysis, able scholars and lovers of the Church are to be found who read the encyclical as placing the death

penalty in the category of defensive action. Professor Charles Rice
tells us that it is the whole point of *Evangelium Vitae* that the death
penalty is now to be interpreted purely in the light of the defense of
society. Hence he wrote the following lines in a letter a year and a
half ago to the *National Catholic Register* (March 24–31, 2002):

> A Catholic can no longer argue for the *use* of the death
> penalty on grounds of retribution, deterrence of others from
> committing crimes, or for any other reason unless the exe-
> cution is "the only possible way" of protecting others from
> *this criminal.*"

This formulation of "defense" is so extreme that it rejects the
jurisprudential legitimacy of the consideration of deterrence – which
is precisely a consideration directly pertinent to social defense. This
interpretation is wholly preoccupied with the individual felon, as
though this concern could justly be separated from concern for the
common good of society.

Similarly, Justice Antonin Scalia concurs with Professor Rice
that the teaching of *Evangelium Vitae* is a formal rupture with the
teaching of the Catholic tradition – although Justice Scalia at least
concedes that there is a social dimension to the type of "defense"
spoken of in the encyclical. In a letter criticizing an editorial in the
National Catholic Register (March 24–31, 2002), Justice Scalia
wrote of papal teaching on the death penalty that:

> This represents a fundamental change from the (infalli-
> ble) universal teaching of the past 2000 years, because it
> proceeds from the premise that the only justifiable purpose
> of the death penalty is to "defend society" in the manner
> that prisons defend it – that is, to disable the offender and
> deter future offenders. Prior teaching, from St. Paul for-
> ward, was that *retribution* is a valid objective. Whereas, St.
> Paul says, individual Christians must "give way to wrath,"
> the government "carries the sword" as "the minister of God
> to execute vengeance upon him that doeth evil."

It is difficult to know what to say to such distinguished critics,
except that they seem to be reading a papal encyclical as though it
were not the work of a profound mind extremely well-schooled *in
the Catholic tradition of theology and philosophy.* Hence, rather than
note the problem within the text of the encyclical itself that is caused
if we read it as each suggests we should, these authors implicitly

allege that the pope *confuses the nature of public penalty with the nature of purely defensive action.* Each must logically hold that Pope John Paul the II cannot distinguish between the nature of defense and the nature of legal penalty, and, consequently, that the pope's teaching logically countenances a legal penalty of death levied upon someone in the absence of a prior judgment of guilt – because, *as Evangelium Vitae* itself teaches, *justified killing in defense need not presuppose any judgment of guilt.* This insuperable doctrinal and logical tangle awaits us within the text of the encyclical itself once we determine to interpret it as annulling the distinction between judicial penalty and defense.

Manifestly, however, papal teaching is not proposing that criminal execution is an essentially defensive act, nor is it suggesting that morally guiltless persons may on occasion be executed. It follows that we must either renounce the position that implies these propositions, or renounce the distinction between defensive action and criminal penalty. But because philosophic reason and the testimony of the Catholic tradition alike support this distinction between penalty and defensive action – and because the denial of this distinction implies manifest absurdity – we should not reject it. It follows that we are logically bound to reject any reduction of criminal penalty to defense and, correspondingly, any interpretation of the encyclical that implies this conclusion.

It should be noted that because these difficulties flow with logical and natural necessity directly from the error of assimilating judicial penalty to the ratio of defense, this is not a matter that easily lends itself to disposal by ad hoc clarificatory statements. There is a reason why the distinction between judicial penalty and defense is so clearly made within the Catholic tradition, and that distinction cannot be undone without ratifying inferences that plainly no one wishes to ratify. Thus the common reading of the encyclical – according to which judicial penalty of death is to be assimilated to the *ratio* of defense – seems the clearest possible manner of negating the encyclical's coherence.

One ought further to recollect that it is, after all, the nearly unanimous opinion of the Fathers and Doctors of the Church[1] that the death penalty is morally licit, and further it is the teaching of past popes (and numerous catechisms) that this penalty is essentially just, and even – as was taught by Pope Pius XII – that the validity of the death penalty is not subject to cultural variation.[2] Whilst the

teaching of many of the Doctors and Fathers of the Church empha-
sizes the role of Christian mercy, their common predilection is well
represented by the case of St. Augustine, who despite virtually
always pleading for mercy, unequivocally affirmed the rational justice of the death penalty in principle. Surely we must presume that
Pope John Paul II *knows this*. In this light, the eagerness to embrace
the proposition that the pope does not distinguish between legal
penalty and defense – especially when other explanations are available – is difficult to fathom.

Of course there is a large antinomian community with a vested
interest in arguing for doctrinal mutation in this case, because it
makes argument for mutation more plausible elsewhere – for example regarding contraception, abortion, homosexuality, or the nature
of the priesthood. But Professor Rice and Justice Scalia clearly are
not what anyone in his wildest dreams could plausibly think to be
card-carrying members of this constituency. Yet one would think that
these and other scholars might think the matter through again rather
than implicitly endorse a mutationist account of moral doctrine sur-
rendering two millennia of Catholic wisdom on the basis of a dubi-
ous exegesis that damages the coherence of an otherwise inter-
pretable encyclical.

It does seem to me that these authors inadvertently sacrifice the
moral intelligibility of the Catholic tradition to a merely surface
reading of papal teaching, and, moreover, to a surface reading which
strains credulity to the breaking point. For this is an account according to which an encyclical titled *The Gospel of Life* must be held logically to imply that persons may justly be executed without prior
judgment of guilt because execution is wholly defensive in nature.
Such a reading is in danger of collapsing the intelligibility of Church
teaching through a positivism that unnecessarily mutiplies ruptures
with tradition. One might think that this is to cross the threshold of
hope in the wrong direction.[3]

III. FIVE PRINCIPLES FROM THE
CATHOLIC TRADITION

Before I try to explain the seemingly anomalous juxtaposition of
defense and *capital punishment* in *Evangelium Vitae* and in the
revised *Catechism of the Catholic Church*, it is important to articulate five essential points from the Catholic tradition – my third
strategic goal in these remarks. As it so happens, these points are

articulated in their most refined form in the work of St. Thomas Aquinas, with whose insights most contemporary legal and moral thought has yet to catch up. But they are widely diffused throughout the writings of the Fathers and Doctors of the Church, and I think it not too much to say that these points are decisive for understanding the virtually unanimous consensus of Catholic tradition on the matter of the death penalty.

The first point concerns the transcendence of the common good. The common good isn't simply a quantitative idea – it isn't merely the private good for many as opposed to the private good for one, as though it were a question of arithmetic. Private goods are by nature particular and limited – if one has a private good then some others cannot have it. For example, if I drink my coffee, you don't – it is by nature an individual good. But common goods are ends that by nature are more shareable, more rationally diffusive, and more communicable. *Bonum diffusivum est*, the good is diffusive. And common good represents an end naturally more diffusive than private good. For instance, if a judge does *justice* in my case, this does not mean that there is less justice left over, that the judge is required to compensate by doing injustice to someone else. The sum of available justice is not diminished by the quantity meted out. Likewise, truth is not merely an individual good. We can simultaneously seek and consequently enjoy the same truth without it being in any way diminished. According to St. Thomas Aquinas, the common good is an end that is the genuinely higher, more universal, and rational good of each individual person. The common good is good for the individual, but it is not merely an individual good. Hence, prior to choice, *the common good is known to be an ethically weightier consideration than the private good – to transcend the individual good, and even at times to call for its sacrifice.*[4,5] *Not everything that is good for the individual is an individual* good – the common good manifests a greater ontological density than does the private good.

St. Thomas does teach that there are common goods more excellent than the political common good: for example, in *Quodlibet* 1, Q. 4, article 3, St. Thomas points out that God is the ultimate extrinsic common good of the entire universe. Nonetheless the political common good is more noble than the private good. It is *the good of right ordering of one thing to another in society called for by justice and truth, the defense of which may require sacrifice of some private good.*[6] Hence St. Thomas writes (*STh*.II-II.25.6.ad2) about imposition of the death penalty that "the judge puts this into effect, not out of hatred for the sinners, but out of the love of charity, by reason of which he prefers the public good to the life of the individual."[7] The part is ordered to the whole, and the whole here is not merely a quantitative amalgam, but the whole *qua* universal good which has formal priority over any merely individual good as such.

The second point concerns the nature of penalty. Penalty is retributive in its essence – as St. Thomas puts it, in the *Summa Contra Gentiles* (*SCG*.III.Part II.Ch. 141): "It is essential not only that punishment be a privation of the good, but also that it be contrary to the will." Elsewhere in the same work (*SCG*.II.Ch. 83), Thomas writes that "punishment is something contrary to a good of nature, and thus is said to be evil." As St. Thomas argues in the *Summa Theologiae* (I-II.87.3.ad1): "Punishment is proportionate to sin in point of severity, both in divine and in human judgments." It is not that one wishes the criminal precisely to suffer, which would render penalty indistinguishable from cruelty or sadism. Rather, it is that the criminal ceases to merit possession of certain human goods, the deprivation of which predictably will be a cause of suffering. Yet one may impose a just penalty out of charity for the common good, without gloating over another's sorrow. Thus Aquinas writes that (*STh* I-II, q. 87, a. 3, ad 3): "God does not delight in punishments for their own sake; but He does delight in the order of His justice, which requires them."

In punishment, the true bitterness of the evil embraced is manifested to the criminal. This always entails some form of banishment from the common ordering of providence and society, involving deprivations contrary to the criminal will. Manifestly the most profound form of such banishment is represented in a sentence of execution, whereby one is declared unfit to participate in the society of the living.

One should note also that penalties are what St. Thomas calls "determinations" rather than "conclusions" of the natural law. This is to say that penalties specify and particularize more general natural law purposes, and are prudentially tailored to circumstances, rather than being determined solely through some strict deduction from natural law.[8]

The third point from the tradition affirms that in addition to the retributive purpose of penalty, penalty is further ordered to medicinal ends for the common good. In this life we are not free to penalize solely with a backwards view to the nature of the crime and its gravity, but we also have a duty to look forward to the effect of any proposed penalty on the common good of society. As St. Thomas Aquinas puts it in the *Summa Theologiae*: "The punishments of this life are more of a medicinal character" (STh.II-II.108.3.ad 2). Considerations of deterrence and rehabilitation or conversion of criminals are further considerations of justice that specify retributive penalty. We may distinguish medicinal ends which are more individual and rehabilitative from medicinal ends which are more social and deterrent. Yet these diverse medicinal considerations all are ordered to the common good.

This directly leads to the fourth point found in the tradition and one which is especially clear in the work of St. Thomas Aquinas. The *primary* medicinal purpose of penalty is *neither deterrence nor rehabilitation*, but rather is *the manifestation of a transcendent norm of justice within society.*

Just as for St. Thomas law is not merely a command backed by force but is a *precept of reason*, so penalty, while coercive and contrary to criminal will, addresses all intelligences with the proportion of justice, revealing the inner misery merited by crime, and to some greater or lesser degree banishing the criminal from normal participation in the goods of society. This medicinal purpose of *manifesting* a transcendent norm of justice might be called a "truth manifestative" function of penalty essential to social healing and solidarity in the good. Inasmuch as the common good of society is a more universal and rational good, the laws and penalties of the state are by nature ordered to serve this good and to manifest the justice essential to it.

One might, after all, live in a society wherein retributive penalties were secretly imposed and never made public. In such a case the retributive end of penalty might be achieved, but such penalty would fail in manifesting justice within society. While penalty has a starkly punitive element, in this life it is more medicinal than retributive, and its highest medicinal purpose is the manifestation of a transcendent norm of justice.

The fifth point from the tradition that we need in order to interpret *Evangelium Vitae* correctly is common to the whole tradition, and is consummately articulated by Augustine and subsequently by Aquinas: namely, that the primal jurisdiction over life belongs by right not to the political state, but to God alone. The forcefulness of

Evangelium Vitae on this point is unassailable. In fact, all authority of the political state to execute, and even to punish, is delegated by God as a function of the participation of genuine human law in the eternal law. As St. Thomas reminds us (*Sth.*I-II.93.3.ad2): "Human law has the nature of law in so far as it partakes of right reason; and it is clear that, in this respect, it is derived from the eternal law."

Some while ago, at the Ave Maria School of Law, I debated the gifted literary editor of *The Weekly Standard*, Jody Bottum, on the question of the death penalty. His instinctive response to this view that God delegates to the state the authority to punish was to construe it as "theocratic." But it is not by some *superadded religiosity* that just government participates the eternal law – rather it is by the very being and nature of just law that it participates eternal law. The essential point is that all just law and government participates the eternal law, and that the state receives its power to judge, to punish, and, indeed, to execute from God. The nature of human society and political government, and the authority to penalize – and to kill – do not originate in any mere social contract, but in that natural law which is nothing other than a rational participation in eternal law.

IV. DEFENSE AND THE DEATH PENALTY IN *EVANGELIUM VITAE*

With these elements understood, we possess the tools we need to understand why *Evangelium Vitae* treats capital punishment in the context of defense. Within a culture of death where wrongful homicide is privatized by the state, the state tacitly assumes to itself the authority to permit that which no state justly can authorize. But when wrongful homicide on a massive scale is legally permitted, the primary medicinal end of the death penalty – to manifest a transcendent norm of justice within society – is seriously impeded. Within such a society it is in a sense an accident that the one being executed is actually guilty, for the state legally permits thousands of wrongful homicides.

Further, within the culture of death, the transcendent referent of the common good is progressively denied. We see a sign of this in the way that the death penalty often is construed in terms of emotional resolution or vengeance rather than in terms of the vindication of justice, as also in the efforts to suppress political discourse which acknowledges the complete truth about the nature and destiny of man. Radical devaluation of life and the loss of any transcendent referent for the common good each cripple the manifestation of justice through the imposition of the death penalty.

Insofar as the prime medicinal end of the death penalty – the manifestation of a transcendent norm of justice – is gravely impeded by the culture of death, the prudential consideration that remains is that of deterrence or defense. Hence both in the encyclical and in the *Catechism* the death penalty is treated in relation to *defensive considerations* – but this is a *prudential* judgment, not a doctrinal shift.

Encyclicals and catechisms often address widespread and determining circumstances that affect the reception of Catholic faith and morals. Clearly in the case of *Evangelium Vitae,* the strategic determining circumstance is that of the culture of death. Subtract this determining prudential factor, and the need for this encyclical at this time is drastically diminished. Accordingly, it is not "reading into" the context of this encyclical to note that the very factor which calls forth the encyclical is also the factor which obstructs the primary medicinal end of the death penalty.

The argument *is not* that only a Christian regime, or a regime healthy in every respect, can justly impose the death penalty. To the contrary, the Roman Empire possessed the just authority to execute criminals for grave crime, even under Nero. Our legal institutions bear the same authority today. But surely any reflective critic will need to admit that the abuse of the death penalty by Nero affected the capacity of this penalty to manifest justice within Roman society. When Christians were lighting up the night sky at Nero's garden parties, burning alive, does anyone really think that this had no affect on the manner in which the death penalty within Roman law of that time could socially manifest justice? *This* is the defining question of prudence.

Similarly, when the political state privatizes, protects, and privileges wrongful homicide, which hence comes to be widely practiced, and when justice itself is publicly framed as a mere command of the state at the behest of a usurpatory court – does anyone truly believe that this widespread and determining circumstance *does not affect* the manner in which imposing death can manifest justice? To deny these points is arguably to fall short of the social realism exhibited by Pope John Paul II's teaching in *Evangelium Vitae* regarding the culture of death.

V. POSTSCRIPT: TWO SOURCES FOR THE ERRONEOUS READING OF *EVANGELIUM VITAE*

By way of postscript, if the common approach to interpreting *Evangelium Vitae* is erroneous, we are well-advised to revisit the chief determinants of this error. Foremost among these is the loss of the perception of the transcendence of the common good of political society. And, as a theoretical matter, this loss is directly related to the teaching that goods denominated as basic are objectively incomparable or "incommensurable" prior to choice.

Because the proponent of moral incommensurability views the common good as no loftier than the private good, the common good of civil society comes to be viewed as purely instrumental in the satisfaction of essentially private desires. Consequently, the justice of the political state comes to be viewed as something less than a species of genuine justice. Whatever we may say about this teaching philosophically – and there is a great deal to say, pro and con, which fills the literature – it must be noted that everyone admits that *Evangelium Vitae excludes* the death penalty from its list of intrinsic evils or *mala per se*, and also that *it defines the death penalty as just under some circumstances*.

This leaves us with a stark fact. Inasmuch as *Evangelium Vitae* teaches that under certain circumstances the death penalty is a legitimate penalty for the sake of the common good – and this *is* what the encyclical holds irrespective how restrictive the circumstances are construed to be – it formally proposes a teaching that is directly contrary to this thesis of the incommensurability of goods denominated as basic. This is unavoidable once we denominate life as a basic good and then judge that it cannot be subordinate to, or sacrificed for the sake of, an essentially nobler good. Hence, for two millennia, up to and including *Evangelium Vitae*, the Church's teaching regarding the death penalty – and by extension, its treatment of the common good of political society – has been incompatible with the doctrine of the incommensurability of basic goods. It follows that we have reason, as Catholics, seriously to doubt this doctrine of the incommensurability of basic goods. When one finds that holding "x" is contrary to the perennial ordinary magisterium of the Church, this normally counts as a reason for the believer not to hold "x" rather than to anticipate the imminent change of a two-millennia-old teaching of the ordinary magisterium.

While one might lobby for a change of the Church's position in these matters, arguably it is more fitting to take another long, hard look at the discourse which leads up to this idea of the objective incomparability or incommensurability of basic human goods. The founding preoccupation of this doctrine of ethical incommensurability of basic goods with the dangers of utilitarian and proportionalist modes of analysis – a preoccupation excluding the consideration of objectively unified moral teleology – seems to doom it to fail to understand the Church's tradition: a tradition which, historically and doctrinally speaking, develops in another intellectual context altogether.

I would also suggest that dignitarian strains emanating from continental personalism may to some extent conduce to confusion regarding the common good. A view of the person as essentially ordered to progressively transcendent ends which are more diffusive common goods, is far different from one which treats the higher rational destiny of the person as implicitly dissociated from such perfective ends. It is not transparently clear that the thought of Levinas or Mounier is consistent with the thought of Augustine or Aquinas on these points.[9]

In any case, the perspicuous question about the Church's teaching on the death penalty is why a consistent teaching of over two millennia should be supposed to be tottering on the verge of non-entity? The teaching of *Evangelium Vitae* regarding the death penalty addresses the *circumstance* of the culture of death in relation to the prudential *determinatio* of penalty, and so clearly is prudential rather than doctrinal. The war of Catholics is not properly with their own tradition, but with the culture of death, and in that conflict of visions *Evangelium Vitae* gives us a direction that is wholly in accord with the deeper wellsprings of the tradition. Thank you.

Steven A. Long received his undergraduate degree from the University of Toledo and his MA in philosophy from the University of Toledo. He pursued postgraduate study at the University of Leuven in Belgium at the Institute of Philosophy, where he also undertook private studies with Fr. Jan Walgrave, O.P., the renowned Newman scholar and Thomist. He pursued further studies at the Catholic University of America in Washington, D.C., receiving his doctorate there in 1993. He has published in the *Revue Thomiste, The*

Thomist, The National Bioethics Quarterly, Communio, The International Philosophical Quarterly, the English language edition of *Nova et Vetera,* as well as in other journals. He lectures widely in both North America and Europe.

Dr. Long is married with four children, and currently teaches at the University of St. Thomas in St. Paul, Minnesota.

Notes

1   The two exceptions are Tertullian, who died outside the Church, and Lactantius.

2   Cf. *Acta Apostolicae Sedis* 47 (1955): 81–82, recounting this teaching of Pope Pius XII within this century. One notes also the high theological note characterizing the profession required of the Waldensians in 1210 in order to re-establish ecclesial communion. The Waldensians were required to acknowledge among other things the essential justice of the death penalty for grave crime. Cf. Denzinger, #425 – "Concerning secular power we declare that without mortal sin it is possible to exercise a judgment of blood as long as one proceeds to bring punishment not in hatred but in judgment, not incautiously but advisedly." Clearly to require this oath for the re-establishment of ecclesial communion at one moment, and then to require its opposite – where what is at stake is not prudential application, but the principled possibility of just penalty of death – would constitute not a development of doctrine, but rather a mutation. Note, again, that the statement directly refers to the death penalty in principle and that it indicates that as such it cannot be a *malum in se.*

3   Quite apart from the problem of confusing judicial penalty with defense, there is a further problem in the encyclical's prudential advisement that in contemporary circumstances the defense of society may be assured without recourse to the penalty. The difficulty is that this suggests a univocal judgment of prudence across extremely different circumstances. But it is not clear that one prudential determination of the efficacy of alternate means of defense can be adequate for all societies, or even within the same society at different times. Further, the claim that social concern for deterrence is unjust or contrary to reason is one that might be taken to presuppose that only the individual, and not the common good of society, is at stake in our legal practices: whereas deterrence is by natural law one of the social functions of penalty, as prior Catholic tradition clearly indicates. Accordingly, it seems more reasonable to read the encyclical as providing a general direction without ruling out the essential variety of circumstances that may affect whether a penalty adequately serves to defend society against the conduct penalized.

4   *STh.* II-II.152.4.ad3: "*Ad tertium dicendum quod bonum commune potius est bono privato si sit ejusdem generis.*" "The common good takes precedence of the private good, if it be of the same genus."

5 *STh.* II-II.117.6.resp.: *"...et in bonis humanis bonum publicum praeeminet bono privato" – i.e.,* "Public good prevails over private good."

6 Food is a particular good (the same steak can be eaten only by one), but that no one be arbitrarily denied food and starved to death pertains to the common good. Bodily life is a particular good, but that it not be subject to arbitrary cruelties and torture belongs to the common good. An airplane trip is a particular good: but the safety of air travel for passenger and non-passenger and the means to provide it pertain to the common good. A particular person's education is a private good, but that a society justly order the means for the discovery and communication of truth pertains to the common good. Justice in society is incompatible with arbitrary subjection to death – hence speed limits, driving on one side of the road rather than the other, laws governing the use or distribution of dangerous explosives or drugs, etc. Justice is utterly incompatible with mass murder imposed on citizen noncombatants – hence police, prisons, fleets, military power, domestic and foreign security and intelligence services, etc. All these considerations are proportioned and refer to the political common good.

7 *Sth.*II-II.25.6.ad2.

8 *STh.* I-II.95.2.resp. Note the following lines of St. Thomas: "Sed sciendum est quod a lege naturali dupliciter potest aliquid derivari: uno modo, sicut conclusiones ex principiis; alio modo, sicut determinationes quaedam aliquorum communium. Primus quidem modus similis est ei quo in scientiis ex principiis conclusiones demonstrativae producuntur. Secundo vero modo simile est quod in artibus formae communes determinantur ad aliquid speciale, sicut artifex formam communem domus necesse est quod determinet ad hanc vel illam domus figuram." – "But it should be noted that something may be derived from the natural law in two ways: first, as a conclusion from the premises, secondly, by way of determination of that which is more universal. The first way is like to that by which, in sciences, demonstrated conclusions are drawn from the principles: while the second mode is likened to that whereby, in the arts, general forms are particularized as to details: thus the craftsman needs to determine the general form of a house to some particular shape."

9 It is clear that certain contemporary dignitarian criticisms aimed specifically at Aquinas mis-portray his teaching, e.g., some would argue that Thomas denies the humanity of the criminal owing to his use of biblical glosses to depict criminals as making themselves like beasts through their crimes (e.g., Psalm 48:21: "Man, though he was honored, did not understand; he has been compared to the stupid beasts, and has been rendered similar to them"; and Proverbs 11:29: "Who is stupid will serve the wise"). But Thomas everywhere insists that the criminal must be treated with charity. While he views the criminal as bereft of that specific dignity which accrues to virtuous life, he does not consider the criminal to be bereft of the dignity accruing to human nature as such. For example, in II-II.64.2 Aquinas argues that we must hate sinners as regards their evildoing, but love them as regards their nature by virtue of

which they are capable of sharing with us in the beatific end. Even the condemned in Hell persist in the dignity of their human nature, which is the source of undying remorse. In this life, it is precisely owing to human dignity that a criminal may justly be held responsible for his action, and it is a sign of this same dignity that execution cannot in itself prevent achievement of the condemned person's last end of beatific vision. What is at stake is rather the nature of charity itself, and whether it is charitable to fail to honor the transcendence of the common good. It is also conspicuous in this regard, that, historically, it is materialists and utilitarian positivists who have argued – owing to their reductionist view of the person and of the common good – that the idea of the death penalty constitutes the cancelling of human dignity. Inveterate provincialism with respect to metaphysics has the predictable effect of obscuring from the mind the gradations of perfection in reality, especially as these delineate the superiority of common good to merely private good.

CATHOLIC MORAL TEACHING AND THE PROBLEM OF CAPITAL PUNISHMENT
E. Christian Brugger

THE PAPAL TEACHING INTERPRETED

Responses to the present papal teaching on the problem of capital punishment have been varying and even conflicting. Steven Long, whose ideas I consider in the second part of this essay, argues that the papal teaching cannot say what it appears to be saying because the Church has never said such a thing; it therefore must be interpreted as saying what the Church has always said. Avery Cardinal Dulles, s.j., tends to agree, arguing that what is new is not the underlying principle regarding the legitimacy of capital punishment but the application of that principle to changing conditions.[1] Gerard V. Bradley, on the other hand, says the treatment is novel; capital punishment, once justified as a means of retribution, is now is being assessed in terms of civil society's right to defend itself.[2] Mark Latkovic agrees but says the novelty does not go so far as to render capital punishment intrinsically evil.[3] Janet Smith suggests the pope might be leaning precisely in that direction.[4] James Hitchcock thinks the pope is trying to elevate the social conversation "to a higher plane . . . by affirming the sacredness of human life in all situations."[5] Charles Rice agrees and thinks the papal teaching has made "obsolete" the traditional view that death is the only fitting punishment for certain very grave crimes.[6] Justice Antonin Scalia thinks that Charles Rice and the pope are flat wrong.[7] And so on.

I think the papal teaching is saying something new.[8] Catholic tradition has argued that legitimate public authority rightly inflicts the death penalty for very grave crimes, and that its infliction, insofar as it serves to redress disorder introduced by a criminal's crime, protects the community from a dangerous influence, and deters others from committing similar crimes, is not only justified, but good. This is not something the present pontificate has taught, nor in my estimation would be willing to teach. The papal teaching as articulated in the 1997 edition of the *Catechism of the Catholic Church* (*CCC*) (which includes the morally relevant elements of the death penalty account of *Evangelium Vitae*) is unprecedented for a magisterial document. A careful examination justifies the conclusion that a theoretical foundation is being laid for a substantive revision in the Church's teaching on the morality of capital punishment. That revision would teach that capital punishment as *punishment* is no longer legitimate; that the state rightly uses lethal force only for purposes of self-defense, which means that inflicting death could not be justified as a means of retribution; that in using lethal force against a dangerous criminal, the state is justified only in using force proportionate to render him incapable of causing harm; if he dies as an consequence, his death would have to remain *praeter intentionem* (i.e., unintended).

This is not the explicit teaching of the *CCC*. But the conclusions follow neatly from a fair reading of the text. I say this for four reasons. First, capital punishment in the 1997 *CCC* (and *Evangelium Vitae*) is not conceived in traditional retributive terms, but rather in terms of self-defense; second, the *CCC* deliberately distances itself from traditional ways of categorizing the death penalty in the Church's tradition of justifiable homicide; third, it frames its discussion of the legitimate infliction of death in terms of double-effect reasoning; and fourth, the 1997 text deliberately suppresses the one statement from the 1992 text warranting the conclusion that death can be rightly inflicted as a punishment *per se*. I will consider each in turn.

The first indication that the papal teaching is proposing something new is found in the title of the subsection in which capital punishment is addressed. The section is entitled "Legitimate Defense." What precedent is there in the tradition for treating capital punishment as a form of legitimate defense? Almost none. Aquinas never uses the term "legitimate defense" *(defensio legitima),* neither in his treatment of the death penalty, nor in any major work on theology or morality. But he does use the related term "blameless defense" *(inculpata tutela).* Asking whether it is morally legitimate to kill a man in self-defense he answers: "It is legitimate to repel force with force provided one does so with the *moderation of a blameless defense*."[9] He adds: "Nor is it necessary for salvation that one omit an act of moderate defense in order to avoid killing another."[10] Aquinas' phrase *moderamine inculpatae tutelae* is repeated continually over the centuries in treatments on lawful killing – only not in regard to the infliction of the death penalty by public authority. Rather, in virtually every instance it is used as Aquinas uses it, that is, to limit lawful killing by private persons in self-defense.[11] When the 1917 and 1983 Codes of Canon Law use the term "legitimate defense" (*legitima tutela*), they too use it in reference to acts of legitimate killing by private persons in *self-defense*.[12] And when Vatican II's *Gaudium et Spes* uses the term its use is more or less the same.[13] In each, the context for the term's usage is self-defense. The *Catechism's* insertion of its treatment of the death penalty under this title is entirely novel.

The second indication that the magisterium intends to distance itself from its traditional justification for the death penalty occurs in the very first line of the subjection. It reads: "The legitimate defense of persons and societies *is not* an exception to the prohibition against the intentional killing of the innocent that constitutes murder" (No. 2263, emphasis added). Why deny at the outset that killing in legitimate defense is an exception to the fifth precept of the Decalogue? Perhaps because the *Catechism's* historical predecessor, the 1566 *Roman Catechism*, issued pursuant a decree of the Council of Trent, locates its teaching on the death penalty in a section explicitly devoted to "exceptions" to the fifth Commandment.[14] The logic is straight forward. The *Roman Catechism* teaches that capital punishment is an exception, the new *Catechism* teaches that it is not.

Third, the theoretical framework for the *Catechism's* treatment of capital punishment, indeed, its treatment of all forms of legitimate killing is double-effect reasoning. Recall Aquinas says that an act can have two or more effects, one intended the other(s) not. Since *intention* is primary, though not always sufficient, for assessing the morality of an act,[15] it can be morally legitimate to perform an act that results in bad effects, like death, provided the bad effects are unintended. The *Catechism*, having denied that killing in legitimate defense is an exception to the Decalogue, continues in its next sentence to quote Aquinas on double effect reasoning indicating that what the Commandment forbids is not all acts that bring about death, but only those that intend death: "The act of self-defense can have a double effect: the preservation of one's own life; and the killing of the aggressor . . . The one is intended, the other is not."[16] The next paragraph, no. 2264, applies double-effect reasoning to a specific form of legitimate defense, namely, the killing of aggressors by private persons in self-defense:

> Love toward oneself remains a fundamental principle of morality. Therefore it is legitimate to insist on respect for one's own right to life. Someone who defends his life is not guilty of murder even if he is forced to deal his aggressor a lethal blow:

> If a man in self-defense uses more than necessary violence, it will be unlawful: whereas if he repels force with moderation, his defense will be lawful... Nor is it necessary for salvation that a man omit the act of moderate self-defense to avoid killing the other man, since one is bound to take more care of one's own life than of another's (Aquinas ST, II-II, 64, 7c).

CCC Paragraph 2265 expands its scope of the term legitimate defense to include the defense that public authority renders on behalf of the community in repelling aggressors, implying that they are foreign aggressors:

> Legitimate defense can be not only a right but a grave duty for one who is responsible for the lives of others. The defense of the common good requires that an unjust aggressor be rendered unable to cause harm. For this reason, those who legitimately hold authority also have the right to use arms to repel aggressors against the civil community entrusted to their responsibility.

This paragraph does not explicitly mention a form of killing and so there is no need to specify limits in terms of double-effect reasoning. But there are two good reasons for concluding that the same context of indirect killing is being maintained. First, the logical relation set by the preceding paragraphs and absence of any indication of a change of context would seem to necessitate that the context of double-effect reasoning be carried over. Second, the defense the paragraph speaks about requires "rendering aggressors unable to cause harm." This is classical language in Catholic moral tradition used to explain the limits of lawful killing by private persons in self-defense. If the aggression of another threatens my life, the tradition from Aquinas very clearly has taught that the natural right to preserve myself in being justifies me in using force against that aggressor proportionate to render him unable to cause harm; and the tradition has unambiguously asserted that the killing that follows from such a defensive act must be unintended.[17]

Having addressed the duty of civil authority to defend the community against external threats in section 2265, we might anticipate that the next paragraph would address civil authority's duty to defend the community against internal threats. And this is what we find in paragraph 2266 in its consideration of just punishment:

> The efforts of the state to curb the spread of behavior harmful to people's rights and to the basic rules of civil society correspond to the requirement of safeguarding the common good. Legitimate public authority has the right and the duty to inflict punishment proportionate to the gravity of the offense. Punishment has the primary aim of redressing the disorder introduced by the offense. When it is willingly accepted by the guilty party, it assumes the value of expiation. Punishment then, in addition to defending public order and protecting people's safety, has a medicinal purpose: as far as possible, it must contribute to the correction of the guilty party.[18]

Is the context for no. 2266 still double-effect reasoning? It would seem not. In setting forth the primary aim of punishment in terms of retribution – "of redressing the disorder introduced by the offense" – the paragraph indicates that it is no longer talking about an act of forward looking self-defense. The defining aim of punishment, it says, is to correct a disorder caused by some crime, to look back, as it were, at something that has already happened, not forward at something that still threatens to happen. This makes sense, since only those who do wrong are rightly punished. Punishment, the paragraph says, *also* serves the purpose of "defending public order" and "protecting people's safety"; but neither of these two purposes makes punishment punishment.

We would expect number 2267, in which the death penalty is taken up, to frame its discussion of the lawful limits of capital punishment in terms of the theoretical framework used to define the nature and purposes of punishment outlined in 2266. But this is not what we find. When turning to the death penalty, the subsection returns to the language of double-effect reasoning:

> Assuming that the guilty party's identity and responsibility have been fully determined, the traditional teaching of the Church does not exclude recourse to the death penalty, if this is the only possible way of effectively *defending human lives against the unjust aggressor.*

> If, however, non-lethal means are sufficient *to defend and protect people's safety from the aggressor*, authority will limit itself to such means, as these are more in keeping with the concrete conditions of the common good and more in conformity with the dignity of the human person.

> Today, in fact, as a consequence of the possibilities which the state has for effectively preventing crime, *by rendering one who has committed an offense incapable of doing harm* – without definitively taking away from him the possibility of redeeming himself – *the cases in which the execution of the offender is an absolute necessity "are very rare, if not practically non-existent"* (Emphasis added).

The act of force referred to here is not an act of "punishment proportionate to the gravity of a criminal's offense"; it does not look back at a disorder introduced by deliberate crime; and it is not, in fact, an act of punishment according to the preceding paragraph's own definition. It is an act of self-defense as described in sections 2263–2265. The text states that it is a defensive act against an "aggressor" aimed at "rendering him incapable of doing harm." If he is safely incarcerated in prison, why refer to him as an aggressor? Why not call him "the condemned," "prisoner," the guilty," or some other term that appropriately describes one who lives under a sentence of death? The papal authors deliberately eschewed a traditional retributive framework and terminology in its treatment of capital punishment in favor of a framework and terminology equally traditional but not in relation to the death penalty, but rather in relation to lawful killing by private persons in self-defense. This is the language and framework of double-effect reasoning. Limiting the death penalty's lawful infliction by conditions traditionally invoked for the guidance of acts of private self defense, number 2267 concludes that "the cases in which the execution of the offender is an absolute necessity {*absolute necessarium*} 'are very rare, if not practically non-existent.'"[19] The last statement is of course taken directly from the papal encyclical *Evangelium Vitae*.

The final – and perhaps the clearest – indication that the papal teaching explicitly intends to re-conceive the death penalty along non-traditional lines is seen when we compare the 1992 version of the *CCC* with the same section in the 1997 *editio typica*. The 1992 version taught:

> For this reason the traditional teaching of the Church has acknowledged as well-founded the right and duty of legitimate public authority to punish malefactors by means of penalties commensurate with the gravity of the crime, *not excluding, in cases of extreme gravity, the death penalty* (Emphasis added).

A retributive justification is proposed here. Punishing someone "by means of penalties commensurate with the gravity of their crime" says they are being punished for what they have done, not for the threat they still pose. Sometimes a person's crime – "in cases of extreme gravity" – merits death. In such a case the death penalty is legitimate. This is a non-controversial re-articulation of a traditional principle of justifiable homicide. Remarkably, however, in the 1997 *CCC*, the clause I highlighted is suppressed. The statement in the 1992 text was the only indication that a traditional retributive justification of capital punishment was being maintained. And that proposition was deleted from the final authoritative text. Moreover, in 1992 the *Catechism* included its treatment of capital punishment in its analysis of punishment generally. In the revisions, the death penalty is moved from the section dedicated to punishment to its own section (2267).

ONE CRITIC

As I said, there is ample reason for concluding that a new doctrinal teaching on the morality of capital punishment is being anticipated in the *CCC*. Not all, however, would agree. Steven A. Long, for example, published an influential article in *The Thomist* in 1999 refuting this claim.[20] His essay is problematic in several respects, however. First, its method of interpretation is flawed, which results in a tendentious interpretation of the text and the explaining away of important assertions about the lawfulness of the death penalty in the modern world. Moreover, its use of Thomistic sources is misleading. Next, it falsely states that there is no precedent in Catholic moral tradition for the plain interpretation of the papal teaching. And, finally, it caricatures terribly the same plain interpretation.

Long's attention is directed exclusively to the treatment of the death penalty found in *Evangelium Vitae*, which, he says, is "the most important modern locus for understanding the Church's teaching on the topic."[21] Because the preparation of the *Catechism of the Catholic Church* (*CCC*) was a collaborative effort of the bishops of the world, and because the morally relevant elements of *Evangelium Vitae's* teaching were incorporated into the 1997 typical edition, I take the *Catechism's* teaching on the death penalty to be equally if not more important for assessing the mind of the present pontificate. I will therefore appeal to both documents in my analysis.

Long's essay revolves around a judgment that the apparent meaning of the death penalty teaching of *Evangelium* Vitae – and by extension the *CCC*, because it diverges from what the tradition has ordinarily taught – cannot be its actual meaning. In other words, the papal teaching should not be interpreted as saying what it appears to be saying, but rather as what the Church has always said. A methodological error at its outset, however, leaves this conclusion unconvincing. Long asserts at the beginning of his lengthy essay that "as a magisterial document, its meaning is *constituted* in relation to tradition."[22] Although appealing to Catholic tradition to help clarify ambiguous or partial magisterial statements is a valid principle of interpretation, to say that a document's meaning is "constituted" by its relation to the tradition (by which I take him to mean constituted by the meaning of past authoritative statements on the subject) is false. The meaning of an ecclesiastical statement or document is constituted in the first place by the intentions of its author(s). This is why it is possible to ask to what degree a particular magisterial assertion corresponds to or departs from the tradition *to which it contributes*. A Catholic scholar's role in the interpretation of ecclesiastical texts, therefore, is to ascertain in the first place, through careful analysis of a text, the precise intentions of its author. Most of the problems with Long's essay stem from his application of his exegetical principle to the papal teaching on capital punishment with the result that the most important elements of that teaching become relativized along lines that Long considers more compatible with the Catholic ethical tradition.

Long asserts that "a more traditional reading" of the encyclical, what he also calls a "prudential" reading, will "not hesitate to give 'defense of society' a rich meaning inclusive of the manifestation of a transcendent order of justice within society" (513–14). The term "defense of society," or more specifically "legitimate defense," deserves unpacking. Both *Evangelium Vitae* and the *CCC*, as I have shown, frame their discussions of the lawfulness of capital punishment in terms of legitimate defense; and in both, legitimate defense is narrowly construed to mean the collective self-defense of society. The death penalty, they teach, may only be inflicted when it is in the interests of societal defense. But as I have stated, the Catholic moral tradition has held that death can be a fitting punishment for a crime whether or not the self-defense of society remains at stake. In other words, the death penalty in the tradition has been justified as a means of retribution, as a means of giving criminals what they deserve. This tension between the present papal teaching and the ordinary teaching of the tradition is the sticking point for Long. It leads him to argue that we ought "not hesitate" to include within the interpretation of "societal defense" a retributive meaning. But that meaning is not sustained by the text. On the contrary, the text sets forth an exclusively non-retributive justification, namely necessary defense: *"The nature and extent of the punishment* must be carefully evaluated and decided upon, and ought not go to the extreme of executing the offender, except in cases of absolute necessity: in other words, when it would not be possible otherwise to defend society" (*EV*, 56). Recall too that the *Catechism's* analysis references Aquinas' discussion of lawful killing by private persons in self-defense. *Evangelium Vitae* does the same. Neither text references Aquinas' article defending the killing of malefactors by the state, an article which has exercised enormous influence on Catholic moral tradition, and with which any scholar familiar with traditional literature on capital punishment – including the drafters of *Evangelium Vitae* and the *CCC* – would be well acquainted. Why not? Why suppress such reference? Why reference instead an argument that says killing is legitimate only when necessary to render an aggressor incapable of causing harm? Why refer to the beneficiaries of this kind of killing, as in the *CCC,* as "aggressors," not "the condemned," "the guilty," etc.? One reason is because you intend to conceptualize lawful killing in capital punishment along lines of lawful killing in self-defense. Long discounts this possibility from the outset, calling it a "reductionist reading" of the papal teaching.[23] He says if we conceive of capital punishment under a paradigm of self-defense, then the papal teaching "will appear to mis-contextualize the teaching of Thomas," that is, it will appear to apply a set of norms to capital punishment that Aquinas only intended to be applied to self-defense. But this is precisely the novelty of the papal teaching, that its analysis applies a non-traditional paradigm to limit the lawful killing of criminals. Long admits that the text tends toward a novel justification: "If we accept a reading of the document as a doctrinal argument *apart from tradition*, it does appear to propose that only those executions are justified which are absolutely necessary to the physical protection of society" (517). But the text does not merely "appear" to say this, it states it outright: ". . . ought not go to the extreme of executing the offender except in cases of absolute necessity." (*EV*, 56).

Long uses fidelity to the tradition as a tool to reshape the meaning of the papal text. He says "we might wish to ask whether the solemn execution of a divine norm of justice might not be described as necessary to a richer conception of social order and the common good that may legitimize the application of the death penalty" (517). Defining capital punishment in these terms may very well lead to a "richer" conception of capital punishment, but whether or not it does is irrelevant to the meaning of the papal teaching, whose texts neither state nor imply such a meaning.

Evangelium Vitae, having established "absolute necessity" as the condition for the lawful infliction of the death penalty, concludes with the now well-known prudential judgment: "Today however, as a result of steady improvements in the organization of the penal system, such cases are very rare, if not practically non-existent." Commenting on the papal judgment, Long argues: "If one incorporates within 'protection of society' not only physical protection, but also the manifestation of transcendent justice in society as constituting a good in its own right . . . then there is no particular *doctrinal* reason why justified uses of the death penalty should be absolutely 'very rare, if not practically non-existent'" (*EV*, 56) (539). Again, there is no textual warrant for concluding that the intentions of the papal authors would tolerate such a conclusion. In so doing, as

Long's statement illustrates, one is forced to explain away the pope's prudential judgment that the condition of absolute necessity effectively eliminates the death penalty in the modern world as a viable alternative. Long's assumptions lead him to propose what he terms "a *more plausible reading,*" namely, that "the encyclical stresses that it is better for contemporary society to avoid the use of the penalty" (546). But the text does not state nor imply that it would merely be "better" to avoid inflicting death; it states that occasions warranting the penalty "are very rare, if not practically non-existent." Long says that "an astute intra-textual reading should see this prudential feature of the argument" (546–47). But such a feature should be seen if the author intended it to be seen. We are not warranted in reading such an intent into the papal teaching.

If it was the pope's intent to stay within the traditional framework, we may presume he would have made his intention clear; at the very least he would have referenced the account in Aquinas that scholars have referenced for centuries in defense of capital punishment. But he didn't. He did what is almost without warrant in the tradition: not only to state the condition of "absolute necessity" as the primary ground for the death penalty's lawful infliction; not only to refer to the beneficiaries as "aggressors"; not only to say that death penalty is lawful for purposes of rendering such aggressors incapable on causing harm; but also to reference Aquinas' account of lawful killing by private persons in self-defense as the basis of his statements.

Long's phrase, "the manifestation of the transcendent order of justice in society," used to describe what he takes to be the primary purpose of punishment in general, and capital punishment in particular, is repeated continually throughout his paper. It deserves a closer look.

Long attributes it to the Church's tradition, which he says stems from Aquinas.[24] But the phrase is neither Aquinas's nor the tradition's, but Long's. Punishment, Aquinas says, not only tends to the emendation of the one punished[25] and the preventing (deterring) of others from choosing wrongly,[26] but it also heals some *defectus* in the order of justice in civil society.[27] The order of justice to which Aquinas refers here is an order established by the just interactions of members of a community based upon naturally created equality and the morally relevant elements stemming from their relationships. It is a *moral* order maintained by the upright willing of the members of a community. The order can be called transcendent to the extent that the moral order is God's ordering of the human person to his proper end, just as divine providence orders all things in the universe towards their proper ends.[28] Deliberate crime disturbs this order to the extent that a criminal deliberately "exceeds the due degree of his measure when he prefers his own will to the divine will by satisfying it contrary to God's ordering."[29] A criminal "has been too indulgent to his will,"[30] has been "inordinate [in his] affection,"[31] "has exceeded in following his own will,"[32] all of which makes him "deserving of punishment".[33]

Because crime entails the immoderate satisfaction of the will, punishment entails the suppression of the wayward will in due proportion: "The nature of punishment consists in being contrary to the will, painful, and inflicted for some fault."[34] "By means of punishment the equality of justice is restored in so far as he who by sinning has exceeded in following his own will suffers something that is contrary to his will."[35] The result is the "restoration of the equality of justice."[36] Long's phrase, "the manifestation of the transcendent order of justice in society," what he calls elsewhere, the "'truth manifestative' function of punishment,"[37] never arises. And though it is intelligible, given Aquinas's conception of the just order of civil society as reflective of a community's conformity to the moral order established by divine providence, its imprecision is misleading. Rather than using the Hegelian notion of punishment as the *manifestation* of justice,[38] Aquinas and the tradition refer simply to punishment as the *correction* – in EV and the *CCC's* words, *redress* – of a disorder introduced into the good order of the community by a deliberate offence.

Even granting the similarity between Aquinas' retributive explanation of punishment and Long's conception of capital punishment as "the manifestation of the transcendent order of justice in society," it should be noted that Aquinas never to my knowledge justifies the infliction of capital punishment explicitly in terms of punishment's retributive function. When Aquinas turns from punishment in general to discuss capital punishment in particular, his justification invariably turns to his Aristotelian conception of the relationship of a part to its corresponding whole. The most prominent example is found in the *Summa Theologiae*, II-II, q. 64, a. 2c. There he writes:

> Now every part is ordered to the whole as imperfect to
> perfect. And therefore every part is naturally for the sake of

the whole. On account of this we see that if it is useful (*expediat*) to the health of the whole body of a man to cut off one of his members, as when it is putrid or corrupting of the other members, it will be praiseworthy and salubrious for it to be cut away. Now every individual person is compared to the whole community just as a part to the whole. Therefore if any one is dangerous and corrupting to the community on account of some sin, it is praiseworthy and salubrious that he be killed, in order to preserve the common good.[39]

He argues that dangerous and harmful men – with danger and harm being precisely specified in terms of "some sin" – may rightly be removed from the community as a diseased limb may be removed from the body whose integrity it threatens. Aquinas does not say here or elsewhere that the death penalty is only lawfully inflicted for purposes of societal defense. And his larger account of punishment makes it improbable that he would have employed such a limiting factor. But he does say that death as a punishment is justified when man's moral state becomes a threat to the community, that is, when the community needs to be protected from a person's harmful influence. But he certainly never says that killing a criminal "manifests a transcendent norm of justice." In fact, an explicitly retributive justification for capital punishment does not figure prominently into Catholic moral tradition until the sixteenth century.[40]

Long asserts that the 'reductionist' premise – that the state only rightly inflicts the death penalty when necessary for the physical protection of society – is not found "anywhere in Catholic sources prior to *Evangelium Vitae*" (539). Catholic theologians, however, back in the nineteenth century were beginning to argue along these lines. Francis Xavier Linsenmann, for example, an influential professor of theology at Tübingen, argued:

The death penalty can only be considered just – and therefore permissible – if it is necessary from the standpoint of self-defense; and it remains legitimate only so long and to such an extent that the need for self-defense remains. Just as war is self-defense writ large against an external threat to the community, so the infliction of *the death penalty is self-defense writ large* against an internal threat to the community, i.e., against a dangerous element in one of the many layers of the community itself. It follows, that if a condition of civil order and safety arises in which it is possible to control individual dangerous elements with lighter coercive means than death, then the death penalty would be rendered superfluous. Indeed, legally limiting the use of the death penalty is a goal well worth striving for. Its abolition by law is simply a political or cultural question; no principle of right stands against it.[41]

A twentieth century example is Jacques Leclercq, professor of moral theology at Louvain, who argued in the 1940s that:

The death penalty, like all punishment, is *legitimate* only *if it corresponds to the legitimate defense of the community.* It is not justified by a right of the state to dispose of the life of its citizens, but only by social necessity. The life of a man is in itself inviolable, for the state as for individuals.[42]

Legitimate defense, he makes clear, refers to self-defense – "unless the person in question poses a serious threat to the lives of others."[43] Leclercq continues: "Supposing there is no other effective means of defending the social order, it seems in practice that the death penalty must be limited to the case where civil authority has no other sure means of incarcerating dangerous offenders."[44] But other means of safely incarcerating criminals have been around for "more than a century (*plus d'un siècle*)." Therefore, he concludes, "today, in the Western world, the death penalty has ceased to be legitimate as states have other effective means (*suffisants moyens*) to defend the social order."[45] This conclusion is repeated by Catholic authors in the years that follow.[46]

By the end of his essay, Long's criticisms of the plain interpretation of the papal teaching become sweeping and farcical. Not only has the "reductionist interpretation," he argues, erroneously subsumed its analysis of the death penalty under a model of self-defense, but its entire rationale for punishment generally, he says, is derived from punishment's utility in defending public order:

The reductionist interpretation of *Evangelium Vitae* appears to place the entire *ratio* of penalty in question, suggesting that inasmuch as penalty is not required for defense of minimum public order it is superfluous. In arguing that mere physical protection is the primary aim of criminal law and penalty – such that a penalty not absolutely required for physical protection of society is to be avoided – the encyclical would then be construed to suggest that there is no question of justice pertinent to the common good beyond physical protection (541).

Evangelium Vitae neither states nor implies that the primary aim of punishment is the physical protection of society. When addressing the question of the justification of punishment in general, it asserts plainly that "the primary purpose of the punishment which society inflicts is 'to redress the disorder caused by the offence'" (*EV*, 56). (The second half of this quotation is taken directly from the *CCC*, no. 2266). The primary rationale for punishment, according to the encyclical, is not "physical protection," but retribution; punishment is punishment, in other words, to the extent that it looks back at a crime already committed and aims to correct the disorder that the crime introduced. This traditional account of punishment, immediately preceding the text's analysis of capital punishment, is what makes the papal teaching so interesting, and Long's interpretation so unsatisfactory. The text sets forth a thoroughly traditional account of the nature and purposes of punishment, and then, when turning to the particular type of punishment the death penalty entails, lays out *another* justification, apparently incompatible with the former; on the one hand, it says that the primary purpose of punishment is retribution, and on the other, that a criminal's crime alone is not a sufficient justification for killing the criminal; that although retribution defines punishment generally, it does not define capital punishment. The papal teaching says in effect that the death penalty may not be inflicted for purposes of retribution, but rather only in cases where it is absolutely necessary to defend civil society. It is not the encyclical's account of punishment, as Long suggests, that departs from the tradition, but the encyclical's failure to subsume its account of capital punishment under *its own* analysis of the nature and purposes of punishment.

Asserting without argument that the plain interpretation follows from an inadequate conception of the common good, which, Long says, has been proposed "in the effort to come to terms with republican political institutions and the old liberalism," he levels the elliptical criticism: "The regnant minimalist interpretation of the teaching of *Evangelium Vitae* constitutes another minimalist epicycle in the to and fro between rich and eviscerated senses of political common life" (543). But paragraph 56 of *Evangelium Vitae* is traditional in its account of punishment, and it is traditional in its conception of the duties of civil authority. It maintains that punishment is primarily ret- ributive and that public authority has the responsibility to inflict ret- ributive punishment – "Public authority must redress the violation of personal and social rights by imposing on the offender an adequate punishment for the crime" (*EV*, 56). It just does not include capital punishment as one of the available expressions of this authority. There is no indication that it maintains an "eviscerated" conception of political common life. Long continues saying that "the reduction- ist major premise (viz, that the State rightly inflicts the death penal- ty only when absolutely necessary for the physical protection of soci- ety) seems to embrace an instrumentalist view of the common good that is, finally, incompatible with the infliction of any punishment save on grounds that appear remarkably utilitarian" (549). It is not clear what Long means by the phrase "instrumentalist view of the common good," or what is particularly problematic in conceiving the common good as instrumental. *Gaudium et Spes*, for example, defines the "common good" as instrumental to the goods of persons, and nothing about this suggests incompatibility with retributive pun- ishment.[47] It does seem fair to say, however, that the encyclical's jus- tification for capital punishment is grounded in empirical considera- tions and devoid of formal (retributive) ones. If this is what Long means by "utilitarian," then, in this respect, his point is granted. But to say that the plain interpretation of *Evangelium Vitae* entails a view of the common good that is "incompatible with the infliction of *any* punishment" save on utilitarian grounds is gratuitous. Not only are some punishments, according to the papal teaching, primarily justi- fied on non-utilitarian, retributive grounds, but *all* punishments are, save capital punishment.

Long concludes by saying that "the reductionist interpretation of *Evangelium Vitae* to this effect is vulnerable to decisive criticism from tradition" (551). While I reject the view that the plain interpre- tation of *Evangelium Vitae* (and the *CCC*) is 'reductionist,' it is fair to say that it departs from tradition and in that sense is subject to crit- icism. I suggest, however, that rather than relativizing the papal teaching along traditional lines, we should be making every effort to fairly formulate that teaching, asking to what degree it is compatible with the Church's traditional teaching on the lawfulness of capital punishment, examining where the present teaching is pointing, and judging whether or not, in light of Catholic tradition, the Church can go there.

WITH WHAT AUTHORITY?

I would like to conclude this essay by asking the question: Is the Church bound by an irreformable tradition not to take the next step in declaring the death penalty wrong *per se*? This question comes down to whether or not the traditional justification of the right of civil authority to inflict death has been infallibly taught by the magisterium of the Catholic Church. Vatican II teaches that the Church's infallibility is exercised when: 1) the pope as successor of Peter intends to solemnly define an article of faith or morals (i.e., makes an *ex cathedra* statement); 2) the bishops in union with the pope gathered together in council intend to solemnly define a dogma; and 3) the bishops scattered throughout the world though preserving a bond of communion amongst themselves and with the successor of Peter agree on a judgment on a matter of faith or morals and teach it as to be definitively held (This latter is called the infallibility of the ordinary and universal magisterium).[48]

Has the proposition "capital punishment is in principle a legitimate exercise of civil authority" ever been solemnly defined by a pope or ecumenical council? The topic of capital punishment has rarely been raised by ecumenical councils. Among those at which it has, no judgement on its morality has ever been taught. Lateran III (1179) speaks of the assistance the Church receives from harsh penal laws, but does not propose any moral judgment on the death penalty *per se*.[49] And Lateran IV (1215) states that clergy are forbidden from participating in bloody punishment, but also makes no positive assertions about the death penalty's morality.

As for papal statements, only two are of such a nature as to merit attention. The first is the famous statement in the Waldensian Oath by Pope Innocent III in the early 13th century. In the context of a profession of faith intended to reconcile members of the heretical sect, he states:

> We declare that the secular power can without mortal sin impose a judgment of blood provided the punishment is carried out not in hatred, but with good judgement, not inconsiderately, but after mature deliberation.[50]

With what authority was this statement proposed, or rather, was the profession of faith in which the statement appears proposed? First, the profession is directed to a particular group and not to the universal Church; and second, it was published in the form of a personal letter to the breakaway sect members and not in the form of a Bull or otherwise universally authoritative document. Not all its assertions therefore should be taken to be Catholic dogmas, binding on the universal Church, even though certain assertions already possess this status. If, therefore, one of its propositions is not already a definitive doctrine of Catholic faith, its presence in the oath to the Waldensians does not alone suffice to constitute it as such. It is my judgement therefore that Innocent's statement does not constitute an infallible definition.

The second papal is a solemn condemnation of an article ascribed to Martin Luther by Pope Leo X in his Bull *Exsurge Domine* (1520). Luther's proposition reads: "That heretics be burned is against the will of the Spirit."[51] With what authority was this condemnation promulgated? *Exsurge Domine* is a papal Bull, a document of high papal authority addressed to the whole Church. Its solemn condemnations single out judgments of faith and morals considered to be dangerous to Christian faith and life.[52] For argument's sake, let us say the censures it contains have been promulgated with the highest degree of papal authority. Should we also conclude that the *falsity* of Luther's proposition has been proposed infallibly, entailing the conclusion that the burning of heretics is *not* contrary, or not always contrary, to the will of the Holy Spirit? To resolve this question we need first to examine the precise language of the papal condemnation. The general censure which follows the list of Luther's 41 condemned propositions reads: "All and each of the above mentioned articles or errors, so to speak, as set before you, we condemn, disapprove, and entirely reject as respectively heretical, or scandalous, or false, or offensive to pious ears, or seductive of simple minds, and in opposition to Catholic truth."[53] The precise formulation warrants us in concluding no more than that the article in question is among a set of articles whose members are either heretical *or* scandalous *or* false *or* offensive to pious ears *or* seductive of simple minds, and are obstructive to Catholic truth. It is reasonable to conclude therefore that the falsity of Luther's proposition has not been infallibly proposed in *Exsurge Domine*.

The question remains however whether the liceity of the death penalty has been infallibly taught by the ordinary and universal magisterium. Vatican II's formulation of this mode of infallibility reads:

> ...the individual bishops. . . proclaim Christ's doctrine
> infallibly whenever, even though dispersed through the

world, but still maintaining the bond of communion among themselves and with the successor of Peter, and authentically teaching matters of faith and morals, they are in agreement on one position as to be definitively held.

It states four conditions that must be met before this mode of infallibility has been exercised: 1) the bishops must remain united amongst themselves and with the successor of Peter; 2) they must teach authentically on a matter of faith or morals; 3) agree on one judgment; and 4) proclaim it "as to be definitively held" (*definitive tenendam*). To resolve the question as to whether these four conditions have been met relative to the Church's tradition defense of capital punishment would involve an in-depth analysis that is beyond the scope of this paper. I have undertaken it elsewhere and have concluded as follows:

> The evidence supports the conclusion that the first three criteria have been met. The writings of Catholic bishops and councils of bishops going back to early Christianity contain an explicit or implicit affirmation of one or more of the propositions summarizing the Church's traditional teaching. These affirmations have remained constant and the bishops have remained united in them among themselves and with the successor of Peter. If chronological scope and the magnitude and firmness of consensus were all that were necessary for the bishops in their ordinary teaching to proclaim doctrine infallibly, there could be little doubt about the status of the Church's traditional affirmation on the lawfulness of the death penalty. But *Lumen Gentium* states that the bishops' judgment on an issue, even their united and firm judgment, is not enough to assure the protection of the Holy Spirit from error. As teachers of the Christian faith, the bishops must teach that judgment to the faithful not simply as a doctrine of Christianity, nor as a probable or very probable conclusion of Christian faith, but as a matter of faith, certainly true, to be definitively held by all. Their act of teaching and the faithful's act of receiving are complementary, and it is in this movement of teaching and receiving that the Holy Spirit secures and advances the right belief of the Church.
>
> [I judge that] the evidence does not warrant the conclusion that this final criterion of the ordinary and universal

magisterium has been met. Scattered episcopal statements assert all or part of the traditional teaching as to be definitively held, but the majority of episcopal statements are not proposed in this manner. More often than not, the lawfulness of capital punishment is directly or indirectly affirmed only in the context of discussions, condemnations, and affirmations of other points of human morality.[54]

This, of course, is a scholarly judgment. If the Church should teach otherwise I would assent to the Church's judgment and encourage others to do the same. But if my conclusion is true, then it implies that the Church's traditional teaching can change. To speak about the changing of a teaching as eminent and long-standing as the Church's defense of the death penalty understandably makes some people uneasy. The concern is that an analysis like the one I propose opens the way to a rejection of other controversial but authoritative moral teachings by those characterized by a disposition of dissent or those who are weak in conscience. This is not my intention. My intention is to provide a fair and honest reading of the present papal teaching and then ask its implications. If the *doubt* regarding the traditional teaching was raised in the first place by me, or by a small group of theologians, or a large group of dissident theologians like the CTSA, then there would be good reason not to entertain serious doubt about the verity of the traditional judgment. Such is the case, for example, with the widespread unjustifiable dissent from the central moral judgment of Paul VI's *Humanae Vitae*.

But the present situation is different. The signs of revision have not arisen in the first place by dissident theologians or disaffected Catholics. Rather, clear signs are found in contemporary doctrinal documents promulgated by the bishops of the world in union with the successor of Peter. Whereas Christian writers from the early Church up through the middle of the twentieth century maintained a relatively consistent attitude towards the death penalty, that attitude began to change in the 1950s and 1960s, and more so in the 1970s and 1980s, so that by the middle of the 1990s, a far-reaching turn in the Church's attitude toward capital punishment had taken place.[55] The attitudinal change alone might be considered sufficient justification for asking questions regarding a *change* in the traditional teaching. But more followed. The attitudinal turn was fused in 1995 and 1997 with formal and universally authoritative doctrinal promulgations of the magisterium (viz., *Evangelium Vitae* and the *CCC*), promulgations that clearly introduce new terminology and a new ethical paradigm for examining an age old problem. In light of this, it seems to me not only justified, but of paramount importance for theologians, to ask questions of the tradition that otherwise might not be warranted to ask.

E. Christian Brugger is an assistant professor of ethics in the Religious Studies Department at Loyola University. He earned his Ph.D. in Christian Ethics from the University of Oxford in England. His thesis was on the problem of Capital Punishment in Catholic Moral Tradition. He also has a Master's Degree in Moral Philosophy from the Harvard Divinity School in Cambridge, Massachusetts, as well as a Master's in Moral Theology from Seton Hall University in South Orange, New Jersey. He is the author of *Capital Punishment and the Roman Catholic Moral Tradition* (Notre Dame Press, 2003). He had published widely on the topic of Christian ethics.

Notes

1   See Avery Dulles, S.J., "The Death Penalty: A Right to Life Issue?" Laurence J. McGinley Lecture, Fordham University (October 17, 2000); reprinted in *First Things* as "Catholicism and Capital Punishment" (April 2001).

2   Gerard V. Bradley, "The Teaching of the Gospel of Life," *Catholic Dossier* 4 (Sept.-Oct. 1998), 43–48.

3   Mark S. Latkovic, "Capital Punishment, Church Teaching, and Morality: What is Pope John Paul II Saying to Catholics in *Evangelium Vitae*?" *Logos* 5:2 (Spring 2002), 82.

4   Janet E. Smith, "Rethinking Capital Punishment," *Catholic Dossier* 4 (Sept.-Oct. 1998), 49–50.

5   James Hitchcock, "Capital Punishment and Cultural Change in American Life," in *Capital Punishment: Three Catholic Views* (Washington, D.C.: Faith and Reason Institute, 2003), 13.

6   Charles Rice, "Avery Cardinal Dulles and His Critics: An Exchange on Capital Punishment," in *First Things*, (August/September 2001), 9.

7   Antonin Scalia, "Justice Scalia's Letter to the Editor," *National Catholic Register* (March 24–31, 2002).

8   *Catechism of the Catholic Church*, nos. 2263–67; *Evangelium vitae*, nos. 55–56.

9   "*Vim vi repellere licet cum moderamine inculpatae tutelage*," *ST,* II-II, q. 64, a. 7c, emphasis added.

10 *"Nec est necessarium ad salutem ut homo actum moderatae tutelae praetermittat ad evitandum occisionem alterius," ST,* II-II, q. 64, a. 7c.

11 A few examples include: Alphonsus Marie de Liguori, *Theologia Moralis,* tom. 1, lib. 3, tract. 4, cap. 1, dub. 3, par.380 (Rome: *Ex Typographia Vaticana,* 1905); M. Zalba, S.J., *Theologiae Moralis Compendium,* vol. 1 (Madrid: Biblioteca De Autores Cristianos, 1958), no. 1591, p. 871; I. Aertnys, C.SS.R. and C. Damen C.SS.R., *Theologia Moralis* (Rome: Marietti Editori Ltd., 1956), tom. I, lib. III, tract. V, cap. III, no. 571, p. 541.

12 *"Causa legitimae tutelae contra iniustum aggressorem, si debitum servetur moderamen, delictum omnino aufert; secus imputabilitatem tantummodo minuit, sicut etiam causa provocationis." Codex Iuris Canonici* (1917), can. 2205, § 4; *"legitimae tutelae causa contra iniustum sui vel alterius aggressorem egit, debitum servans moderamen"; "ab eo, qui legitimae tutelae causa contra iniustum sui vel alterius aggressorem egit, nec tamen debitum servavit moderamen"; Codex Iuris Canonici* (Vatican City: Libreria Editrice Vaticana, 1983), can. 1323, 5⁰, 1324, 6⁰.

13 In its treatment of warfare it teaches: "Once all means of peaceful negotiations are exhausted," governments cannot be denied the right of legitimate defense." It is the responsibility of civil authority, it continues, to "protect the safety of people," to provide "a defense that is just," and should never use means which "far exceed the limits of legitimate defense {*legitimae defensionis*}" (GS 79, 80). The context is still self-defense, not, however, the private defense of an individual, but rather the self-defense of the community.

14 The catechism itemizes five exceptions: 1) the killing of animals; 2) the execution of criminals; 3) killing in a just war; 4) killing by accident; and 5) killing in self-defense.

15 John Finnis, *Aquinas* (Oxford University Press, 1998), 27.

16 *ST,* II-II, q. 64, a. 7c.

17 See Aquinas *ST,* II-II, q. 64, a. 7c; although Aquinas only refers to aggressors, not *unjust* aggressors, it is not uncommon for authors to refer to the status of the aggressor's aggression as *unjust,* if not formally, at least materially; e.g., Henry Davis writes: "Everyone has a natural right to defend himself against unjust aggression even to the death of the assailant . . . But the assailant's death is a secondary result of my act, the primary result being my own defense. The doctrine is justified on the universally valid principle of the double effect. (nt. II-II, q. 64, a. 7c)"; H. Davis, S.J., *Moral and Pastoral Theology,* 5th ed , (London: Sheed and Ward, 1946), 152–53; see also *EV,* no. 55, p. 28 below.

18 I consider this paragraph in greater depth in the next chapter and so my comments here are limited to the context of the discussion at hand.

19 It should be noted that this claim is a matter of sociological and technological fact, not a matter of faith and morals. Since the teaching author-

ity of the Church extends only to matters of faith and morals (cf. LG, no. 25), it cannot be said to form part of the Church's authoritative teaching on capital punishment, but must be held to be incidental to it.

20 Steven A. Long, *"Evangelium Vitae*, St. Thomas Aquinas, and the Death Penalty," *The Thomist,* 63, 4 (October 1999), 511–52.

21 *Ibid.,* 511.

22 *Ibid,* 513, emphasis added.

23 Long says the same in another essay: "Yet careful reading of the document itself shows that *Evangelium Vitae* cannot intend to declare that the formal doctrinal reason for capital punishment is some species of mere defense." See *"Evangelium Vitae* and the Death Penalty," in *Capital Punishment: Three Catholic Views* (Washington, D.C.: Faith and Reason Institute, 2003), 29.

24 In the same essay, Long asserts that "the *primary* medicinal purpose of penalty is *neither deterrence nor rehabilitation,* but rather is *the manifestation of a transcendent norm of justice within society.*" This, he states, "is especially clear in the work of St. Thomas Aquinas." See *"Evangelium Vitae* and the Death Penalty," 33.

25 *Commentary on Aristotle's* Nicomachean Ethics (*Eth.*), bk. II, lecture III, n. 4, 270; *ST,* II-II, q. 108, a. 4c; *SCG,* III, c. 158, n. 6; *ST,* I-II, q. 87, a. 6, ad. 3; *In Lib. III Sent.,* d. 19, q. 1, a. 3, sol. 2.

26 See *SCG,* III, c. 140, n. 7, *In Lib. IV Sent.,* d. 46, q. I, a. 2, sol. 3, ad. 2, *ST,* I-II, q. 87, a. 8, ad. 2, II-II, q. 33, a. 6c.

27 *Commentum In Lib. II Sententiarum Magistri Petri Lombardi (In Lib. II Sent.),* d. 42, q. 1, a. 2, sol.; see also *In Lib. III. Sent.* d. 19, q. 1, a. 3, sol. 2. See also *Summa Contra Gentiles (SCG),* III, ch. 144, 9–11.

28 *SCG,* III, c. 140, n. 2–4

29 *SCG,* III, c. 140, n. 5.

30 *ST,* III, q. 86, a. 4c; I-II, q. 87, a. 6c.

31 *ST,* I-II, q. 87, a. 1, ad. 3.

32 *ST,* II-II, q. 108, a. 4c.

33 *ST,* I-II, q. 87, a. 1, ad. 2.

34 *ST,* I-II, q. 46, a. 6, ad. 2; "The nature of punishment is that it is contrary to the will." *On Evil,* q. 1, a. 4c, tr. Jean Oesterle (University of Notre Dame Press, 1995); see also SCG, III, c. 140, n. 5, c. 141, n. 1, 4, 6; *In Lib. II Sent.,* d. 42, q. 1, a. 2, sol.; ST , I, q. 48, a. 5c, I-II, q. 87, a. 6c.

35 *ST,* II-II, q. 108, a. 4c.

36 *ST,* I-II, q. 87, a. 6c.

37 See Steven Long, *"Evangelium Vitae* and the Death Penalty," 33.

38 *Hegel's Philosophy of Right,* tr., T. M. Knox (Oxford: Oxford University Press, 1967), 69–73.

39 *"Omnis autem pars ordinatur ad totum ut imperfectum ad perfectum. Et*

ideo omnis pars naturaliter est propter totum. Et propter hoc videmus quod si saluti totius corporis humani expediat praecisio alicuius membri, puta cum est putridum et corruptivum aliorum, laudabiliter et salubriter abscinditur. Quaelibet autem persona singularis comparatur ad totam communitatem sicut pars ad totum. Et ideo si aliquis homo sit periculosus communitati et corruptivus ipsius propter aliquod peccatum, laudabiliter et salubriter occiditur, ut bonum commune conservetur", my translation; cf. *SCG*, III, c. 146, nos. 4–5; see Aristotle, *Politics*, bk. 1, ch. 2, 1253a, 19–29.

40 See chapter 6 of my forthcoming book, *Capital Punishment and Catholic Moral Tradition* (Notre Dame, IN: University of Notre Dame Press).

41 *"In der Tat muss man vom Wesen und Zweck der Strafe als solcher absehen und darauf recurriren, dass die Todestrafe nur als gerecht erkannt wird, wenn sie aus einem andern Grunde für nothwendig erklärt werden muss; mit andern Worten: Die Todestrafe ist nur zulässig, wenn dieselbe unter den Gesichtspunkt der Nothwehr gebracht werden kann; und sie ist es nur so lange und in solcher Ausdehnung, als die Nothwehr vorliegt. Gleichwie der Krieg eine Notwehr im Grossen ist gegen Bedrohung der Gesellschaft von Aussen her, so ist Ausrechthaltung der Todestrafe eine Nothwehr im Grossen gegen die Bedrohung der Gesellschaft durch innere Feinde, durch gemeingefährliche Elemente in den verschiedenen Schichten der Gesellschaft selbst. Hieraus folgt, dass es ganz wohl einen Zustand bürgerlicher Ordnung und Sicherheit geben könnte, in welchem einzelne gemeingefährliche Elemente mit leichteren Zwangsmitteln, als die Hinrichtung ist, niedergehalten werden könnten, die Todestrafe also entbehrlich wäre; ja, dass es ein zu erstrebendes Ziel sei, die Anwendung der Todestrafe gesetzlich einzuschränken. Die gesetzliche Abschaffung der Todestrafe ist einfach eine politische oder Culturfrage, ein Rechtsgrund steht ihr nicht entgegen."* F. X. Linsenmann, *Lehrbuch der Moraltheologie* (Freiburg im Breisgau: Herder, 1878), 473, emphasis added.

42 *"La peine de mort, comme toute peine, n'est légitime que si elle correspond à la légitime défense de la collectivité. Elle ne se justifie pas par un droit de l'État à disposer de la vie des citoyens, mais seulement par la nécessité sociale. La vie de l'homme prise en elle-même est invi-olable pour l'État comme pour les particuliers."* Jacques Leclerq, *Lecons De Droit Naturel* vol. IV- *"Les Droits Et Devoirs Individuels"* (Louvain: Société D'Études Morales, 1946), 89.

43 *". . . un danger grave pour celle des autres." Ibid.*, 89.

44 *"La peine de mort supposant qu'il n'y ait pas d'autre moyen efficace de défendre l'ordre social, il semble qu'en pratique, il faille la limiter aux cas où les pouvoirs publics ne disposent pas de moyens sûrs d'incarcérer les malfaiteurs.."*

45 *"Dans le monde occidental, la peine de mort a cessé d'être légitime, les*

États disposant sans elle de moyens suffisants pour défendre l'ordre social." Ibid., 90.

46 E.g., "The theologians' acceptance of the state's right to inflict capital punishment does not rule out a divergence of opinion on the appropriateness of exercising that power in given conditions. It seems that a growing number of moralists would like to see the power of the sword in abeyance, a power to be exercised should the need arise but otherwise resolutely kept in the background." M. B. Crowe, "Theology and Capital Punishment," *The Irish Theological Quarterly,* 31, no. 1 (Jan. 1964), 102; "There will always be criminals, but modern society has other means of protecting itself from them than this . . ." Jean Imbert, *La Peine de Mort: Histoire-Actualité* (Paris: Armand Colin: 1967), English quote in James J. Megivern, *The Death Penalty: An Historical and Theological Survey* (New York: Paulist Press, 1997), 297; "The death penalty for murder in this country [i.e., England] at present is unnecessary and therefore unjust." M. Tidmarsh, O.P., et al., *Capital Punishment: A Case for Abolition* (London: Sheed and Ward, 1963); see also "Statement of Rhode Island's religious leaders," *Origins,* vol. 5, no. 40 (25 March 1976), 629, 631; Declaration of the Administrative Board of the Canadian Catholic Conference, 1976, in Thomas G. Daily, "The Church's Position on the Death Penalty in Canada and the United States," *Concilium,* 120 (10 October 1978), p. 122; before the 20th century, see Beccaria, *On Crimes and Punishments,* ch. 28, par. 3.

47 "Interdependence (between nations) . . . is leading to an increasingly universal common good, the sum total of the conditions of social life enabling groups and individuals to realize their perfection more fully and readily," *Gaudium et Spes,* 26. "And the common good comprises the sum of the conditions of social life which enable individuals, families and associations to reach their own perfection more completely and more readily." *Ibid,* 74.

48 *Lumen Gentium,* 25.

49 It is actually a quote from St. Leo the Great; *"Sicut (ait beatus Leo,) licet ecclesiastica disciplina, sacerdotali contenta iudicio, cruentas non efficiat ultiones, catholicorum tamen principum constitutionibus adiuvatur, ut saepe quaerant homines salutare remedium, dum corporale super se metuunt evenire supplicium."* Third Lateran Council (1179), ch. 27 (*DEC-I,* 224). This statement appears again in Decretal. Gregor. IX, lib. V, tit. VII- *De Haereticis,* cap. VIII (*CIC-2,* cols. 779–80).

50 *"De potestate saeculari asserimus quod sine peccato mortali potest judicium sanguinis exercere, dummodo ad inferendam vindictam, non odio, sed judicio, non incaute sed consulte procedat."* (PL, tom. CCXV, col. 1512a), my translation; the entire revised 1210 profession is translated in Denziger, *The Sources of Catholic Dogma,* tr. Roy J. Deferrari (London: B. Herder Book Co., 1954), nos. 420–27, esp. no. 425.

51 *Denz.* 773.

52 It is not uncommon for the authoritative condemnations of papal bulls to
    be judged to have been promulgated with infallible authority. Francis A.
    Sullivan S.J., for example, claims that theologians Louis Billot, in his
    work *Tractatus de Ecclesia Christi* (1898), and Edmond Dublanchy, in
    his article on infallibility in the *Dictionnaire de Théologie Catholique*
    (1927), judged that *Exsurge Domine* (1520) contains "dogmatic defini-
    tions." Sullivan does not specify to which propositions he refers. His
    own judgment is that *Exsurge Domine* "does not meet the requirements
    for a dogmatic definition." See Sullivan, *Creative Fidelity: Weighing
    and Interpreting Documents of the Magisterium* (Dublin: Gill &
    Macmillan, Ltd, 1996), 84–85.

53 *Denz.* 781.

54 E. Christian Brugger, *Capital Punishment and Catholic Moral Tradition*
    (Notre Dame, IN: University of Notre Dame Press, forthcoming), 151.

55 A few examples of national conferences going on record in the past
    twenty five years in opposition to the death penalty include: Canadian
    Catholic Conference (press release, March 4, 1976); Irish Bishops (see
    Irish Commission for Justice and Peace, "Capital Punishment," *The
    Furrow* 27 (1976), 697–8, *La Documentation Catholique*, 78 (1981),
    581–4); French Bishops (see Social Commission of the French
    Episcopate, "*Éléments de Réflexion sur la Peine de Mort*," *La
    Documentation Catholique*, 75 (1978), 108–15); Philippine Bishops (see
    "Restoring the Death Penalty: 'A Backward Step'," *Catholic
    International* 3 (1992), 886–88); Bishops of England and Wales (see
    "Bishops Say "No" to the Re-introduction of Capital Punishment,"
    Briefing of the Catholic Information Service, 15 July 1983, vol. 13, no.
    22); the U.S. Catholic bishops individually or in state or national con-
    ferences have issued over 130 statements in opposition to the death
    penalty since 1980 alone (see Catholics Against Capital Punishment,
    *Bibliography of Statements by U.S. Catholic Bishops on the Death
    Penalty: 1972–1998*; (CACP, P.O. Box 3125, Arlington, Va 22203,
    USA).

FORMAL AND MATERIAL
COOPERATION WITH EVIL

LAWYERS AND COOPERATION WITH EVIL IN DIVORCE CASES
Rev. John J. Coughlin, O.F.M.

Please permit me to begin my remarks by expressing my admiration for the Fellowship of Catholic Scholars. One of the benefits of this Fellowship is that we gather as Catholic intellectuals and attempt to articulate in an intelligent and faith-filled way the truth of the Catholic tradition. We are often faced with the difficult task of explaining and defending a counter-cultural truth. The task is also sometimes a thankless one. In this regard, I would like to take this opportunity to express my gratitude to two of the founding members of this society, Monsignor William Smith and Father Donald Keefe, S.J., who are in the audience. For seven years, I was privileged to serve as a spiritual director and fellow member of the teaching faculty with these two fine priests at St. Joseph's Seminary, Dunwoodie, in Yonkers, New York. Both of them in their own ways represent the scholar-priest, an indispensable tradition in the life of the larger ecclesiastical communion.

My topic today is lawyers and cooperation of evil. Specifically, I shall limit my remarks to lawyers and divorce cases. I have addressed this issue previously in a published article, and it is not my intention simply to repeat the analysis offered elsewhere.[1] Although some of the previous analysis is presented here in abbreviated form, I shall also discuss several new issues which are related to the problem posed by lawyers and cooperation in divorce cases. The new issues include the state's view of marriage as a contract created and terminated on the basis of subjective choice, the impact of unilateral no-fault divorce laws, and the application of number 73 of

Evangelium Vitae. After describing the present cultural context in which we consider the issues of cooperation in divorce, I shall discuss formal cooperation and necessary material cooperation respectively.

I. THE CULTURAL CONTEXT

Statistical information confirms that American society at the turn of the twenty-first century constitutes a culture of divorce.[2] The long-term negative consequences of the divorce culture for the spouses and their children have also now been well established. Married people are in general significantly better off in terms of physical, emotional, financial, and spiritual well being than divorced persons.[3] The same kind of comparison has been established through longitudinal studies with regard to children from intact families as compared to children whose parents are divorced; and the difficulties for children of divorced parents can continue for years, even long into adulthood.[4] For those of us who accept the traditional Catholic understanding of marriage as a natural and supernatural institution, the data drawn from these scientific studies can only confirm our deeply held anthropological, social, and religious assumptions.

In accord with out fundamental anthropological assumptions, marriage constitutes a most basic from of human participation and solidarity. It represents the profound justification for the expression of sexual intimacy between a man and woman. It affords the stable form of life in which children learn of human love and trust from their parents.[5] Socially, marriage is understood as the basic building block for culture and civilization. As an objective social reality, the family unit formed around marriage remains an essential element of the common good. A society's health depends directly upon the health of marriage and the family.[6] From a religious perspective, the teaching of Jesus in the Gospels constitutes a clear and radical affirmation of the indissolubility of marriage.[7] Consistent with the teaching of the Lord, traditional Catholic doctrine considers divorce a grave evil against the natural and divine law. Marriage is first a natural institution intended by the Creator for the love of the spouses and procreation of children. The inseparable unitive and procreative properties of marriage were instituted as a sacrament by Christ. In its natural and supernatural indissolubility, marriage remains indispensable for the flourishing of the spouses, their children and the general societal well being.[8]

This traditional Catholic teaching met major resistance during the Protestant Reformation, when Martin Luther rejected the sacramental nature of marriage. Even for Luther, however, the family remained critical to his social philosophy. He permitted divorce only in cases of malicious desertion or adultery, which he viewed as subversive of family solidarity. In such cases, only the innocent party was free to remarry following a divorce.[9] The Enlightenment theory of marriage as a civil contract that could be entered into and broken through the will of the parties presented the most serious threat to the Catholic understanding of marriage. A central feature of the theory focused on individual autonomy to the detriment of participation, solidarity and the common good.[10] The Enlightenment theory, however, would only gradually supplant the theological understanding of marriage as an indissoluble and objective social reality.

At the time of the American Revolution, the diverse laws of the original states to the new nation tended to reflect that of the English ecclesiastical courts which had maintained the canonical tradition of granting not an absolute divorce but a permanent separation (*a mensa et thoro*). The only possibility for an absolute divorce which permitted remarriage (*a vinculo matimoni*) was through an act of the legislature.[11] During the nineteenth century, state legislatures increasingly enacted statutes that vested the judiciary with jurisdiction over divorce cases. Until the second half of the twentieth century, the laws of the vast majority of the states granted divorce only on the ground of some serious fault. In response to the legislative delegation, the courts developed elaborate evidentiary laws and defenses around the concept of fault. This led to serious abuses of the judicial process.[12] Additionally, the full faith and credit clause of the United States Constitution required that the states with strict divorce laws (the vast majority of the states) recognize the final judicial orders of the few states that ran so-called divorce mills on the basis of more liberal approaches.[13] Pursuant to the doctrine of comity, a divorce granted in foreign country could also be recognized as valid by a state court in the United States.[14] State courts responded by embracing the legal doctrine of divisible divorce under which the decision about the granting of the divorce is severable from the issues of the financial consequences and custody and care of the children.[15] The cumulative impact of these various legal developments was to relegate *de facto* the decision about the termination of the marriage to the subjective choice of the individual who had the resources to obtain a divorce in a permissive jurisdiction.

Starting in the 1960s, a momentum grew to deemphasize the role of fault in determining whether to dissolve a marriage. Emphasis shifted from blame to the determination of whether a marital relationship was broken to the point of no hope for repair. The so-called no-fault divorce was a statutory provision adopted by many state legislatures that permitted divorce through an uncontested court proceeding.[16] As initially envisioned by state legislatures, the new approach typically permitted legal dissolution of the marriage following a brief living apart period. Most recently, many state legislatures have passed unilateral no-fault divorce provisions pursuant to which either party may obtain dissolution of the marriage even without the consent and cooperation of the other. The sea change in divorce regimes has meant that the state's interest remains solely in the economic distribution and custody issues.[17] In accord with Enlightenment theory, liberal divorce regimes have thus reduced marriage to an economic partnership based on subjective options.[18]

The contemporary view of marriage thus undermines the traditional natural and supernatural understandings of marriage. First, the focus of contemporary view sees marriage as an agreement between autonomous individuals based upon subjective preferences. This perspective contrasts with the natural law understanding of marriage as an objective social reality which is good for the spouses, children, and for general societal stability and well-being. As previously mentioned, reliable statistical data drawn from longitudinal studies confirm the truth of the natural law theory.

Second, the contemporary view of marriage rejects indissolubility as a restriction on the autonomy of individuals. It adopts a negative definition of freedom as the absence of constraint on subjective desire. The contemporary view privileges "freedom from" over and against "freedom for" some set of values. According to the traditional view, the life long and exclusive commitment of marriage represents a positive freedom consistent with the human capacity for enduring trust and love. Natural law theory posits the development of the human capacity for trust and love as essential to individual and societal flourishing. Negative freedom, with its insistence on individual autonomy and subjective choice, also conflicts with positive freedom and its emphasis on marriage as an objective social reality.[19]

Third, the contemporary view leads to a redefinition of marriage by the state in a way that is contrary to the natural law tradition. The reduction of marriage renders it difficult to offer persuasive public policy arguments against same sex marriage. If marriage is fundamentally based on subjective choice, one may be hard pressed to argue why official state recognition must be limited to traditional marriage. This is not to suggest that efforts to preserve the special social and legal status of traditional marriage as a natural institution ought to be abandoned. However, from a legal perspective, the reduction has paved the way for judicial recognition of same sex marriage as a fundamental constitutional right.[20] The reduction of the state's understanding of marriage to individual subjective preference should be a concern to all citizens and attorneys. The natural law understanding of marriage is not dependent upon religious revelation or theological doctrine.

Finally, the contemporary view of marriage contradicts the Judeo-Christian religious tradition about the status of marriage in society. In particular, it denies the Catholic understanding of marriage as a Sacrament instituted by Christ. This supernatural view of marriage complements the natural law understanding and only strengthens the understanding of the indissolubility of marriage. The theological integration of the natural and supernatural properties of marriage has no doubt served as the bedrock for Western culture.

In his 2002 Allocution to the Officials of the Roma Rota, Pope John Paul II reaffirmed the principle of the indissolubility of marriage. The Holy Father specially addressed the role of lawyers with regard to divorce cases:

> Lawyers, as independent professionals, should always decline the use of the profession for an end that is contrary to justice, as is divorce. They can only cooperate in this kind of activity when, in the intention of the client, it is not directed to the break-up of marriage, but to the securing of other legitimate effects that can be obtained through such a judicial process in the established legal order (cf. *Catechism of the Catholic Church*, n. 2383). In this way, with their work of assisting and reconciling persons who are going

through a marital crisis, lawyers truly serve the rights of the person and avoid becoming mere technicians at the service of any interest whatever.[21]

The Pontifical advice to lawyers reflects the traditional criteria of Catholic moral theology for issues raised by cooperation in divorce.

II. LAWYERS AND FORMAL COOPERATION

The first of the criteria prohibits formal cooperation in the evil intent of another.[22] Unfortunately, for us lawyers, opportunities for cooperation in the evil intent of a client who seeks a civil divorce are all too abundant. Examples would include, *inter alia*, the client who seeks the break-up of a marriage as a matter of personal convenience, finds another person more attractive at the given moment, is no longer in love with his or her spouse, refuses to attempt forgiveness, or wants personal financial gain as a result of the equitable distribution of the marital assets. Subjective motivations are by their very nature as numerous as the virtually limitless variations of human desire and emotional states. In the absence of some legitimate intent based on objective evidence, these kinds of subjective motivations for seeking the dissolution of one's marriage would involve the lawyer in prohibited formal cooperation.

In contrast, the *Catechism of the Catholic Church* identifies several legitimate effects of a civil decree of divorce:

> If civil divorce remains the only possible way of ensuring certain legal rights, the care of the children, or the protection of inheritance, it can be tolerated and does not constitute a moral offense.[23]

It must be stressed that civil divorce is justified only when all other avenues such as reconciliation or permanent separation are simply not possible resolutions. In calling attention to this provision of the *Catechism,* the Holy Father is obviously aware of the tragic circumstances in which a married person sometimes finds him or herself.[24] When a lawyer encounters a client who seeks a divorce to secure a legitimate effect, the lawyer may in good conscience represent the client.

In this regard it should be noted that in the United States, the diocesan tribunals require civil divorce prior to granting an annulment.[25] In his 2002 Allocution, Pope John Paul II affirmed the "pastoral service" of the ecclesiastical tribunals as a work of "authentic charity."[26] If I may be so bold as to add the voice of a simple Franciscan friar to that of the Successor of the Apostle Peter, I must say that my experience as a judge in the inter-diocesan appeal tribunal in New York afforded me a much deeper appreciation of the legitimacy of the annulment process. Prior to assuming responsibilities as a judge, I was well aware of the criticism of the annulment process.[27] While some of the criticism is well-founded, my experience suggests that the majority of the declarations of nullity granted by the tribunal are justified. The frequency of tragic factual situations that seriously compromise one or both of the individual's capacity to consent to the marriage covenant is perhaps more a statement about our culture than the fault of the tribunal process. In this regard, the civil lawyer who assists a client for whom divorce is the only alternative to secure a legitimate effect may be preparing the way for the healing work of the ecclesiastical tribunals.

In addition to the legitimate effects recognized by the *Catechism,* I believe that the current situation of no-fault divorce laws must also be considered. The vast majority of the fifty states now permit some form of no-fault divorce. Although some of these jurisdictions such as New York require bilateral agreement of the spouses, the current trend favors unilateral no-fault divorce. In a unilateral no-fault divorce, the marriage may be dissolved through the intention of only one spouse even where the other spouse opposes the divorce. This legal arrangement thus may leave a spouse in the position of being forced into participating in a divorce proceeding in order to secure some legitimate effect. In representing a client who does not intend the dissolution of the marriage, but who is the respondent to a petition for a unilateral divorce, a lawyer may proceed with a fair degree of moral certainty. The lawyer represents the client in order to safeguard legal rights, secure the custody and care of children and protect financial interests. Given the secular trend in favor of the unilateral divorce, lawyers are more and more likely to encounter such clients.

According to the traditional understanding of the lawyer's responsibilities as a member of the legal profession, the representation of a client in the unfortunate circumstances just described may constitute a professional responsibility. It remains true that a lawyer may refuse a given case for any reason, even a banal one.[28] From the perspective of an individual practitioner, professional autonomy must always be understood against the background of the ethical commitment to make legal counsel available. To the individual spouse faced with a unilateral divorce, the lawyer may be the only hope for a just resolution. The profession as a whole has an obligation to insure that persons in this situation are not left without legal representation.

To summarize the situation of lawyers and formal cooperation, the attorney as an autonomous agent may represent a client in a divorce proceeding when the intention of the spouse is not an evil one and divorce is the only option available to secure a legitimate legal effect. Among the legitimate effects are included the defense of legal rights, custody and care of children and protection of financial interests such as inheritance. The prevalence of unilateral no-fault divorce means that lawyers may often be faced with a client who does not seek divorce but requires competent legal representation.

III. LAWYERS AND MATERIAL COOPERATION

Certain attorneys such as judges sometimes enjoy diminished independence in the selection of their cases. Continued employment, financial security for family and opportunities to advance professionally may require that they be involved in divorce cases by necessity. Unlike the lawyer as an independent professional who is free to limit his or her service to clients with good intentions, judges and other legal professionals may be required to handle cases without regard to the intention of the parties. When it is practically possible, lawyers in this situation should refuse to cooperate in divorce cases. The refusal constitutes a form of conscientious objection against a legal system that propagates the culture of divorce. When refusal of a case is not a practical option, the doctrine of necessary material cooperation applies. In his 2002 Allocution to the Roman Rota, Pope John Paul II acknowledged the application of the principles of material cooperation to lawyers and divorce cases.[29]

Pursuant to the doctrine of necessary material cooperation, the object and motivation of the cooperator's action must remain distinguishable from that of the wrongdoer. Additionally, the cooperator's reason for acting must be proportionate to the gravity of the wrong doing and to the closeness of the assistance.[30] In the application of these conditions, all of the concrete facts of a specific case must be considered. Because the application of the conditions remains so fact-specific, no magic formula guarantees a resolution to the case. Given the grievous injury caused to spouses, children and society as a whole by the culture of divorce, the countervailing reasons for cooperation would have to be of a significant gravity. At the same time, the total elimination of judges and lawyers who appreciate the function of traditional marriage from the legal system does present an attractive alternative.

This raises the problem of an unjust law and the application of *Evangelium Vitae*, 73.[31] To the extent that one participates in the legislative, executive, and judicial powers of a system of law, one has an obligation to endeavor to render the law as just. The legislator would seem to have the most serious obligation in rendering just laws. To a more limited extent, those with executive and judicial power also have an obligation to execute and interpret existing law in ways that are consistent with natural justice.[32] With the primary responsibility on the legislator, it is fundamental that one may not vote in favor of a new divorce law that permits divorce for unjust reasons. The legislator, for example, should not vote to introduce unilateral no-fault divorce into a jurisdiction where it does not already exist as a legal option. It is perhaps more realistic, however, to discuss the situation of the legislator who confronts an already existing regime of statutory law that has led to the deterioration of the traditional concept of marriage as an objective social reality with all of the good that it promises. According to *Evangelium Vitae, 73*, it seems permissible for the legislator to vote in favor of new legislation that restricts divorce but which legislation does not represent the ideal law through which to regulate divorce. During the process, it seems helpful for the legislator to explain publicly when possible his or her reason for the affirmative vote. It other words, it is licit to vote in favor of legislation that restricts a more permissive statute. The new law obtains the most protection for the sanctity of marriage in the here and now. This kind of cooperation does not imply any necessary approval or responsibility for that which can not be prevented.

To summarize: some lawyers enjoy less independence in the selection of their cases. When a legal professional must of necessity handle such a case, the traditional principles of material cooperation apply. *Evangelium Vitae* 73 serves as a reminder that lawyers, especially those who are members of legislative bodies, have an obligation to strive for just divorce laws. Voting in favor of new legislation that restricts an already existing too liberal statute constitutes acceptable moral cooperation without necessarily implying approval of any unjust provision of the new statute.

CONCLUSION

The present culture of divorce in the United States is causing serious injury to individuals and to society as a whole. The increasing availability of unilateral no-fault divorce has tended to reduce the state's notion of marriage to a contract created and terminated in accord with the individual's subjective preference. This trend flies in the face of the traditional natural law and religious understandings of marriage and the family. The disturbing developments oblige a lawyer to observe caution in the handling of divorce cases. Lawyers should not act as mere technicians who facilitate divorce but as wise stewards of a legal tradition that reflects the highest possibilities for individuals and the common good.

A lawyer may never facilitate a divorce case based on the mere subjective preference of the client to terminate the marriage. The lawyer's action would constitute a formal cooperation in the evil intent of the client which is morally impermissible. When divorce is the only means available to assist a client to secure some legitimate legal effect, it is morally permissible for a lawyer to assist the client. This rule also applies to a situation of a unilateral no-fault divorce.

A legal professional, such as a judge, who has some degree of decreased autonomy in the selection of cases may participate in an action for divorce in accord with the traditional rules of material cooperation. The rules require that the object and motivation of the cooperator's action be distinguishable from that of the wrong-doer, and that the cooperator's reason for acting be proportionate to the gravity of the wrong doing and to the closeness of the assistance. The application of the rules on material cooperation necessitates an *ad hoc* approach. All lawyers vested with government responsibilities, but especially legislators, have an obligation to work for just laws with regard to marriage, family life and divorce. In the face of an overly liberal divorce law, *Evangelium Vitae* 73 permits a legislator to vote for a less than ideal but more restrictive provision. Whether in the handling of an individual case or in the making of public policy, the lawyer should endeavor only to bolster marriage as an objective social reality which fosters the flourishing of the spouses, children and society as a whole.

Rev. John J. Coughlin, O.F.M., is a Professor of Law at the University of Notre Dame. He holds J.C.D. and J.C.L. degrees from the Pontifical Gregorian University; a J.D. degree from the Harvard Law School; a Th.M. degree from the Princeton Theological Seminary; an M.A. from Columbia University; and a B.A. from Niagara University. He received his Harvard Law School degree in 1987 and his Gregorian Doctorate in Canon Law in 1994. He was ordained to the priesthood in 1983, and has served as a retreat director for priests and religious throughout the United States.

Fr. Coughlin was formerly a Spiritual Director as well as a Professor of Canon Law at St. Joseph's Seminary at Dunwoodie in Yonkers, New York. He also served the archdiocese of New York as a judge, as the Vicar for the Canonical and Legal Aspects of Health Care, and as a member of the boards of directors of several Catholic hospitals and educational institutions. He currently teaches Administrative Law, Canon Law, Family Law and Professional Responsibility, and has also published numerous articles in these fields.

Notes

1   See John J. Coughlin, O.F..M., "Divorce and the Catholic Lawyer," *The Jurist,* 60 (2001), 290–310.

2   See Bureau of the Census, *Statistical Abstract of the United States,* 117th ed. (Washington, D.C.: Government Printing Office, 1997), tbl. 145. The data indicates that the national divorce rate has leveled-off at approximately fifty percent of all marriages, and may be in a slight decline.

3   See Linda J. Waite and Maggie Gallagher, *The Case For Marriage:Why Married People Are Happier, Healthier, and Better Off Financially* (New York: Doubleday, 2000), 82–83, 123. On the basis of statistical surveys, Waite and Gallagher conclude that married persons and their children in general are emotionally and financially better-off than divorced persons and their offspring.

4   See Judith S. Wallerstein, Julia M. Lewis and Sandra Blakeslee, *The Unexpected Legacy of Divorce: A 25 Year Landmark Study* (New York: Hyperion Press, 2000), 294–316. On the basis of a twenty-five year longitudinal study, the authors conclude that divorce has left damaging social, psychological, and financial effects on spouses and children.

5   See Karol Wojtyla, *Love and Responsibility* (San Francisco: Ignatius

Press, 1993), 125–40.

6   See Christopher Lasch, *Haven in a Heartless World* (New York: W. W. Norton, 1977), xxiii–xxiv.

7   See John P. Meier, *A Marginal Jew, Companions and Competitors,* vol. 3 (New York: Doubleday, 2001), 337.

8   See Theodore Mackin, s.j., *The Marital Sacrament* (New York: Paulist Press, 1989), 517–533.

9   See John Witte, Jr., *From Sacrament To Contract: Marriage, Religion, and Law in The Western Tradition* (Louisville: Westminster Press, 1997), 42–73.

10 See *id.,* 194–215.

11 See Walter Wadlington, "Divorce Without Fault Without Perjury," *Virginia Law* Review, 52 (1966), 32, 35–38.

12 See Glenda Riley, *Divorce: An American Tradition* (New York; Oxford, 1991), 40–49, 135–55.

13 See *Sherrer v. Sherrer,* 334 U.S. 343 (1948).

14 See *e.g., Perin v. Perin,* 408 F.2d 107 (1969).

15 See *e.g., Newport v. Newport,* 245 S.E.2d 134 (1978).

16 See Riley, *Divorce: An American Tradition,* 161–168.

17 See Wadlington, "Without Fault Without Perjury," 66–80.

18 In his 2001 Address to the Rota officials, John Paul II focused on the idea of marriage as a natural institution. He contrasted the metaphysical understanding of nature with the historical and existential reality of culture. See Pope John Paul II, 2001 Address to the Roman Rota: *AAS,* 92 (2000), 350–355. Availableat http://www.vatican.va/holy_father /john_paul_ii/speeches/2001/february/documents/hf/jp-i_20010201_roman-rota_en.html.

19 See Pope John Paul II, 2002 Allocution to the Roman Rota, January 28, 2002, at 2, 4, & 9. Available at http://www.vatican.va/holy_father /john_paul_ii/speeches/2002/january/documents/hf/jpii_20020128_rom an-rota_en.html.

20 The primacy of the subjective self is a constitutive aspect of the "substantive due process" right of privacy designed by the United States Supreme Court. In *Griswold v. Connecticut,* 405 U.S. 438 (1972), the Court struck down a state statute that criminalized the use of contraceptives "for the purpose of preventing conception." Appealing to the "sacredness" of marriage, the Court described the statute as "repulsive to the notions of privacy surrounding the marriage relationship." The privacy right protecting the distribution and use of contraceptives was extended to non-married individuals in *Eisenstadt v. Baird,* 405 U.S. 438 (1972). This legal reasoning then supplied the justification for the right of a woman to have an abortion in *Roe v. Wade,* 410 U.S. 113 (1973).

Thus, the privacy right, which the Court initially justified on the "sacred character" of marriage, was extended to include constitutional protection for individuals to distribute and use contraception outside marriage as well as to perform and have abortions. In *Bowers v. Hardwick*, 488 U.S. 186 (1986), the majority of the Court refused to extend the privacy right to homosexual activity in that such activity was neither "implicit in the concept of ordered liberty," nor "deeply rooted in this Nation's history and tradition." By a five to four vote, the Supreme Court reversed its hold in *Bowers,* in the 2003 case of *Lawrence v. Texas*, 123 S.Ct. 2472 (2003). The trend towards redefinition of marriage through the recognition of the legal right was apparent in *Baker v. Vermont*, 744 A.2d 864 (Vt. S.Ct 1999), where the Vermont Supreme Court held that a same-sex couple may not be deprived of the statutory benefits and protections afforded to heterosexual married couple pursuant to the Common Benefits Clause of the Vermont Constitution. In *Goodridge v. Department of Public Health*, 2003 WL 22701313 (Mass. 2003), the highest court in Massachusetts held that prohibiting the granting of marriage licenses to same sex couples violated the Commonwealth's constitution.

21 See Pope John Paul II, 2002 Allocution to the Roman Rota, 9.

22 St. Alphonsus Liguori articulated the classic statement about cooperation: "That [cooperation] is formal which occurs in the bad will of the other, and it cannot be without sin . . ." *Idem, Theologia Moralis,* L. Gaudé ed., 4 vols. (Rome: Ex Typographia Vaticana, 1905–1912), 1:357 (lib. II, §63), cited in Germain Grisez, *The Way of the Lord Jesus,* Vol 3, *Difficult Moral Questions* (Quincy, Illinois: Franciscan Press, 1997), 876.

23 *Catechism of the Catholic Church* (Vatican City: Libreria Editrice Vaticana, 1994), 573, n.2383.

24 Pope John Paul II has urged pastoral sensitivity towards divorced persons. He has also spoken forcefully about the dignity and equality of women as well as against the abuse and abandonment of children. See e.g., John Paul II, Apostolic Constitution, *Familiaris Consortio,* November 22, 1981, no. 84, 23–24: *AAS,* 74 (1982), 81–191.

25 See Grisez, *Difficult Moral Questions,* 179, who suggests that the reason for this approach is that the tribunals do not want to encourage separation of the spouses or open the diocese to a lawsuit as a result of the annulment process.

26 John Paul II, *2002* Allocution to the Roman Rota, 1.

27 See Robert H. Vasoli, *What God Has Joined Together: The Annulment Crisis in Ammerican Catholicism* (New York: Oxford University Press, 1998), 200–213. He criticizes the tribunals in the United States for not adequately safeguarding the indissolubility of marriage.

28 See Canon 1, EC 1-1; and Canon 2 of the *American Bar Association*

Model Code of Professional Responsibility (1981).

29 See Pope John Paul II, 2002 Allocution to the Roman Rota, 9

30 St. Alphonsus Ligouri, *Theologia Moralis*, 1905–12, 1:357 (lib. I, §63), cited in Grisez, *Difficult Moral Questions,* 876: "That [cooperation] is material which occurs only in the bad action of the other, apart from the cooperator's intention. But the latter [material cooperation] is licit when the action is good or indifferent in itself; and when one has reason for doing it that is both just and proportioned to the gravity of the other's sin and to the closeness of the assistance which is thereby given to the carrying out of that sin."

31 See Pope John Paul II, *Evangelium Vitae, 73 in* J. M. Miller, C.S.B., ed., *The Encyclicals of John Paul II* (Indiana: Our Sunday Visitor Press, 2001), 682, 739.

32 See Robert P. George, *In Defense of Natural Law* (Oxford: Oxford University Press, 1999), 107–111.

COOPERATION WITH EVIL IN THE MILITARY PROFESSION
John P. Hittinger

PREFACE

As a preface to a discussion of the issues pertaining to formal and material cooperation with evil in the military profession, I must state some general considerations about military service; they may be obvious, but they are important assumptions for a proper framing of the issues.[1] The first relates to the basic moral standing of the military profession; the second relates to the special conditions that attach to moral agency within that profession.

First, members of the armed forces must be prepared to face and battle evil in its most hideous forms – political brutality and tyranny, torture and executions, forced starvation, and even genocide. It is difficult enough to withstand the corrosion of war and combat; and it takes moral vigilance to insure that the use of force be restrained or limited to a moral scope. It would therefore be useful to review the charter for military service laid out in *Gaudium et Spes*. This document is characterized by a simplicity and a subtle balance. It affirms the right and duty of a nation to maintain a military force; but it also condemns the unjust and indiscriminate use of force. The document strikes a subtle balance between national and international points of view, between force and non-violence, and between principle and prudential application.

Every Catholic who is a member of the Armed Services should find encouragement in the following words: "Those who are pledged to the service of their country as members of its armed forces should regard themselves as agents of security and freedom on behalf of their people. As long as they fulfill their role properly, they are making a genuine contribution to the establishment of peace" (#79). This fundamental truth is rooted deeply in both empirical and moral judgment. Human affairs require some amount of force to maintain order and promote justice; violence must be restrained through force and its threat. The love of peace and justice require that such a force be maintained. The neglect of such matters is foolish and morally wrong.[2] Thus the document states unequivocally that "governments cannot be denied the right to legitimate defense"; and they have a "duty to protect the welfare of the people entrusted to their care" (#79). The military has a clear role in establishing peace by defending the nation from attack and deterring would-be aggressors.

This direct affirmation of the positive role of the soldier is balanced by the phrase, "as long as they pursue this role properly." Blind obedience does not excuse unjust actions. The fundamental rule which must guide the actions of soldiers is that they avoid the direct killing of non-combatants. The document forbids the methodical extermination of peoples, nations or minorities (#79); and it condemns the indiscriminate destruction of cities and populated areas (#80). Such acts are condemned as "a crime against God and man himself." A soldier, an army, and a nation should acknowledge this sacred principle in speech and deed. Restraint must be built into policy, rules of engagement, international agreements, and world opinion. It warns against the unique hazard of total war: "Those who possess modern scientific weapons are provided with a kind of occasion for perpetrating such abominations, and through an inexorable chain of events, it can urge men on to the most atrocious decisions" (#80). It is just these evils that concern the limit of cooperation in a material or formal way. Military service is a moral enterprise, a noble profession, indeed a service a Catholic may perform in good conscience, if performed within moral parameters.

Second, members of the Armed Forces serve under oath.[3] The officer receives a commission and by the oath he promises to "support and defend the Constitution of the United States against *all enemies*"; and he promises to "faithfully discharge the duties of the office." By the oath of enlistment one also promises to obey orders "according to regulations and the Uniform Code of Military Justice (UCMJ)." Promulgated laws and policies delimit the possibilities for action within a military setting. The warrior lives and acts out of a "code."[4] The chain of command insures by definition a formal participation in the operations. Thus, formal cooperation constitutes part of the very distinction between the military and the civilian, or rather the "combatant" and the "non-combatant." Military status is determined by the fact that a member of the military stands in a formal chain of command such that orders for action may be implemented. A member of the military is formally connected to the planning and execution of war. A non-combatant is one who is not formally bound by orders. Non-combatant status also derives from the sphere of action or service – that is, whether the action pertains to military operation as such or rather serves the interests of the human concerns such as food service, medical service, housing, and the like. Thus, a medic and a chaplain have a non-combatant status. But the overall point to be made here is that the military person has very little leeway in making the distinction between formal and material cooperation precisely because one is bound by the formal system of command. Normally, a member of the armed services may not recuse himself or somehow segment spheres of action, as one may do in the legal or medical profession. On the other hand, the limits of action should be clearly defined by law and regulation.

THE POTENTIAL EVIL IN MILITARY OPERATIONS

We should consider the potential evils of military service in two broad categories: those involving actual combat operations, and those involving everyday or routine administration of military affairs such as personnel, training, procurement, and the like. The potential evils involving military operations may be about the justice of the war or the conduct of the war. *Gaudium et Spes* states that it is wrong to use armed force for "the subjugation of other nations," a violation of the *jus ad bellum*. We already noted the condemnation on the use force for indiscriminate destruction of areas or peoples, a violation of the *jus in bello*. In addition to these potential evil actions on the side of military operations, we could also add potentially evil actions on the side of the administration of military operations in the unfair or abusive treatment of people under the military command, complicity in covering up incompetence, or dishonesty in the procurement and development of weapons. The recent U. S. Air Force Academy scandal falls in this latter category, as would other instances of coercion, or unfair treatment of military personnel in day to day operations of combat operations.

UNJUST WAR/*JUS AD BELLUM*

What if a particular war is an unjust one? Many critics of the just war approach claim that it is too easy to ignore the rigor of its application. But one must remember that for a member of the armed services, it is not a decision made out of the blue or in an academic setting. Normally one can judge from the direction of national foreign policy what type of engagements will be faced. The military is a volunteer service. One should have some grasp of the possibilities and policies of American foreign policy and military operations prior to enlistment or accepting a commission. A disagreement over the particularities of the war may require that one cooperate with the effort. The ground of judgment is important. That is, if the problem of justice of the war pertains to last resort or proportionality, prudence comes into play. Men and women of goodwill may disagree. Deference to authority in a matter of prudence is essential to a sound political order; the guilt will be on the king. However, this is different from blatantly unjust wars where refusal of service may be required. Obviously the gravity of injustice is at stake here. But as mentioned above, the oath requires formal participation. Thus, the options for military personnel are limited. An enlisted man must serve for his term of commitment. One can refuse to serve and face a court martial and spend time in the brig. At what point does one do this? One can wait out one's term of service and then simply not re-enlist. Terms of service are normally four years. Officers can offer a resignation – they may give up any benefits they may have accrued and suffer some stigma. Their resignations may be refused. And then they can refuse orders and face court-martial. Each branch of service has rules and procedures for withdrawing from service on the basis of conscientious objection. A related issue may be raised here concerning selective conscientious objection (CO). At present, our law does not allow selective CO but only CO to all wars. Would a selective CO make it better for the protection of conscience in cooperation with an unjust war, since formal cooperation is demanded of the member of the military? It undoubtedly would, but given the volunteer basis of the military, promulgation of procedures, and the democratic basis for political decision making, the option for selective CO seems to be unnecessary as well as impractical.

ILLICIT MEANS OF WARFARE/*JUS IN BELLO*

The conditions for the right conduct of warfare are not quite as elaborate or complex, but for that matter they are more vital and obliging in their simplicity. The overriding precept guiding the conduct of war is the principle of non-combatant immunity from direct attack. Simply put, this means that the fighting should be aimed directly at the military and not at the civilian portions of the population. The failure to observe this rule constitutes a war crime. As Professor Anscombe has pointed out, this provision of the just war theory grounds the significant moral difference between murder and the legitimate use of lethal force. The danger of pacifism, according to Professor Anscombe, is that it teaches people to make no distinction between the shedding of innocent blood and the shedding of any human blood.

As for means of warfare, again there are policies and regulations in place to inform military personnel about methods and means of warfare. Are they consistent with the laws of war? Do they observe non-discrimination and proportionality? The actual moral value comes down to the right use of the weapons systems. So what if the operation which one is commanded to perform or assist is illicit or immoral? If the command violates the law or morality, one may refuse to cooperate. This brings in the risk of court martial. But there are cases in which such refusal is deemed appropriate. If the action is a legal order, but judged to be immoral, the soldier faces a dilemma. Air Force lawyers make assurances that all legal orders are moral orders, such that the moral and the legal are co-extensive. But that may not always be so. Refusal to cooperate will take tremendous courage and willingness to endure negative consequences for one's career.

Strategic nuclear weapons pose a special problem. The moral teaching is clear: "Any act of war aimed indiscriminately at the destruction of entire cities of extensive areas along with their population is a crime against God and man himself. It merits unequivocal and unhesitating condemnation" (*Gaudium et Spes*, #80). But even nuclear weapons are not per se evil – it is their use. Deterrence is a special form of possession, with the ultimate intention of non-use. The nuclear threat is complicated by the threat of use of nuclear weapons as a means to avoid using them. There is a complex dilemma here, one of the most challenging in theory and practice. The deterrent force has established a kind of peace; but the threat to kill civilians is also immoral and not transformed by the greater intention of peace. One may resolve the dilemma through the concept of bluff or through a policy of not targeting civilian areas. The bluff deterrent is not credible. American policy makers claim that the targets are not directly on civilian sites. But the principle of proportionality must be applied at this point; the extent of damage to civilian areas and the environment would be so great as to undermine its moral warrant. The Vatican and the U.S. Bishops have issued a "conditional acceptance" of deterrence, calling for good faith efforts at disarmament.[5] Other thinkers have extended this concern about proportionality to cover any modern war, questioning whether any modern war can be just because of the extensive collateral damage done to civilians and the environment. No doubt, weapons of mass destruction, by definition, are likely to be used in an immoral fashion, i.e., indiscriminately. A soldier, sailor, or airman must refuse cooperation with these acts. It is not possible to envision formal cooperation with any chain of command leading to the launching of massive strikes. How could one in good conscience ever stand by for the launch? General Tibbets has not made his case persuasive for the bombing of Hiroshima. Because there is no selective conscientious objector status, the best one can do is attempt to segment service and seek service in units or commands not directly involved with potentially illicit means of war.

With the demise of the Soviet Union, and the progress made in reducing the weapons of mass destruction, there are more urgent and pressing dangers facing the members of the armed services. There is talk of a "revolution in military affairs" (RMA).[6] According to Andrew Marshall, director of the Office of Net Assessments in the Office of the Secretary of Defense, an "RMA" is a major change in the nature of warfare brought about by the innovative application of new technologies which, combined with dramatic changes in military doctrine and operational and organizational concepts, fundamentally alters the character and conduct of military operations."[7] The current military revolution goes back to World War II and the development of nuclear weapons and ballistic missile delivery systems; the associated and resultant revolutions include: precision reconnaissance and strike; stealth; computerization and computer networking of command and control; and massively increased lethality of "conventional" munitions. According to McKitrick et al., the revolutionary impact of future changes in the conduct of warfare will come from the intersection of precision strike, information warfare, dominating maneuver, and space warfare. Precision strike will hold an enemy at a distance and "blind and immobilize him by destroying operationally and strategically crucial, time-urgent targets"; information warfare will deny an enemy "critical knowledge of his own- as well as our-forces and turn his 'fog of war' into a wall of ignorance"; dominating maneuver, will deploy the right forces at the right time and place to cause the enemy's "psychological collapse and complete capitulation"; and space warfare will enable the United States to "project force at dramatically increased speeds in response to contingencies while denying the enemy the ability to do the same." The promise of this RMA is that the fog of war will be lifted and the United States will have strategic superiority for the foreseeable future. There are significant moral hazards in this much heralded revolution in military affairs. It sounds as if the superiority will tempt its holder to redefine the purpose of war to be domination and "bending the will" of others, no longer the more rough goals of defense and balance of power. Also there are moral dangers concerning non-combatant immunity from direct attack. Some new doctrines of war, such as John Warden's "ring" tactic, seem to countenance and even encourage the targeting of non-combatants.[8] And finally, by a great and tragic irony there may be more collateral damage with the advent of precision weapons. Precision weapons could encourage greater risk in collateral damage or lead to denial of the risks involved. These are matters under the control and planning of American military officers, and subject to policy making rules. As John Courtney Murray said: "Policy is the hand of the practical reason set firmly upon the course of events. Policy is what a nation does in this or that given situation. In the concreteness of policy therefore the assertion of the possibility of limited war is finally made and made good. Policy is the meeting place of the world of power and the world of morality, in which there takes place the concrete reconciliation of the duty of success that rests upon the statesman and the duty of justice that rests upon the civilized nation that he serves." It is up to Catholic members of the U.S. armed services to bring morality to bear on the world of power so that one need not face the prospect of cooperation with these potential evils that may emerge with the "revolution in military affairs."

Finally, members of the armed forces may face the phenomenon of "moral numbing" due to the high tech, virtual war.[9] "Virtual War" is a term used by Michael Ignatieff and others to refer to modern wars fought from a distance and with sophisticated weaponry. These wars use the revolution in military affairs to the full advantage of the United States, such that the conflict is near one-sided, or at least "asymmetric." Ignatieff says: "Virtual reality is seductive...We see war as a surgical scalpel and not a bloodstained sword. In so doing we mis-describe ourselves as we mis-describe the instruments of death. We need to stay away from such fables of self-righteous invulnerability. Only then can we get our hands dirty. Only then can we do what is right."[10] "Moral numbing" is what can happen when people no longer feel the true moral weight of their actions – when they become insensitive to the pain and suffering of others and when they no longer place a high value on human life. Other military psychologists have spoken out about this moral danger.[11] So the greater moral challenges to members of the armed services may now be in the more hidden areas of the revolution in military affairs, and less in the more expected or explicit dangers in violating the laws of war.

ADMINISTRATIVE DISHONESTY

For the last item of discussion I wish to consider those situations in which the chain of command may be used to implement unjust deeds or to cover up unjust deeds. Silence is a form of material cooperation. There are some cultural factors in play here such as careerism, deference to authority etc. But what if one does know about sexual abuse or rape within ones unit or area of responsibility? Or what if one knows about unsafe equipment? It takes a willingness to risk failure to advance in the career, social acceptance, even monetary rewards in order to speak the truth about these situations. Formal involvement could be signing off on untruthful disclosures or lying by omission. The material cooperation involves silence and the willingness to look the other way. Isn't this a form of material cooperation which may lead to the continuation of abuse and protection for those who deserve punishment? A reckless officer crashed a B-52, after a number of people had observed his previous reckless behavior, but they were afraid to speak out about his bad character. The recent scandal uncovered at the Air Force Academy indicates a corrupt culture in which silence up the chain of command and implicit cooperation with abuse of position is tolerated. Efforts must be made to inculcate the moral courage needed to refuse such material cooperation by speaking out or blowing the whistle despite repercussions to one's career.

CONCLUSION

Military service is an important and honorable profession. A moral framework and a moral code structure the very profession. The range for disengaging from formal participation are quite limited. But this discussion helps to remind us of the moral burden and heroic decisions which must be faced by every member of the armed services. The role of the military must be placed in a larger perspective. The soldier does not exist in isolation from the citizen, just as military strategy does not exist in isolation from political purpose. *Gaudium et Spes* states that peace cannot be reduced to a sheer balance of power. Peace is "an enterprise of justice" (#78). The build up of arms and revolutions in military affairs, we might add, do not produce a "steady peace" (#81). In light of the great stakes for humanity, the document takes an international perspective and encourages much greater international cooperation. In fact, it calls for "the establishment of some universal public authority acknowledged as such by all, and endowed with effective power to safeguard on behalf of all, security, regard for justice, and respect for rights" (#82). This is a tall order indeed and a high hope for the earthly city; it may not be realistically possible. But it does serve as an upward pull on the thoughts and actions of the citizens of each nation. It may help to check corporate selfishness and ambition and "nourish a respect for humanity as a whole" (#82). It can lead citizens to be honest in their appraisal of the causes of tension and war. The document mentions for our consideration "excessive economic inequalities, the quest for power, and contempt for personal rights" as injustices upon which wars thrive (#83). It also raises the problems caused by "excessive desire for profit, nationalistic pretensions, lust for political domination, militaristic thinking, and intrigues designed to impose and spread ideologies" (#85).

The upward pull which serves to qualify the right and duty of a nation to self-defense is itself qualified by a sober realism. For example, the call for disarmament is not unilateral and must be "backed up by authentic and workable safeguards" (#82). Those who are willing to forsake the use of force for non-violent solutions are praised only insofar as they do no "injury to the rights and duties others or of the community itself" (#78). The work of peace actually extends beyond the order of justice and requires charity and love of neighbor

(#78). And indeed, the deepest explanation for violence and war lies in "human jealousy distrust, pride, and other egotistic passions" (#83). The real problem is human sinfulness and the solution is divine redemption. So the document states that: "Insofar as men are sinful, the threat of war hangs over them, and hang over them it will, until the return of Christ. But to the extent that men vanquish sin by the union of love, they will vanquish violence as well" (#78). The goal of true peace will be accomplished only in proportion to the advance of love. This is more an object and hope for prayer and grace than it is for political action as such.

The members of the armed services must be realistic about the evils they face; they must be courageous in their willingness to sacrifice for the common good; and they must be ready to withstand the corrosion of evil upon their own character. They deserve our support and prayers.

John P. Hittinger is a Professor of Philosophy at Sacred Heart Major Seminary in Detroit, Michigan. Prior to that, he served as the Provost and Academic Dean at St. Mary's College of Ave Maria University in Michigan. Dr. Hittinger has also held faculty positions at Benedictine College in Atchison, Kansas and at the College of St. Francis at Joliet, Illinois, where he served as chairman of the philosophy and theology department. In 1994, he accepted a position as the first civilian professor in the philosophy department at the United States Air Force Academy, where he held the rank of full professor.

Dr. Hittinger has published articles and essays and presented papers on a variety of topics, including just war theory and military ethics, John Locke, Jacques Maritain, liberal education, political philosophy, and the thought of John Paul II. He recently published a collection of essays entitled *Liberty, Wisdom, and Grace: Thomism and Modern Democratic Theory* (Lanham, MD: Lexington Books, 2002).

Notes

1 See my "Just War and Defense Policy," In *Natural Law and Contemporary Public Policy*, edited by David F. Forte, pp. 333–60. Washington, D.C.: Georgetown University Press, 1998. Also "Symposium on the Christian Soldier," in *Catholicism in Crisis*, March, 1984.

2   See G. E. M. Anscombe, "War and Murder," found in *War and Morality,* ed. Richard A. Wasserstrom (Belmont: Wadsworth, 1970), pp. 42–53: Professor Anscombe says that it is both necessary and right that there should be this exercise of military power, because through it the world is much less of a jungle than it could possibly be without it. One should in principle be glad of the existence of such power, and only take exception to its unjust exercise.

3   See Anthony E. Hartle, *Moral Issues in Military Decision Making* (Lawrence: University of Kansas Press, 1989) and James Toner, *True Faith and Allegiance: The Burden of Military Ethics* (The University Press of Kentucky, 1995).

4   See Shannon French, *The Code of the Warrior: Exploring Warrior Values, Past and Present* (Lanham: Rowman and Littlefield Publishers. 2002). Foreword by Senator John McCain.

5   Compare Michael Novak, *Moral Clarity in the Nuclear Age* (Nashville: Thomas Nelson, 1983) and John Finnis, Joseph Boyle, and Germain Grisez, *Nuclear Deterrence, Morality and Realism* (Oxford: Oxford Univ. Press, 1987).

6   *Dynamics of Military Revolution, 1300–2050* edited by MacGregor Knox and Williamson Murray. (New York: Cambridge University Press, 2001).

7   Jeffrey McKitrick *et al.,* "The Revolution in Military Affairs," in *Battlefield of the Future: 21st Century Warfare Issues,* edited by Barry R. Schneider and Lawrence E. Grinter, revised edition (Air University: Maxwell Air Force base, AL: 1998), pp. 65–99. See also Daniel Goure and Christopher M. Szaara, editors, *Air and Space Power in the New Millennium* (Washington, D.C.: CSIS, 1997).

8   See John A. Warden III, *The Air Campaign* (Washington: Brassey's 1989); David R. Mets, *The Air Campaign: John Warden and the Classical Airpower Theorists* (Maxxwell Air Force Base, Alabama, 1998); and John Warden, "Air Theory for the Twenty First Century," in *Battlefield of the Future,* pp. 103–124.

9   See Michael Ignatieff, *Virtual War: Kosovo and Beyond* (New York: Metropolitan Books, 2000).

10 *Ibid.,* pp. 214–215.

11 Jonathan Shay, *Achilles in Vietnam: Combat Trauma and the Undoing of Character* (New York: Scribner's, 1995); and Lt. Col. Dave Grossman, *On Killing: The Psychological Cost of Learning to Kill in War and Society* (Boston: Little Brown, 1995).

PACIFISM AND JUST WAR

JUST WAR PRINCIPLES
J. Brian Benestad

One of the most urgent tasks of Catholic social teaching is to keep the principles of the just war doctrine before the eyes of government leaders and citizens. This essay lays out the fundamental tenets of just-war principles and shows the roots of these principles in the thought of St. Augustine and St. Thomas Aquinas. Familiarity with the thought of Augustine on peace is especially important to understand both the necessity for a just-war teaching and the preconditions for a just peace.

ST. AUGUSTINE

Augustine argues that the practice of justice preserves the peace. He understands justice primarily as order in the soul of individuals, which contributes to the proper ordering of society, and thus to peace. Ernest Fortin's summary of Augustine's reflection on justice is helpful: "It exists when the body is ruled by the soul, when the lower appetites are ruled by reason, and when reason itself is ruled by God. The same hierarchy is or should be observed in society as a whole and is encountered when virtuous subjects obey wise rulers, whose minds are in turn subject to the divine law."[1] This means that citizens and rulers must strive to achieve order in their soul by the practice of all the virtues. So, Augustine is talking about justice as a general virtue that encompasses all the virtues that produce order in the soul.

Augustine's description of peace is closely related to his definition of justice:

> Thus, the peace of the body is the ordered proportion of its parts. The peace of the irrational soul is the ordered repose of the appetites. The peace of the rational soul is the

ordered agreement of knowledge and action... The peace
between a mortal man and God is an ordered obedience, in
faith, under the eternal law.

The peace among human beings is ordered concord.
The peace of the household is an ordered concord concerning commanding and obeying among those who dwell
together. The peace of the city is an ordered concord concerning commanding and obeying among the citizens. The
peace of the heavenly city is a fellowship perfectly ordered
and harmonious, enjoying God and each other in God. The
peace of all things is the tranquility of order [*tranquiltas
ordinis*].[2]

Augustine is arguing that the achievement of peace in the city
and among nations depends heavily on the dispositions in the souls
of rulers and ruled. Peace within individuals is disrupted when they
fail to act according to their knowledge of the good and indulge disordered appetites. Concord in the family or the city is, of course, disrupted by the disordered passions in the souls of individuals. For
example, the inordinate desire for pleasure, power, gain, glory,
honor, or revenge could lead individuals to disrupt the concord of the
household or the city. The peace between man and God depends on
obedience to God's will. Peace among human beings also depends
on the universal obedience to God's will. Insofar as human beings
disobey God, they will be at odds with each other. The very first
pages of Genesis emphasize this point with unmistakable clarity.
Cain's killing of Abel quickly follows Adam's and Eve's disobedi-
ence of God. John Paul II reflects on this truth in his 1995 encyclical, *Evangelium Vitae*.[3]

Political communities can not be rightly ordered if individuals,
especially the leaders, don't have order in their souls produced by the
practice of virtues. What caused World War II in Europe, if not the
disorder in the soul of Adolph Hitler? Hitler's lust to dominate and
his hatred of the Jews led to terrible consequences for vast numbers
of people, especially the Jews. What is the principal cause of Al
Qaeda's terroristic acts, if not the disordered passions of its leaders
and members?

I believe it is a misreading of Augustine to think that *tranquilitas
ordinis* refers only to a "dynamic and rightly ordered political community," that can be achieved without justice in the souls of individ-

uals, as George Weigel argues.[4] Augustine, of course would recognize that the desire for gain or the threat of force might induce a bad state or an individual tyrant to forsake evil public purposes. So, a "peace process" might yield some results, even if no effort is made to overcome the vices of the principal antagonists in a conflict. But any peace process will have great difficulty in forging a peace between bitter enemies, if the anger and hatred of many individuals do not lessen. Given Augustine's understanding that peace within and among nations depends on peace or order in the souls of individuals, it comes as no surprise that Augustine believes that war will never disappear from the face of the earth. Because of sin, war is inevitable. The sin or disorder in the souls of individuals leads one state to make war on another. In the words of Ernest Fortin: "However much one may dislike and regret it, war is unavoidable, not because good men want it, but because it is not within their power to avoid it altogether, since it is imposed on them by the wicked ..."[5] Augustine has no doubt that wicked people will always threaten the peace. Of course, they may be more or less numerous or more or less able to disturb the peace in certain periods of time. In some moments of history, peaceful nations may be able to keep the wicked in check by the judicious use of force.

Augustine believes that the evil purposes of the wicked must be resisted out of love, love for them and their victims. Summarizing Augustine's position, Fortin writes: "Nothing is more injurious to mankind than that evil-doers should be given free reign to prosper and use their prosperity to oppress the good."[6] Obviously, unjust aggressors are resisted so that they can not overthrow nations and inflict harm on innocent people. But they are also resisted in order to stop them from doing harm to themselves by doing evil to others. Evil people receive a benefit when their license for wrongdoing is wrested away.

> When, however, men are prevented, by being alarmed, from doing wrong, it may be said that a real service is done to themselves. The precept, "resist not evil," was given to prevent us from taking pleasure in revenge, in which the mind is gratified by the sufferings of others, but not to make us neglect the duty of restraining men from sin.[7]

Augustine's advice to political leaders on war follows logically from his position on the love required of political leaders. In Letter

138 Augustine says: "If this earthly republic kept the Christian precepts, wars themselves would not be waged without benevolence, so
that, for the sake of the peaceful union of piety and justice, the welfare of the conquered would be more readily considered."[8]
Augustine wants political leaders to protect the innocent from unjust
aggression, and he wants the victorious leaders to benefit the souls
of the conquered, who disrupted the peace. In a similar vein, he says
in a letter to Boniface, the Roman governor of the province of
Africa: "Be a peacemaker, then, even by fighting, so that through
your victory you might bring those whom you defeat to the advan-
tages of peace...Let necessity slay the warring foe, not your will. As
violence is returned to one who rebels and resists, so should mercy
be one who has been conquered or captured, especially when there is
no fear of a disturbance of peace..."[9] Augustine wants political leaders to declare war only out of *necessity*, and to show love to their
enemies by resisting their evil-doing and by showing mercy after
they have been conquered. Necessity means there is no other way of
protecting innocents and resisting aggressors. As a way of inculcat-
ing in leaders a reluctance to see necessity where there is none,
Augustine tells leaders to look at just wars as lamentable necessities.

> They say, however, that the wise man will wage only
> just wars – as if, mindful that he is human, he would rather
> lament that he is subject to the necessity of waging just
> wars. If they were not just, he would not be required to
> wage them, and thus he would be free of the necessity of
> war. It is the iniquity on the part of the adversary that forces
> a just war upon the wise man.[10]

If leaders reluctantly come to the conclusion that lethal force has
to be used to protect their community and to restrain evil-doers, then
they are less likely to lie to themselves and declare a war to be necessary when it clearly is not.

Augustine's recommendation to leaders even goes so far as to ask
them to lament the existence of all iniquity, even when it doesn't
require a decision to go to war.

> Even if it did not give rise to the necessity of war, such
> iniquity must certainly be lamented by a human being since
> it belongs to human beings. Therefore, let anyone who
> reflects with sorrow upon these evils so great, so horrid, and
> so savage, confess that he is miserable. Anyone, however,
> who either permits or considers these things without sorrow

in mind is certainly much more miserable, since he thinks himself happy, because he has lost human feeling.[11] Augustine is asking a lot of political leaders. If they rise to this standard, there will be many fewer wars.

Augustine realizes that he has to justify his position on the permissible use of lethal force against evildoers by finding a basis in the New Testament. He points out that the New Testament writings show that soldiers serving in the military were recognized as pleasing to God. In response to the Roman centurion, who expressed his belief that he could heal his paralyzed servant, Jesus said: "Amen, I say to you, I have not found such faith in Israel" (Mt 8:8–10). If Jesus disapproved of the profession of arms, Augustine implies, surely he would have said something to the soldier. Augustine also mentions the centurion Cornelius, to whom an angel said: "Cornelius, your alms have been accepted and your prayers heard" (Acts 10:4). In Letter 138, Augustine says: "Indeed, if Christian teaching condemned all wars, then the advice given in the Gospel to the soldiers asking for salvation would have been to throw down their arms and quit the military completely. What they were told, however, was "terrorize no one, accuse no one falsely, and be content with your pay" (Lk 3:14). "With these words," writes Augustine, "[John the Baptist] commands them to be content with their own pay: he certainly does not prohibit them from serving as soldiers."[12] Augustine interprets this statement of John to be the mind of Christ.

If the teaching of Jesus allows just wars to be fought, that doesn't mean that political leaders and soldiers fighting in a just war need not worry about their attitudes and dispositions during the war. Augustine explains: "The desire for harming, the cruelty of revenge, the restless and implacable mind, the savageness of revolting, the lust for dominating, and similar things – these are what are justly blamed in wars."[13] In other words, belligerents must observe various norms while fighting in a just war. In later times such norms will be discussed under the rubric of *ius in bello*.

In summary, Augustine set the stage for the development of just war doctrine by his rich notion of peace, his understanding of war as inevitable because of sin, and his teaching that rulers have an obligation to protect their fellow citizens from unjust attack, even by the judicious use of force. These Augustinian themes remain an important part of modern Catholic teachings on just war, to which we now turn.

THOMAS AQUINAS AND CLASSIC
JUST WAR PRINCIPLES

John Courtney Murray provides a good introduction to thinking about war by posing two questions: "First, what are the norms that govern recourse to the violence of war? Second, what are the norms that govern the measure of violence to be used in a war? In other words, when is war rightful, and what is rightful in war?"[14] Today, theologians ask when is there a *ius ad bellum* and what is *ius in bello*.

In the thirteenth century, Aquinas identified three things to be necessary for a rightful or just war: a decision by a sovereign authority; a just cause; and a rightful intention. These categories are still used today, although a just cause is usually listed first. The criterion of a competent public authority means that private individuals cannot declare war or summon others to fight in a war. Aquinas gives three reasons for this position. Private parties have the option of asking their superiors or even the sovereign for a redress of their grievances. It belongs to the lawful ruler alone to protect the commonweal both against internal disturbances and against foreign enemies. To that end, the ruler may punish evil-doers and even use lethal force when necessary. James Turner Johnson provides an interesting explanation why competent authority came first for Aquinas and other medieval theorists. Many private individuals were claiming the authority to use arms, which "led to a high level of social violence and fragmented – often unjust – rule by local warlords or armed gangs." Secondly, the question arose whether the pope and diocesan bishops had the authority to use armed force. Thomas followed the canonists of the late twelfth and thirteenth centuries in holding that only the sovereign rulers of sovereign political entities had the authority to use armed force.[15]

In his own name, Johnson offers additional reasons why a competent authority is so important: "The requirement that there must be a right authority for the use of force means that we must inquire whether there is any authority who can control the employment of force so as to limit its effects, and behind that to inquire as to the breadth and depth of popular support this authority possesses."[16] Johnson is referring not only to the head of a legitimate government, but also to the heads of revolutionary groups.

John Courtney Murray recommends an initial deference to a war decision made by the competent political authorities. "In the just-war theory it has always been maintained that the presumption stands for the decision of the community as officially declared. He who dissents from the decision must accept the burden of proof." Murray objects to the view that the spirit of just-war principles "'demands that every war be opposed until or unless it can be morally justified in relation to these principles.'" This especially makes sense when people are not conversant with just-war principles. "The citizen is to concede the justness of the common political decision, made in behalf of the nation, unless and until he is sure in his own mind that the decision is unjust, for reasons that he in turn must be ready convincingly to declare."[17] Even though Murray advocated deference to authority, he was in favor of legalizing selective conscientious objection with the proviso that the objector give an account of his reasons before "a competent panel of judges."[18] Such a requirement, he thought, could raise the level of political discourse in the country and, in my mind, could help political leaders keep in mind relevant moral norms in their decisions about war. Murray's position both serves to heighten respect for political authority and to encourage thoughtfulness on the part of citizens.

Thomas explains the criterion of just cause by citing a passage from Augustine: "A just war is wont to be described as one that avenges wrongs, when a nation or state has to be punished, for refusing to make amends for the wrongs inflicted by its subjects, or to restore what it has seized unjustly."[19] Self-defense is, of course, the third criterion of a just cause. Johnson summarizes Aquinas's understanding of just cause "in terms of three responsibilities" of political leaders: "To maintain order by defending against internal wrongdoing and external attack, to restore justice by punishing those responsible, and to retake any persons, properties or powers wrongly seized by evildoers."[20]

Today, international law seems only to recognize self-defense as a just cause. Yet, Johnson wisely notes that the two other reasons still enter into the determination of a just cause although under the rubric of self defense. He explains: "A retaliatory second strike, for example, would classically have been called 'punishment for evil'; today it is categorized as 'defense.' The use of force to retake Kuwait from Iraq would have classically been called 'retaking something wrongly taken'; in the language of contemporary international law, however, it was 'defense' against 'armed attack' that remained in progress so long as Iraq occupied Kuwait."[21]

The question naturally arises whether the just cause of self-defense includes a pre-emptive strike. Yes, it does, but great caution is needed. In 1967, Israel correctly determined that its enemies were about to attack and, arguably, did the right thing by taking pre-emptive measures to protect its citizens. The United States launched a pre-emptive attack against Iraq in March of 2003 because the administration determined that Saddam Hussein had weapons of mass destruction and was planning either to use them or to pass them on to terrorists. Whether the U.S. administration was correct in its assessment has yet to be definitively confirmed.

The determination of a just cause also requires a comparison of the regimes in nations about to go to war. Writing when the Soviet Union was still in existence, William O'Brien gave an illustrative example: "Specifically, one must ask whether the political-social order of a country like the United States is sufficiently valuable to warrant its defense against a country like the Soviet Union, which, if victorious, would impose its political social order on the United States."[22] One could also ask whether the regime of South Vietnam was good enough to merit a defense by the United States? That scholars have answered both yes and no to that question indicates that recognizing a just cause will not always be easy.

Other criteria entering into the determination of a just cause are proportionality of ends, last resort, and reasonable hope of success. Only leaders with political prudence will be good at assessing these criteria. Everyone in the state of grace has sufficient prudence to work out his salvation, but not necessarily the political prudence that would enable a leader to do what is best for the common good. Aquinas explains: "There is also another diligence which is more than sufficient whereby a man is able to make provision both for himself and for others, not only in matters necessary for salvation, but also in all things relating to human life; and such diligence as this is not in all who have grace."[23] What this means is that even leaders of enormous good will may not be astute enough to determine whether it is right or wrong to use armed force in a particular situation.

"The concept of proportionality [or proportionality of ends] in just war tradition," explains Johnson, "means the overall balancing of the good (and evil) a use of force will bring about against the evil of not resorting to force. It begins with the recognition that a loss of value has already occurred (the just cause) prior to the consideration whether force is justified to restore that value."[24] O'Brien insists that "calculation of proportionality between probable good and evil must be made with respect to all belligerents, affected neutrals, and the international community as a whole before initiating a war and periodically throughout a war to re-evaluate the balance of good and evil that is actually produced by the war."[25] Paul Ramsey notes that this calculation is very difficult and can be violated both by acts of omission and commission: "But, of all the tests for judging whether to resort to or participate in war, this one balancing an evil or good effect against another is open to the greatest uncertainty. This, therefore, establishes rather than removes the possibility of conscientious disagreement among prudent men."[26] As Aquinas implies, some people are better at making a prudential decision when many variables have to be considered. Ramsey even refers to the principle of proportionality as the "principle of proportion or prudence."[27]

The criterion of reasonable hope of success doesn't mean that you necessarily have to win the war. "Even if a nation has good reason to think that it will be defeated ...," explains James Childress, "its vigorous resistance may preserve significant values beyond number of lives and retention of territory or sovereignty."[28] But it would be imprudent to undertake a defensive war that could only end in defeat with no prospect of achieving any worthwhile goals. A stalwart, heroic resistance, however, could bear witness to beliefs and inspire future generations. Again, this is a prudential calculation.

The requirement that war be a last resort means that "every reasonable peaceful alternative should be exhausted."[29] I would put the emphasis on "reasonable." Prudence can determine that some alternatives are unreasonable or fruitless without actually trying them. This criterion is a logical corollary that war should only be undertaken as a lamentable necessity.

The third major condition for a just war is right intention. Aquinas says the belligerents should intend to promote good or to avoid evil. Then, he quotes two passages from Augustine to indicate more specifically what kinds of things should be avoided and promoted: "True religion looks upon as peaceful those wars that are waged not for motives of aggrandizement, or cruelty, but with the object of securing peace, of punishing evildoers, and of uplifting the good."[30] The second passage indicates only what attitudes are to be avoided: "The passion for inflicting harm, the cruel thirst for vengeance, an unpacific and relentless spirit, the fever of revolt, the lust of power, and such like things, all these are rightly condemned in war." In order to have the kind of intention required by Aquinas, political leaders and the body politic would have to possess various virtues in order to stay focused on pursuing a just peace without succumbing to the temptation of indulging disordered passions. For example, it would have been wrong for President George W. Bush to declare war on Iraq because Saddam Hussein made plans to kill his father. O'Brien further explains right intention by adding that just belligerents must prepare themselves for reconciliation after the fighting is over and maintain the virtue of charity toward their enemies throughout the conflict and in the aftermath. This, at least, means that you don't fight the war is such a way as to make reconciliation impossible or very difficult. For example, you don't use disproportionate force or weapons of mass destruction, and you don't display "perfidy, bad faith and treachery."[31]

The proper conduct of the war, or *ius in bello,* depends on observing the principle of proportion and the principle of discrimination. O'Brien succinctly explains the former in two brief sentences.

> In summary, the principle of proportion deals with military means at two levels: (1) tactically, as proportionate to a legitimate military end, *raison de guerre*; and (2) strategically, as proportionate to the just-cause ends of the war, *raison d'etat.* The definition of *legitimate military end* and the calculation of the proportionality of means to such an end is a matter of the pre-existing standards set by the international law of war and of judgments of reasonableness in the light of accepted practices.[32]

Johnson says that "proportionality of means" means "avoiding needless destruction to achieve justified ends."[33] Otherwise stated, "proportionality imposes a further positive obligation to seek to accomplish justified military objectives by the least destructive means."[34] Weapons of mass destruction would violate the principle of proportionality and the principle of discrimination as well.

The principle of discrimination requires belligerents to avoid "direct, intentional harm to non-combatants."[35] The *Catechism of the Catholic Church* quotes Vatican II to explain this principle with this frequently cited statement: "Every act of war directed to the indiscriminate destruction of whole cities or vast areas with their inhabitants is a crime against God and man, which merits firm and unequivocal condemnation."[36] Many would argue that the carpet bombing of German cities in World War II by Great Britain and the

U.S. and the atomic bombing of Hiroshima and Nagasaki violated the principle of discrimination. Johnson rightly points out that the intentional killing of the innocent has now become standard policy in many conflicts: "Intentional, direct targeting of civilians has been the pattern in much warfare since World War II, and it is a particular problem in the form that armed conflicts have taken since the end of the cold war."[37] For a long time the United States and the Soviet Union targeted their strategic nuclear weapons against one another's population centers. Contemporary terrorism is directed at non-combatants on purpose.

Michael Walzer gives a thought-provoking account of the terror bombing that the British decided to inflict on the civilian population in German cities between 1942 and April of 1945. These bombing raids killed about 300,000 people – most of whom were civilians – and seriously wounded another 780,000. The attack on Dresden alone killed 100,000 in the spring of 1945. The purpose of this kind of bombing was to undermine the German morale and thus shorten the war and, ultimately, save lives. Arthur Harris, chief of the British Bomber Command, argued that the bombing of German cities "was the only force in the West...which could take offensive action...against Germany, our only means of getting at the enemy in a way that would hurt at all."[38] Harris thought that the destruction of German cities was the only thing that could stop Hitler. Another motive for the bombing of German cities was revenge for the German bombing of Coventry and other British cities. Walzer mentions that, according to many historians, Churchill had to satisfy the British desire for revenge in order to maintain their fighting spirit. But opinion surveys done as late as 1944 revealed that a majority of the British thought their bombers were only attacking military targets. Since evidence was available indicating that this was not the case, Walzer judges that British saw "what they wanted to believe."

By mid-1942, the Russian and American participation in the war offered other ways of fighting the war besides the bombing of cities. Winston Churchill grants this, but still said: "All the same, it would be a mistake to cast aside our original thought...that the severe, ruthless bombing of Germany on an ever-increasing scale will not only cripple her war effort...but will create conditions intolerable to the mass of the German population."[39] Walzer maintains that Churchill only had "second thoughts" about this policy after the devastating bombing of Dresden.

To the argument that the terror bombing would shorten the war and save lives, Walzer echoes just-war teaching in saying that "the deliberate slaughter of innocent men and women cannot be justified simply because it saves the lives of other men and women."[40] He also notes that the British bombing policy "had further consequences: it was the crucial precedent for the fire-bombing of Tokyo and other Japanese cities and then for Harry Truman's decision to drop atomic bombs on Hiroshima and Nagasaki."[41]

The Jesuit theologian, John Ford, reflected on the bombing of German cities by the British and American Bomber Commands in his famous 1944 article, "The Morality of Obliteration Bombing." He conclusively shows that both Great Britain and the United States violated the principle of discrimination by targeting the civilian populations of 90 German cities with obliteration bombing, otherwise known as area bombing. His explanation of the key term is as follows:

> Obliteration bombing is the strategic bombing, by means of incendiaries and explosives, of industrial centers of population in which the target to be wiped out is not a definite factory, bridge, or similar object, but a large area of a whole city, comprising one-third to two-thirds of its whole built-up area, and including by design the residential districts of workingmen and their families.[42]

Ford quotes American and British leaders to show that they intended to launch direct attacks on civilians. For example, on May 10, 1942, Churchill, reflecting on the bombing of innocent civilians, said:

> The civilian population of Germany have an easy way to escape from these severities. All they have to do is leave the cities where munition work is being carried on, abandon the work [as if the majority were engaged in it] and go out into the fields and watch the home fires burning from a distance. In this way they may find time for meditation and repentance.[43]

Ford cites statements by the bishops of France and the Primate of Belgium, Cardinal Van Roey, respectively calling upon the British and Americans to stop the indiscriminate bombing of civilians in France and Belgium. For example, the French hierarchy made this statement in May of 1944:

Almost daily we witness the ruthless devastation inflicted upon the civilian population by air operations carried out
by the Allied Powers. Thousands of men, women and children who have nothing to do with war are being killed or
injured; their homes re wiped out; churches, schools and
hospitals are destroyed...We are convinced that it should be
possible to distinguish with greater care between military
objectives and humble dwellings of women and children
with which they are surrounded.[44]

Ford's judgment: "It is fundamental in the Catholic view that to
take the life of an innocent person is always intrinsically wrong, that
is, forbidden by natural law."[45]

The only thorny question, Ford argues, is this one: *"Who are to
be considered non-combatants in a war like the present one?"* Some
military leaders claim that they can now attack civilians "because
modern industrial and economic conditions have changed the nature
of war radically and made them all aggressors."[46] Other arguments
used to justify direct attacks on civilians are military necessity,
reprisals, "the enemy did it first," "the situation is abnormal," and
"the whole nation is the aggressor and not just the army." In a country like the United States, Ford estimates that at least three fourths of
the population have nothing to do with the war effort and, therefore,
should not be attacked. Ford also rejects the argument that relying on
the principle of double effect could justify the bombing of German
civilians. By quoting authoritative government sources, Ford shows
that the terrorization of civilians was the direct object of Allied
bombing policy and not the indirect effect of attacks on military targets. Ford's conclusion: "Now I contend that it is impossible to make
civilian terrorization or the undermining of civilian morale, an object
of bombing without having a direct intent to injure civilians."[47] Even
if the killing of civilians were an indirect effect of the bombing, there
is no proportionate reason that could justify the evil of civilian
deaths, not the shortening of the war, nor the saving of soldiers'
lives. "The alleged proportionate cause," Ford concludes, "is speculative, future, and problematical, while the evil is definite, widespread, certain and immediate."[48]

Many moralists distinguish carefully the direct, intentional
killing of noncombatants from unintended harm to civilians resulting
from attacks on military targets. The so-called "collateral damage" is
justifiable if belligerents are only intending to hit military targets and

take reasonable measures to avoid the killing of civilians and the destruction of their property. If the principle of non-combatant immunity could never be violated, even unintentionally, no just war could ever be fought. For, war will always bring about some civilian casualties. In classic just-war theory, what is crucial is 1) the intention not directly to attack non-combatants; and 2) the adoption of military means that can be controlled. In other words, weapons to be avoided are those "broadly destructive or incapable of consistent discriminating use even under the best of conditions. Heavy megatonnage nuclear and thermonuclear weapons fall into the first category, while chemical and bacteriological weapons fall into the latter."[49] If these weapons have long-term effects, such as the spread of radiation, the moral case against them is even stronger.

In thinking about the principle of non-combatant immunity, moralists necessarily make use of the principle of double effect. The direct intention of a belligerent is to hit a military target. That is a morally good act in a just war. An unintended, though foreseen, consequence of his action is the killing innocent civilians. So, there is a double effect of his action, one intended, the other unintended. This is a justifiable action if the belligerent only intends to hit the military target, does his best to avoid hitting innocent civilians, and simply tolerates the inevitable collateral damage. Killing civilians cannot be part of his intention and not the means to accomplish his end. The good achieved, the striking of the military target must outweigh the unintended evil, namely, the death of civilians. In other words, "the good effect must be sufficiently desirable to compensate for the allowing of the bad effect."[50]

The emergence of revisionist or proportionalist moral theology has induced some theologians to look at the principle of discrimination in another way. "The essence of the revisionist effort," writes J Bryan Hehir in his essay on the just-war ethic, "is to recast the moral calculus for decision-making in conflict situations. The principle move is to devalue the role of direct vs. indirect intentionality and to place at the center of the calculus the concept of proportionate reason." Nothing is intrinsically evil in itself. The moral calculus depends on the object of the act as well as on the intention, circumstances, and consequences. The revisionist argues that a person can do evil to achieve good for a proportionate reason. So, a belligerent can kill civilians during war time if there is a "proportionate reason." According to the revisionists, there is no need to make use of the direct-indirect distinction. It is right to attack the military target if there is a proportionate or commensurate reason for killing innocent civilians as well. In Richard McCormick's words: "If one examines carefully all the instances where the occurrence of evil is judged acceptable in human action, a single decisive element is at the heart of the moral analysis: proportionate reason..." This is one of the positions determined to be incompatible with Catholic teaching by Pope John Paul II in his encyclical, *Veritatis Splendor* (The Splendor of Truth).

The revisionist perspective, introducing a sea-change in moral theology, increases the difficulty of discerning a proportionate reason for tolerating the death of innocent civilians. When the principle of double effect is observed, certain kinds of actions are ruled out a priori before the deliberation about proportionality even begins. According to that principle:

> (1) The act itself must be morally good or at least indifferent. (2) The agent may not positively will the bad effect but may merely permit it. If he could attain the good effect without the bad effect, he should do so. (3) ...the good effect must be produced directly by the action, not by the bad effect. Otherwise, the agent would be using a bad means to a good end, which is never allowed. 4) The good effect must be sufficiently desirable to compensate for the allowing of the bad effect.[51]

Observing the first three requirements of the principle of double effect automatically eliminates some alternatives that could come to the mind of a person attempting to discern a proportionate reason for an action. These requirements are really rules of prudence to be welcomed and followed by a prudent person. Discernment in difficult circumstances is easier when the range of alternatives is reduced by following reliable guidelines. The revisionist perspective increases the chances of erroneous judgment about the presence of a proportionate reason for permitting a bad effect to occur.

APPLYING THE JUST WAR ETHIC

In 1993, the United States Conference of Catholic Bishops[52] (known then as the National Conference of Catholic Bishops) published a statement in which they briefly addressed the difficulty of applying just-war criteria:

Moral reflection on the use of force calls for a spirit of moderation rare in contemporary political culture. The increasing violence of our society, its growing insensitivity to the sacredness of life, and the glorification of the technology of destruction in popular culture could invariably impair our society's ability to apply just-war criteria honestly and effectively in time of crisis.

In the absence of a commitment of respect for life and a culture of restraint, it will not be easy to apply the just war tradition, not just as a set of ideas, but as a system of effective social constraints on the use of force.[53]

The bishops talk about the culture because they know that the opinions of citizens will affect the way political leaders make decisions about war and peace. Given the reality of abortion, surreptitious euthanasia, and the lack of restraint with respect to sex, alcohol, and money, many citizens will not be in a position to reflect carefully about the use of lethal force. Back in the 1960s John Courtney Murray observed that "the American attitude toward war has tended to oscillate between absolute pacifism in peacetime and extremes of ferocity in wartime."[54] As examples of ferocity, he mentioned the fire bombing of Tokyo, the atomic bombing of Hiroshima and Nagasaki, and the saturation bombing of German cities. Murray contends that Americans easily put aside *ius in bello* in seeking the defeat of Japan and Germany. Recently, Jean Bethke Elshtain remarked that just-war thinking presupposes a certain kind of citizen, "one attuned to moral reasoning and capable of it; one strong enough to resist the lure of seductive enthusiasms of violence; one laced through with a sense of responsibility and accountability; in other words, a morally formed character."[55] To sum up what the bishops, Murray, and Elshtain are saying: citizens in a democratic nation need to be virtuous and capable of moral reasoning in their political discourse. This is a high standard, which will surely not always be met. What could save a democratic nation from violating *ius ad bellum* and *ius in bello*? I would suggest the quality of its leaders. But since the election of such leaders will not always happen, a nation will fail, at times or often, to grasp and apply just-war principles. This is a sobering thought.

George Weigel has argued that "the just war tradition remains alive in our national cultural memory."[56] Certainly, it does inform American mores, but there have been violations of just-war teachings in America's wars, and there will be more in the measure that education and character formation are deficient. One form of education is that given by the president from his "bully pulpit" and by other spokesmen for the nation. Writing about the morality of the first Gulf War, Elshstain addressed the question of the many, unintended civilian deaths caused by errant bombing in Baghdad. She rightly commented: "This tragedy should have been addressed by the President and our military spokesmen in language of deep regret and acknowledgment of responsibility – a responsibility ironically magnified precisely *because* our bombs were so smart."[57] I vividly remember the wild cheering when President George Bush senior addressed Congress shortly after the first Gulf War ended. There was no mention of regret for the unintentional killing of civilians. By his silence, President Bush passed up a valuable opportunity to educate the citizenry by apologizing for killing Iraqi civilians while attacking military targets. Saying such things from the heart on momentous occasions would teach many Americans a valuable lesson about the just-war ethic and help insure its preservation.

In writing about the first Gulf War, Elshtain brought up another important topic: the role of women soldiers in war. She expressed misgivings about sending young mothers off to the war zone, separating them from their infants and young children: "A society that puts the needs of its children dead last," she writes, "is a society 'progressing' rapidly toward moral ruin."[58] Even Israel, Elshtain points out, exempts married women from all military service. Israel does have women soldiers, but they don't participate in combat on land, sea or in the air. In the first Gulf War, American women were in the war zone, but didn't participate in combat, although an NBC/*Wall Street Journal* poll revealed that "74 percent of women and 71 percent of women...favored sending women on combat missions."[59] 64 percent of Americans were, however, against sending mothers of young children into combat. Given the emphasis on rights, equality of opportunity, careerism, and individualism in American culture, it is not surprising to see a majority of Americans in favor of giving women the opportunity to earn their spurs by participating in combat. The desire of 64 percent of Americans to spare mothers of young children from combat, however, showed that the culture had not completely overwhelmed common sense. Even during the recent war with Iraq, Americans reacted differently when women soldiers were taken prisoner. Today new mothers will be deployed in the war zone, but still not in ground combat. Women, however, are now eligible to fly attack planes and attack helicopters.

In a recent interview, Cardinal Ratzinger made pointed comments about the growing tendency to recruit women as soldiers:

> Personally, it still horrifies me when people want women to be soldiers just like men, when they, who have always been the keepers of the peace, and in whom we have always seen a counterforce working against the male's willingness to stand up and go to war, now likewise run around with submachine guns, showing that they can be just as warlike as men.[60]

Ratzinger implies that to have about half the human race as a force for peace is a good thing for nations. Excepting women from combat is a reminder that fighting in a war, however just, is an exceptional and undesirable activity. Even though soldiers can do righteous deeds by participating in a just war, they do not hope and pray that all their friends and relatives can join them. War is always a lamentable necessity even when it is a righteous deed.

One last point: the responsibility of applying the just war ethic belongs to political leaders, not to religious authorities. The latter can lay out the principles, and even make a judgment about their application, but political leaders must assume the final responsibility for particular judgments about whether to go to war and how to fight it. George Weigel explains:

> If the just war tradition is indeed a tradition of statecraft, then the proper role of religious leaders and public intellectuals is to do everything possible to clarify the moral issues at stake in a time of war, while recognizing that what we might call the "charism of responsibility" lies elsewhere – with duly constituted public authorities, who are more fully informed about the relevant facts and who must bear the weight of responsible decision-making and governance. It is simple clericalism to suggest that religious leaders own the just war tradition in a singular way.[61]

PACIFISM

Vatican II's Pastoral Constitution on the Church in the Modern World *Gaudium et Spes* addresses the subject of pacifism in two oftquoted passages.

> We cannot fail to praise those who renounce the use of
> violence in the vindication of their rights and who resort to
> methods of defense which are otherwise available to weak-
> er parties too, provided that this can be done without injury
> to the rights and duties of others or of the community
> itself.[62]

> It seems right that laws make provision for the case of
> those who for reasons of conscience refuse to bear arms,
> provided however, that they accept some other form of
> service to the human community.[63]

Vatican II thus recognizes that some individuals "for reasons of
conscience" cannot personally participate in the defense of their
country by bearing arms. This is a legitimate and praiseworthy moral
choice for individuals to make, argues Vatican II, as long as their
conscientious decision doesn't harm other individuals or the community itself. The Council further argues that "it seems right"
(*aequum videtur*) that the laws allow individuals to be conscientious
objectors to all wars provided that they perform some other service
for the community. It is interesting to note that Vatican II takes pains
to qualify its endorsement of conscientious objection in two ways: 1)
it must not do injury to other individuals or to the political community; and 2) the conscientious objectors must perform some kind
service for their fellow citizens. If members of the armed forces are
"agents of security and freedom on behalf of their people," then it is
fitting and necessary for conscientious objectors likewise to serve
their country in some way. In no way does Vatican II call into question the right of a state to defend itself from unjust attack.
Immediately after expressing its approval of state-sanctioned conscientious objection, Vatican II reaffirms Church teaching on the legitimacy of just defense.

> As long as the danger of war remains and there is no
> competent and sufficiently powerful authority at the inter-
> national level, governments cannot be denied the right to
> legitimate defense once every means of peaceful settlement
> has been exhausted. Therefore, government authorities and
> others who share public responsibility have the duty to pro-
> tect the welfare of the people entrusted to their care and to
> conduct such grave matters soberly.[64]

The question naturally arises today whether Vatican II authorizes conscientious objectors to believe as Catholic doctrine that no state may legitimately defend itself with armed force against an unjust attack? The answer is clearly no.

The Council doesn't make clear in what circumstances conscientious objection of some individuals would pose a danger to others or to the nation itself. Noteworthy too is the Council's way of endorsing the legalization of conscientious objection. It "seems right" for government to exempt conscientious objectors from military service by law. Vatican II doesn't *urge* governments to enact such legislation. The *Catechism of the Catholic Church*, however, does encourage governments to grant exemption to military service in these words: "Public authorities should make equitable provision for those who for reasons of conscience refuse to bear arms."[65]

In line with Vatican Council II, the *Catechism* doesn't teach that it is acceptable for a Catholic to believe that the state is forbidden to defend itself with force of arms against an unjust attack. Official Church teaching only recognizes the right of individuals to recuse themselves from bearing arms for reasons of conscience. The Council and the *Catechism* expect conscientious objectors to serve their country in some other way when they are unable to bear arms. Catholic citizens are, however, encouraged to use just war criteria to determine whether or not a particular war is justified. The very existence of just war doctrine implies that, in some instances, Catholics will have to refuse to fight in what they deem to be unjust wars. This is what is called selective conscientious objection, and it is the necessary consequence of just-war reasoning. By endorsing the concept of a just war, Vatican II implicitly gives moral approval to selective conscientious objection, but doesn't call for its legalization or even mention it by name.

In the 1960s, the National Advisory Commission on Selective Service took up as one of its topics the question of selective conscientious objection (SCO). Only a minority on the commission, including John Courtney Murray, S.J., as mentioned, voted in favor of its legalization. Commenting on the minority report, Paul Ramsey made several revealing observations on implementing legal provisions for SCO in the United States: "Its acceptability depends first of all upon whether there exists in the ethos of this country a moral consensus or doctrine on the uses of military force" that could be used in determining the statutory grounds on which individuals could base their objections to a particular war the United States was waging or planning to wage.[66] Ramsey believed this moral consensus is indispensable as a basis for deliberation and judgment. Without it the decisions of individuals would be arbitrary or simply the result of a partisan political judgments. He believed that no nation should exempt its citizens from participating in a particular war for merely "political" reasons.

One of the main reasons why Congress should not legalize SCO, according to Ramsey, is the disappearance of common theological and philosophical principles in the nation and within religious communities:

> The first [trend] is the steady erosion, for at least three or four decades, of shared basic convictions concerning normative structures in social ethics having for religious people final theological warrant. There has been a flight from the use of rational principles of analysis, and a lack of political philosophy or norms governing our deliberation upon moral questions. This means that there can be no fundamental moral consensus among or within the religious communities of our nation...The name of the game is casuistry without principles, decision-making that is believed to be more responsible because situations are so unique that there are no relevant, specific norms.

Writing in the late 1960s, Ramsey believed that the "refinement in moral judgment" would be very rare in the discussion of every moral matter, "including the morality of war." As a result, individuals appearing before a government panel to argue their case for the status of SCO would hardly be in a position to elevate the discourse of the nation either on the decision to go to war or on the conduct of the war. Ramsey hoped that SCO might be possible in the United States, because thoughtful individuals, objectors to a particular war, would engender "the state's acknowledgment of some transcendence over its particular decisions on the part of this juridical order, resident within its own body politic, even when it does not agree or think it possible to act in accord with these claims."[67] In other words, public recognition of well thought-out conscientious objection to a particular war would remind political leaders and the entire body of citizens that policy and laws are subject to transcendent moral norms. That kind of reminder is important for the health of political life.

Murray's endorsement of SCO was not without some caveats.

Like Ramsey, he was concerned about the ignorance of selective conscientious objectors. They could have an erroneous conscience, which would have to be respected by the government if SCO were legalized. Consequently, Murray argued that "the political community cannot be blamed for harboring the fear that if the right to selective objection is acknowledged in these sweeping terms [necessary deference to decisions of an erroneous conscience], it might possibly lead to anarchy, to the breakdown of society, and to the paralysis of public policy."[68] The only way SCO would work, Murray argued, is if there were enough "political and moral discretion" in the body politic. The consciences of citizens would have to be formed and informed. Murray did not say, like Ramsey, that such discretion doesn't exist on a wide scale in America., but he did say that "to cultivate this power of discretion is a task for all of us."[69]

In 1968, three years after the close of Vatican Council II, the U.S. bishops expressed their approval of conscientious objection, and then called for the legalization of selective conscientious objection – although with none of the caveats mentioned by Ramsey and Murray.

> We...recommend a modification of the Selective Service Act making it possible, although not easy, for so-called selective conscientious objectors to refuse – without fear of imprisonment or loss of citizenship – to serve in wars which they consider unjust or in branches of service (e.g., the strategic nuclear forces) which would subject them to the performance of actions contrary to deeply held moral convictions about indiscriminate killing. Some other form of service to the human community should be required of those so exempted.[70]

In both 1971 and 1983 the bishops reiterated their support of conscientious objection and their call for the legalization of selective conscientious objection.

In 1983 the bishops also begin to talk about a tradition of nonviolence that complements just-war teaching: "Both find their roots in the Christian theological tradition; each contributes to the full moral vision we need in pursuit of a human peace. We believe the two perspectives support and complement one another, each preserving the other from distortion."[71] This last sentence makes one pause and ask whether the bishops understand by the tradition of non-violence the belief that no state may take up arms to defend itself. Subsequent episcopal statements *seem* to clarify their position. In their reflection on the tenth anniversary of their 1983 "peace pastoral" the bishops have a subheading entitled "Two Traditions: Non violence and Just War." There they say that there are diverse and valid approaches in the Catholic Church on the use of force. One group rightly believes in the just-war ethic. "Others object in principle to the use of force, and these principled objections to the just-war tradition are sometimes joined with other criticisms that just-war criteria have been ineffective in preventing unjust acts of war in recent decades and that these criteria cannot be satisfied under the conditions of modern warfare."[72] These words seem to mean that Catholics may validly embrace the just-war teaching *or* object to the use of force by states. That the bishops do indeed embrace the latter position seems to be confirmed by a statement they made on November 14, 2001. In a section discussing the use of military force in Afghanistan, the bishops make clear that they adhere to the just war ethic, but they affirm that other Catholics may legitimately reject it. The key sentence is as follows: "Some Christians profess a position of principled non-violence, which holds that non-military means are the only way to respond in this case [the effort by the United States to fight terrorists in Afghanistan]. This is a valid Christian response."[73] Are the bishops, then, really saying that Catholics may validly hold that the use of force, meeting just-war criteria, is either right or wrong? It wouldn't make sense for them to undermine their own endorsement of the just war ethic and raise a serious theological difficulty. If the bishops ever taught that Catholics can validly believe that the just-war ethic is either moral or immoral, soon theologians and others would reasonably say why don't you say the same thing about contraception, same-sex marriage, divorce, etc.? To my mind, the bishops were, at the very least, careless in their choice of words. According to episcopal advisers, the bishops only meant to endorse personal conscientious objection, as the quotations in the appendix of their statement imply. The rush of deadlines for issuing timely statements sometimes produces inexact language in episcopal statements.

No theological difficulty exists if the Church teaches both the just war-ethic and the right of individuals not to bear arms for reasons of conscience. When people decide to become conscientious objectors, they could still believe that their country could defend itself in a just war. An analogy may clarify this point. Individuals can both believe that it is right for them to live a life of celibacy and right for others to enter into the state of matrimony. Likewise, people can believe that it would be wrong for them to participate in a just war because of their chosen way of life, but right for others because it is their way of fulfilling duties to God and country. Thomas Aquinas both taught that war can be just under certain conditions, and that bishops and priests cannot participate in just wars because of their way of life. He first argues that "warlike pursuits are full of unrest, so that they hinder the mind very much from the contemplation of Divine things, the praise of God, and prayers for the people, which belongs to the duties of the cleric." Secondly, he says that it is not fitting for clerics to shed blood, even in a just war, because they have the duty to enact the memorial of Christ's death and resurrection. He adds that it is "more fitting that they should be ready to shed their blood for Christ, so as to imitate in deed what they portray in their ministry." Aquinas gives a third reason in a reply to an objection. He says: "Although it is meritorious to wage a just war, nevertheless it is rendered unlawful for clerics, by reason of their being deputed to works more meritorious still. Thus the marriage act may be meritorious; and yet it becomes reprehensible in those who have vowed virginity, because they are bound to a greater good."[74] If clerics should be exempt from military service because of their work, one could argue that the same exemption should be extended to lay persons who make special commitments to follow Christ more closely in some way. The Church could then teach that there is a special kind of life that goes along with being a pacifist, that is, a greater than average dedication to the highest level of perfection demanded by the Gospel.

What about Catholic conscientious objectors who deny that there is such a thing as a justifiable use of force by a state? It seems to me that Catholics should not embrace absolute pacifism, because of the Church's longstanding support of the just-war ethic. To deny a state the moral authority to defend with military force its own people from unjust attack or innocent victims in other countries is a failure to love one's neighbor. It may also be an implicit denial that sin can have devastating effects if not resisted by force of arms when the conditions for a just war are met. (At other times the effects of sin will have to be borne with patient endurance, as the Bible teaches.)

Thirdly, the acceptance of both absolute pacifism and the just war ethic as authentic Catholic teaching lends support to those theologians who advocate the legitimacy of dissent from longstanding Catholic moral teaching by means of proportionalism or historicism.

J. Brian Benestad is professor of theology at the University of Scranton, a Jesuit institution in northeast Pennsylvania. He is the editor of a three-volume collection of Ernest Fortin's essays, published by Rowman & Littlefield. He is also the author of numerous articles on topics pertaining to the discipline of Catholic social thought.

Notes

1   Ernest Fortin, *Classical Christianity and the Political Order: Reflections on the Theologico-Political Problem,* edited by J. Brian Benestad (Lanham, MD: Rowman & Littlefield, 1996), 7. Cf. Augustine, *The City of God*, XIX.21.

2   The City of God, XIX, 13.

3   Evangelium Vitae (The Gospel of Life), numbers 7–10.

4   George Weigel, "Moral Clarity in a Time of War," First Things, no. 129 (2003): 24.

5   Classical Christianity and the Political Order, 46.

6   Classical Christianity and the Political Order, 46.

7   Augustine, Letter 47, 5, quoted from Herbert A. Deane, The Political and Social Ideas of St. Augustine (New York: Columbia University Press, 1963), 164.

8   Augustine, Political Writings, Edited by Ernest L. Fortin and Douglas Kries (Lanham, MD: Rowman & Littlefield, 1996), 209.

9   Augustine, Political Writings, 219.

10 The City of God, XIX, 7.

11 The City of God, XIX, 7.

12 Augustine, Political Writings, 209.

13 Augustine, Political Writings, 221–222.

14 John Courtney Murray, "War and Conscience," in A Conflict of Loyalties:The Case for Selective Conscientious Objection, ed. James Finn (New York: Pegasus, 1968), 21.

15 James Turner Johnson, Morality and Contemporary Warfare (New Haven and London: Yale University Press, 1999), 46–47.

16 James Turner Johnson, Can Modern War Be Just? (New Haven and London: Yale University Press, 1984), 24.

17 Murray, "War and Conscience," 27.

18 Murray, "War and Conscience," 28.

19 Summa Theologiae, II-II, qu. 40, a. 1.

20 Morality and Contemporary Warfare, 48.

21 Morality and Contemporary Warfare, 31.

22 William V. O'Brien, The Conduct of Just and limited War (New York: Praeger Publishers, 1981), 20.

23 Summa Theologiae, II-II, qu. 47, a.14.

24 Morality and Contemporary Warfare, 35.

25 The Conduct of Just and Limited War, 28.

26 Paul Ramsey, The Just War: Force and Political Responsibility (New York: Charles Scribner's Sons, 1968), 195.

27 Paul Ramsey,"Is Vietnam a Just War? in War in the Twentieth Century: Sources in Theological Ethics, Edited by Richard. B. Miller (Louisville, Ky: Westminster/John Knox Press, 1992), 189.

28 James F. Childress, "Just-War Criteria," in War in the Twentieth Century, 360.

29 The Conduct of Just and Limited War, 33.

30 Summa theologiae, II-II, qu. 40, art.1.

31 Childress, "Just-War Criteria" in War in the Twentieth Century, 362.

32 O'Brien, The Conduct of Just and Limited War, 42.

33 Johnson, Morality and Contemporary Warfare, 36.

34 Johnson, Morality and Contemporary Warfare, 157.

35 Johnson, Morality and Contemporary Warfare, 36.

36 Catechism of the Catholic Church, quoting Gaudium et Spes, no. 80.

37 Johnson, Morality and Contemporary Warfare, 120.

38 Michael Walzer, Just and Unjust Wars: A Moral Argument with Historical Illustrations (New York: Basic Books, 2000), 258.

39 Walzer, Just and Unjust Wars, 261.

40 Walzer, Just and Unjust Wars, 262.

41 Walzer, Just and Unjust Wars, 255.

42 John C. Ford, S.J., "The Morality of Obliteration Bombing." Theological Studies 5 (1944), 267.

43 Ford, "The Morality of Obliteration Bombing," 274.

44 Ford, "The Morality of Obliteration Bombing," 266.

45 Ford, "The Morality of Obliteration Bombing," 272.

46 Ford, "The Morality of Obliteration Bombing," 281.

47 Ford, "The Morality of Obliteration Bombing," 294.

48 Ford, "The Morality of Obliteration Bombing," 302.

49 Johnson, Can Modern War be Just, 71.

50 F. J. Connell, "Principle of Double Effect," New Catholic Encyclopedia, (1981), 1021.

51 F. J. Connell, "Double Effect, Principle of," New Catholic Encyclopedia, volume 4, 1021.

52 United States Conference of Catholic Bishops.

53 NCCB (Now USCCB): The Harvest of Justice is Sown in Peace: A Reflection of the National Conference of Catholic Bishops on the Tenth Anniversary of The Challenge of Peace. This quotation is from page 12 of the statement, which can be found on the web site of the USCCB (www.usccb.org).

54 Murray, "War and Conscience," 20.

55 Jean Bethke Elshtain, "Just War as Politics: What the Gulf War Told Us About Contemporary American Life," in But Was It Just? Reflections on the Morality of the Persian Gulf War (New York: Doubleday, 1992), 46.

56 George Weigel, "Moral Clarity in a Time of War," First Things, no 129 (2003): 21.

57 Elshtain, "Just War as Politics: What the Gulf War Told Us About Contemporary Life," 51.

58 Elshtain, "Just War As Politics: What the Gulf War Told Us About Contemporary Life," 58.

59 Elshtain, "Just War as Politics: What the Gulf War Told Us About Contemporary Life,"57.

60 Joseph Cardinal Ratzinger, God and the World: A Conversation with Peter Seewald (San Francisco: Ignatius Press, 2002), 82.

61 George Weigel, "Moral Clarity in a Time of War," First Things, no. 129 (2003): 27.

62 Gaudium et Spes, 78.

63 Gaudium et Spes. 79.

64 Gaudium et Spes, 79.

65 Catechism of the Catholic Church, no. 2311.

66 Paul Ramsey, "Selective Conscientious Objection: Warrants and Reservations," in A Conflict of Loyalties: the Case For Selective Conscientious Objection, edited by James Finn (New York: Pegasus, 1968), 39.

67 Paul Ramsey, "Selective Conscientious Objection," 73–74.

68 John Courtney Murray, "War and Conscience," 30.

69 John Courtney Murray, "War and Conscience," 30.

70 "Human Life in Our Day," in Pastoral Letters of the American Hierarchy, 1792–1970, # 152, p.704.

71 The Challenge of Peace, 120.

72 The Harvest of Peace is Sown in Peace, p. 8 on USCCB website.

73 USCCB, A Pastoral Message: Living With Faith and Hope After September 11, p.5 on USCCB website.

74 Thomas Aquinas, II-II, qu. 40, art. 2.

A "PACIFIST" PERSPECTIVE
IN SEVEN POINTS
Rev. Michael J. Baxter, C.S.C.

Having been asked to speak from a pacifist perspective, I should state right away that I have misgivings about the word "pacifism." Not only does it have connotations of an unreasonable refusal to take up arms to defend the innocent, like your wife or daughter or grandmother who is being raped. It also implies a moral position, the substance of which is intelligible without reference to Christian belief and practice. This is not the kind of "pacifism" (if one must use the word) that I espouse. Placing the qualifier "Christian" before the word "pacifism" helps to correct this problem to some extent. But the implication still remains that pacifism is a coherent position, the core of which is the same in spite of its many varieties.

Nevertheless, in spite of these misgivings, I want to fulfill the assignment I've been given by explaining what a Christian, and more specifically, a Catholic, understanding of pacifism might be; then by drawing out continuities between a Catholic understanding of pacifism and a Catholic understanding of just war; then by offering a series of comments on the present state of Catholic teaching on war and peace in the United States; and then, in conclusion, by re-stating my so-called "pacifist" perspective in the light of all this.. All of it comes by way of seven points.

1.

As I see it, Catholic pacifism is rooted in the gift of peace that Christ gave to his disciples on the night before he died (Jn 14:27); and gave to them again, so to speak, in a renewed and more powerful form in the upper room, with the greeting "peace" (Jn 20:19–20).

What is noteworthy about these episodes is the apparent connection between Christ's peace and the forgiveness of sins which, in Gospel of John, the apostles are to bring to others through binding and loosing. Indeed, as we see from the Book of Acts, they are to bring this peace to the whole world. Thus, "peace" through the forgiveness of sins lies at the heart of the apostolic mission of the Church.

This reality is also at the heart of the theological vision of the least of the apostles, the apostle Paul, as can be seen in his Letter to the Romans. At the outset of Romans 5, we read: "So then, now that we have been justified by faith, we are at peace with God through our Lord Jesus Christ" (Rom 5:1). In this context, "justified by faith" means "being admitted into God's favor in which we are living" (v. 2). This favor was puzzling because we were "still helpless," "godless" (v. 6), "still sinners" (v. 8), "enemies" (v. 10). As the text reads: "For if, while we were enemies, we were reconciled to God through the death of his son, how much more can we be sure that, being now reconciled, we shall be saved by his life?" (v.10).

For Paul, a fundamental and far reaching reconciliation has been accomplished in and through Christ, the reconciliation of God and humanity. We, who were God's enemies, have been brought into God's peace. This is not a reconciliation of individual Christians with God, as understood in certain strands of the Lutheran and Evangelical traditions. Rather, it is a reconciliation that is inherently social. It dissolves the enmity between Jew and Gentile. In this sense, the cross of Christ forges a new people, who live in a new way, made possible by Christ.[1] Peace is thus, first and foremost, an ecclesial reality, and inasmuch as the Church is, in traditional Catholic ecclesiology, a perfect society, it is also a social reality.

The irreducibly social character of peace, in the Catholic theological tradition, is illustrated in the great anti-Arian treatise *On the Incarnation*, where Athanasius declares that the truth of the divinity of Christ has been demonstrated in Egypt inasmuch as the spread Christianity has brought that land peace, true peace, God's peace.[2] If we were to inquire as to how this peace is established, the answer would have to be that it is through the lives of those claimed by Christ in baptism, confirmation, and the Eucharist – lives that are so transformed that Christians may be described as "partakers of Christ" or, simply, as "Christs."[3]

The connection between the Christ-life imparted by the sacraments and the peace of Christ is also reflected in the prohibition, in our moral and canonical traditions, of those who have shed blood, who have taken the life of another with their own hands, to be ordained priests.[4] Similarly, there is the witness of those in the monastic and religious life whose obligations to follow the evangelical counsels included a refusal to participate in any kind of killing. Most notable among these, perhaps, are the follower of Francis of Assisi, who, like their founder, renounced violence as part of pursuing the imitation of Christ.[5] There are many other elements in Catholic tradition that reflect the Church's abhorrence for bloodshed (in keeping with the longstanding principle that "the Church abhors bloodshed"); or, to put it in positive terms, the Church's presumption for peace. All of this indicates that – and this is the first point I want to make – the peace embodied in the followers of Christ, in the Church, is a peace that is intrinsically, inherently *social*.

2.

This leads to my second point, which is that the formulation in *The Challenge of Peace* in which pacifism as an option for individuals is fundamentally distorting.[6] No one receives the gift of peace as an individual, any more than they receive the Body of Christ as an individual. Rather, we receive the gift of peace as members of a body (I Cor 12:12–30, Rom12:4–5), as branches on a vine who remain in God's love and lay down their lives for their friends (Jn 15:1–17). In this sense, Francis of Assisi was not "an individual"; he was a saint, a member within a communion, who took into his body the marks of Christ, and was thus shown to be a sharer in the body of Christ.

The same is true of Franz Jägerstätter, the Austrian Catholic who refused to be drafted into the Army to fight in defense of the Nazi German regime. Here we should note that he refused over and against the counsel of several priests and his bishop, all of whom told him he had an overriding duty to his wife and three children, and that he could participate in the Nazi-controlled Austrian military in good conscience, as did so many Catholics in Austria. Jägerstätter saw this for the lie that it was. He persevered in his refusal to be inducted. He was tried, convicted, sentenced to death, and beheaded on August 9, 1943. He was thoroughly Catholic. In a kind of last-will-and-testament letter to his godson, Franz Huber, Jägerstätter makes clear that his refusal to participate in an unjust war was equaled by his refusal to participate in pre- or extra-marital sex. He describes his life on a journey to his true home, the Eternal Home.

At this point, Jägerstätter's cause for canonization has been introduced, but it has not proceeded with the alacrity of some of the glitzier candidates, whose road to holiness was not impeded by misguided bishops. Jägerstätter is often depicted as an individual, as a "solitary witness," as in the account of his life and martyrdom by Gordon Zahn. But in fact, he himself was a member of the body of Christ, one who, daily, ate the body of Christ and felt called to be a saint, and who – this comes out in his writings – regarded his death as an atonement for the sins of the world.

Now, Jägerstätter is a hero for pacifists, including Gordon Zahn, the man who has done more than any author to publicize his story and promote his cause.[7] Zahn himself was a conscientious objector during World War II. He spent several years in Camp Simon, the alternative service for Catholic conscientious objectors, many of whom were involved in the Catholic Worker Movement, and many of whom (though not all) were Catholic.[8] But – and this is important – Jägerstätter himself embraced the just war tradition. The record indicates that his reasoning was clearly consistent with that of just war theory.[9]

What does this mean? I suppose some might suppose that it lends credibility to the just war tradition of the Church, which was embraced by this hero, this saint. But I submit that it also, and at the same time, signifies quite the opposite, that it diminishes credibility in the just war tradition. For if Jägerstätter was right in refusing to participate in this war, then we should ask: What about the others? Where were his Catholic brothers and sisters, fellow members of the body of Christ in Austria? If we read the story of Jägerstätter, we know that many dismissed him as a religious fanatic or as psychologically deranged. Others condemned him for being a traitor to his country. Still others referred to him as a saint, but insisted that his stance was not something to be expected from most Catholics. And these judgments were made not only during the war, but years later.[10]

3.

This story leads to my third point, which is that there is a continuity between just war and pacifism, in that when the just war tradition is faithfully theorized and practiced, it calls for a politically disruptive witness on the part of its practitioners. The fact that such faithful practice is rare and exceptional should not obscure the demands of this tradition, but should make us press it upon the

Church all the more urgently, precisely because, as the experience in Austria showed, it has had so little impact on the moral discernment of Catholics. One would hope that there would be a long record of careful moral discernment on the part of Catholics regarding their participation in war, in particular, regarding whether or not participating in a particular war would be unjust and thus an instance of co-operating with evil; and whether or not participating in particular actions or operations within a war would be unjust, and thus an instance of co-operating with evil.

But the fact of the matter is that there is very little record of this kind of discernment among Austrian Catholics or German Catholics during these years.[11] Moreover, there is very little record of this kind of discernment among American Catholics either. Catholics in the United States had little or no problem with the obliteration bombing inflicted upon Germany and Japan in the Second War, culminating, of course, in the use of the atomic weapons. Most Catholics approved, and still approve, of the use of that weapon of mass destruction on the flatly utilitarian grounds that it ended the war, as powerfully articulated by Paul Fussell in his morally dangerous essay, "Thank God for the Atom Bomb."[12]

What I am saying is that there was a dearth of serious just war reflection among Catholics in allied countries when it came to the Good War. But, thankfully, this was not entirely the case, as there were some voices of protest against the coming war on just war grounds. Most notably among these was the voice of Elizabeth Anscombe, a student of Ludwig Wittgenstein, and for most of her life a philosopher at Oxford and Cambridge.

In the fall of 1939, shortly after England declared war on Germany, she wrote a brief, very powerful essay entitled: "The Justice of the Present War Examined." Arguing on the basis of traditional just-war principles, Anscombe stood against the war waged by British government for three reasons: (1) the government's intentions were not just but clearly opportunistic; (2) it was planning to murder large numbers of civilians by means of indiscriminate obliteration bombing; and (3) the probable evil effects of the war outweighed the probable good effects given that the Allies were bent on waging a war without a clear goal. The essay begins with a statement that is worth quoting at length given its pertinence, in my view, to our post-9/11 situation in the United States. "In these days," she writes, the authorities claim the right to control not only the policy of the nation but also the actions of every individual within it; and their claim has the support of a large section of the people of the country, and of a peculiar force of emotion. This support is gained, and this emotion caused, by the fact that they are "evil things" that we are fighting against. That they are evil we need have no doubt; yet many of us still feel distrust of these claims and these emotions lest they blind men to their duty of considering carefully, before they act, the justice of the things they propose to do. Men can be moved to fight by being made to hate the deeds of their enemies; but a war is not made just by the fact that one's enemies' deeds are hateful. Therefore it is our duty to resist passion and to consider carefully whether all the conditions of a just war are satisfied in this present war, lest we sin against the natural law by participating in it.[13]

I quote this text because it was, as was Jagerstatter's witness, so exceptional. Indeed, Anscombe's essay was published as a pamphlet, but before it could be widely disseminated, a bishop ordered the pamphlet withdrawn from publication, an order with which she complied, remarking later that, back then, people did what their bishops told them to do.[14] But *her* words, rather than those of her bishop, remain in our memory. So, when it comes to the just war tradition, it can, and often does, emerge as a protest against the waging of modern warfare; and it can and should generate a kind of heroic stance, indeed a prophetic witness – the kind that is often associated with pacifism.

4.

My fourth point is related to this. Most critics of pacifism contend that it is either unrealistic, or irresponsible, or both. But if one takes this strict understanding of just war theory, then it too can be criticized on similar grounds. Take, for example, the argument advanced by Finnis, Boyle, and Grisez in *Nuclear Deterrence, Morality, and Realism* (which by the way has a long section in the footnotes that confirms Anscombe's view of the immoral intentions of Allied Commanders in planning how to wage war against Nazi Germany).[15] They argue that deterrence strategy is immoral in that it entails a willingness to take innocent life, or if not, then it entails lying. But, the question arises, if we reject deterrence strategy, what are we supposed to do? Let the Soviet Union conquer the West? In the final chapter of the book, they provide an answer to such questions by offering some "concluding Christian thoughts" including a "profession of faith" in Jesus Christ whose life, death, and resurrection shows to humanity the path of righteousness and true freedom. This path requires Christians to pay many costs, and one of those costs in the context of the nuclear rivalry of the early 1980s is a sacrifice of the notion that the fate of Christianity depends on the future of the Christian West, which must not, they point out, be confused with the kingdom of God. Christians must, in other words, have faith in Divine Providence, which calls them to greater detachment from the Christian West.[16]

A similar emphasis on Divine Providence can be found in the encyclical *Veritatis Splendor* by Pope John Paul II, who argues that one should avoid evil no matter what the consequences, trusting that any and all consequences will be enveloped into God's mysterious plan.[17] This profound belief in Divine Providence is deeply rooted in Catholic tradition, which holds that God is capable of bringing forth good from any kind of horrifying evil.

On this score, a strict understanding of just war tradition resonates with the central themes in a "pacifist" stance. Take, for example, the stance put forth by Daniel Berrigan in his book, *Isaiah: Spirit of Courage, Gift of Tears,* that we should not recoil from the attempt to do the impossible because God never commands the impossible; rather, what seems impossible, or morally ill-advised because of deleterious consequences, such as unilateral nuclear disarmament, turns out in God's providence to be possible and good.[18] What is important to note is that Berrigan's position on obeying God's command come what may, like the position of Finnis, Boyle, and Grisez, is set against a consequentialist ethic on the basis of a radical trust in God's providence. It is also important to note that both of these positions, the pacifist and strict just war positions, are regularly rejected on pragmatic grounds by exponents of a more lax, more corrupt, version of just war theory; this phenomenon of regular rejection on pragmatic grounds of both the pacifist and the just war positions brings me to the fifth point of the seven original points which I am aiming to set forth here.

5.

This more corrupt, lax version, which can be called "nation-state pragmatism," came to dominate Catholic social thought in the modern period. As the Church was struggling to retain its temporal power in modern Europe, it forged concordats with numerous modern states, and it justified this by resorting to a utilitarian or proportionalist logic, a logic given theoretical legitimization in the thesis-hypothesis distinction formulated by Monsignor Dupanloup of France. The history is subtle and complex and cannot be delved into here.[19] For our purposes, suffice it to say that that this proportionalist logic was carried forward in Catholic social thought in the United States by such eminent figures as Jacques Maritain, and, more importantly, by John Courtney Murray.[20] Moreover, this nation-state pragmatism, featuring a corrupt utilitarian or proportionalist logic, was reinforced in the post-conciliar era when Catholic social thinkers, now calling themselves "Catholic social ethicists," appropriated the so-called "realism" of liberal Protestant thinkers, particularly Reinhold Niebuhr and Paul Ramsey, though the latter sought to offset the utilitarian drift in the former.

One well known Catholic thinker on war and peace has been deeply shaped by this trajectory. I refer to George Weigel, whose thought is governed by an ideal/real antinomy that produces this same kind of pragmatism or utilitarianism. In the Second Gulf War – or better yet, in the latest phase of the Present-and-Ongoing Gulf War – George Weigel has wielded strong influence among Catholics in the United States. In several columns and brief articles, Weigel has stated that the decision to go to war against Iraq was a matter of prudential judgment, and that this judgment is the responsibility of the president, as indicated in the *Catechism of the Catholic Church*, para. 2309.[21] In one respect, such statements, of course, are indisputable. It *is* a matter of prudential judgment, and it *is* the responsibility of the president to make this judgment. But in another respect, these statements simply beg the question. They beg two questions in particular: Has the president actually fulfilled his responsibility well? Was his judgment a sound prudential judgment? And along with these two questions, there arise a host of others: Was going to war against Iraq in March truly a last resort? Was it truly in the service of creating a more stable peace in that country and in the region? Was the information used by the president reliable? Was there any distortion of the facts by policymakers? By those who disseminated the information?

What was the role of the media (which, as traditionally-minded, conservative commentators often note, has such a corrosive effect on our moral lives, especially of the young) in shaping public perceptions of this war? All of these questions pertain to the quality of the judgment to go to war. Was it truly a "prudential judgment" to go to war, or was it rather the work of some false simulation of "prudential judgment," such as cleverness or craftiness or fraud, which as Aristotle and Aquinas note, can look like prudence but is not.[22]

Perhaps the most dangerous element in this view is the idea that we should *trust* the president, simply because he is the president. I see no reason to do so in regard to U.S. policy in regard to this war, any more than I saw a reason to trust President Clinton in regard to policymaking on the matter of abortion. This is not to say that abortion and war are moral equivalents. Abortion is evil in itself and can never be ordered to the good, whereas war is evil only when waged unjustly. But this was precisely the judgment of some of the highest leaders in the Catholic Church: that *this* war – not war in general, not some other war, but the war waged by the United States against Iraq in the early months of 2003 – that this particular war was unjust. And yet, the war was waged. To be honest, I thought there would be more skepticism among Catholics in the United States regarding the Bush Administration's push to go to war when, last fall and winter, deep reservations about its plans were expressed by various leaders of the Holy See: by Cardinal Ratzinger, for example, Prefect of the Congregation for the Doctrine of the Faith; by Cardinal Sodano, Vatican Secretary of State; by Cardinal Martino, President of the Pontifical Council for Justice and Peace; and by the Holy Father himself, who repeatedly referred to war as a human failure, with the clear implication that such a failure with regard to war in Iraq would be in part the responsibility of the United States. I am aware that scholars and pundits differ as to who said what when; whether or not the pope was really against the war (as the plain sense of his words indicate), whether or not he said Catholics should not fight in this war; what degree of authority is to be given to this or that statement, given this context or that context, and on and on.

In the face of all this hair-splitting, I simply want to state my view that the President Bush and his Administration were not prudent in going to war against Iraq because of a lack of docility (a crucial ingredient in the virtue of prudence[23]) in relation to the Holy See; because the Bush Administration had decided some two years ago now to go to war against Iraq; because it, in large part, fabricated the link between al-Queda and Saddam, and thus fabricated a "crisis"; and because, in response to this fabricated crisis, it articulated a specious rationale for going to war, called "preventive war." This rationale is fit for a Hobbesian state, a state that goes to war when deemed advantageous to serve its own interests over and above the interests of rival states. This rationale is also fitting for the description of the modern state as an *imperium*, an Empire. (Admittedly, this sounds like the heightened rhetoric of the Radical Left, but one result of having George W. Bush as president is that we now have a foreign policy that that warrants such heightened rhetoric).

All of this is to say, yes, the decision to go to war was a matter of prudential judgment, a judgment of particulars that cannot be captured in general formulation of universal principles; but no, *this* decision to wage *this* war was an instance of bad judgment. And this decision has had, and will have, many costs attached to it, much suffering, of Iraqi civilians and soldiers, and U.S. civilians and soldiers, which leads to my sixth point.

6.

There is a strand in just war theory that holds that because the responsibility for waging war falls to the head of state – in this case, the president functioning as commander-in-chief – moral responsibility is removed from those in the Armed Services who actually fight the war. This in my view is mistaken, gravely mistaken. It is simply not true that, because the president has the responsibility to determine when to wage war, all others involved are relieved of moral culpability, any more than it is true that because the president of a hospital is responsible to determine when to turn off the ventilator of a patient, the rest of the staff has no moral responsibility as to the degree of cooperating with the act. Of course, we hope that hospital presidents and medical authorities are formed well enough to make sound moral judgments, but we cannot assume that this is the case, which is why families and friends must take it upon themselves to make these judgments, with the help of the Church. So too, regarding war.

Judgments about war are the responsibility of members of the Armed Services, of officers and soldiers, of their pastoral leaders, of their bishops and priests, of the Church. And the duty to follow orders never excuses one of the overriding obligation not to cooperate with evil by participating in an unjust war, as stated by the Fathers of the Second Vatican Council: "Actions which deliberately conflict with these [just war] principles, as well as orders commanding such actions, are criminal. Blind obedience cannot excuse those who yield to them." Or to state this in positive terms: "The courage of those who openly and fearlessly resist men who issue such commands merits supreme commendation kind" (*Gaudium et Spes*, n. 79). Now, this raises a host of issues in moral theology, having to do with the degrees of cooperation with evil, and I take it as a sign of hope that moral theologians are beginning to use again the mode of analysis surrounding the matter of the nature and degrees of cooperation.[24]

The catechetical task involved in translating these complex matters into pastoral action is demanding. How are we to form Catholics that they may be conversant with and adept at making these moral discernments? What resources will be required? And so on. I think it is pastorally irresponsible to avoid that task; or to cut it short, as did the head of the military vicariate, Bishop Edwin F. O'Brien, earlier this year when he wrote to the 375,000 or so Catholics in Armed Forces, assuring them that they were morally permitted to fight in this war, because the president said so – the standard line of the pro-war Catholics.[25]

This letter assured many officers and soldiers, certainly. But many others were not so assured by it, from what can be gathered. The stories are only now trickling in…Stories, for example, of deception on a high level, such as the high ranking officer whose job it was to write speeches for an even higher ranking officer who provided European audiences with a rationale for U.S. policy so as to generate political support for the planned attack on Iraq, a rationale filled with half-truths and deceptions…Stories of horror on the ground, such as those recorded by soldiers engaged in heavy fighting on the way from Basra to Baghdad, making their way into the streets of some cities and finding themselves knee-deep in body parts…Stories heard by a friend of mine by the name of Cathy Breen, who remained in Baghdad throughout the war, and who said that one soldier came to her, a fifty-something American woman, to talk and to share with her, and he said, in a confession-like fashion, "I've seen terrible things…"

A lot of people have seen a lot of terrible things. And they are going to have to live with that. And they are going to have to live with themselves, if they think that the terrible things they have seen, and perhaps have done, were done for an unworthy, immoral cause. And all the accolades, commendations, medals, and ticker-tape parades, all the tough sounding rhetoric from a president who wears a flack jacket for the TV cameras – all of this will do nothing to salve their consciences. What about the soldiers in psych wards? What about the soldiers who are committing suicide in inordinately high numbers? What about the wives who will have to sit up with their husbands, because their husbands are afraid to fall asleep and see what they see in their nightmares? What about the kids who come back and just aren't the same anymore? Another generation...

I know I am not telling anyone anything not already known. But I think we need to keep reminding ourselves that there are real lives of actual people at stake, and it does not do them justice to suppose that their turmoil will cease by waving a verbal magic wand that says, "Paragraph 2309 in the *Catechism* states that the responsibility lies with the president..." What I am trying to emphasize here is the pastoral character of the Church's teaching on the morality of war, which brings me to my seventh and final point.

7.

The Church's teaching on the morality of war originated out of a pastoral concern. As historians have told us, the just war tradition is a set of conditions or principles used to determine when it is just to go to war, and what it is just to do within a war. These principles emerged in the fourth and fifth centuries, and were expanded and elaborated over time, especially during the Middle Ages, largely in order to determine if, in going to war, a person had sinned. We can see this in canon law. No violence and bloodshed on certain days, e.g., Sundays, certain feast days, or during certain times of year, e.g., Lent. Certain weapons were outlawed as too hideous, too lethal, e.g., the crossbow, because it could pierce armor. People coming back from war would confess their sins, and it was necessary to determine the gravity of the sin in order to come up with the appropriate penance. And this led to an accumulation of guidelines, bits of wisdom, rules and regulations, and penitential practices, such as the practice of soldiers returning from war doing forty days of penance.[26] In this context, the teaching on just war was, first and foremost, a form of pastoral reflection and discernment. And it was in this respect an ecclesial discourse.

But a shift occurred in modern times, around the time of Grotius, such that "just war theory" came to be seen primarily as a set of norms for managing the affairs of modern states in the arena of international politics. At length, it came to be seen almost exclusively in this way. In this later context, just war teaching was transmuted into an ethical theory, tied to a theory of statecraft, wherein the state, and politics, is depicted as inherently violent. One of the most influential propagators of this theory was the German sociologist Max Weber. And Weber, as it turns out, was formative of the thought of the Ernst Troeltsch, whose thought, in turn, was formative in the discourse of Catholic social ethics in the United States.[27]

I have already alluded to the way that this legacy paved the way for a utilitarian method of doing social ethics, a method devised by professional ethicists in order to mitigate the violent dynamics of modern nation-states. But another feature in this development is that things associated with religion are relegated to, and cordoned off within, a different sphere of life. It is a sphere of ultimate ends, rather than means, a sphere of the Absolute rather than the Relative. In this thinking, the last thing we want involved in politics is someone who believes in an absolute ethics, such as set forth in the Sermon on the Mount. Also in this thinking, pacifism gets seen as an Absolute, which means it is irrelevant for politics.[28] Thus pacifists, according to Richard John Neuhaus, in his emotional editorial in the December 2001 issue of *First Things*, are nothing more than a reminder of the Kingdom to come and have nothing to say about the morality of war among the kingdoms of this world.[29] Hence my misgivings about being identified as a "pacifist." Hence too my wariness of questions such as, "Are you an absolute pacifist?"

So let me answer that question before the question period begins. I am not an "absolute pacifist." Rather, I am an absolute Nicean and Chalcedonian Christian, that is, I believe absolutely that the Son is one in being with the Father, and that the fullness of God's will and the fullness of God's life, is revealed and made possible in Jesus Christ, through the power of the Holy Spirit, which He gave to us, along with His gift of peace. And it is only by thinking more critically about, and distancing ourselves from, the waging of war by modern nation-states, that we will worthily receive that Gift of Peace.

Rev. Michael J. Baxter, C.S.C., is a priest in the Congregation of Holy Cross and a faculty member of the Department of Theology at the University of Notre Dame. He worked for four years at Andre House, a house of hospitality serving the homeless of Phoenix, and then matriculated at Duke University in 1989 and received a Ph.D. in Religion there in 1996. After a Fellowship with the Center for the Study of American Religion at Princeton University for the 1995–96 academic year, he went to the University of Notre Dame as Visiting Assistant Professor of Theology, and was appointed Assistant Professor there beginning in the fall semester of 1999. Father Baxter is the author of several articles in scholarly journals and books, including most recently "Dispelling the 'We' Fallacy from the Body of Christ: The Task of Catholics in a Time of War," in *Dissent from the Homeland*, edited by Stanley Hauerwas and Frank Lentricchia (Duke University Press). He is currently working on a book on Catholic social ethics in the United States, entitled *No Abiding City*.

Notes

1   John Howard Yoder, The Politics of Jesus, 2nd ed. (Grand Rapids: Eerdmans, 1995), 212–27.

2   Athanasius, On the Incarnation, trans. and ed., A Religious of the C.S.M.V. (Crestwood, New York: St. Vladimir's Orthodox Theological Seminary, 1946), 90–1.

3   Cyril of Jerusalem, Lectures on the Christian Sacraments, ed. F.L. Cross (Crestwood, New York: St. Vladimir's Orthodox Theological Seminary, 1986), 63–4.

4   Ronald G. Musto, The Catholic Peace Tradition (Maryknoll: Orbis Books, 1986), 59.

5   Musto, Catholic Peace Tradition, 83, 89–90.

6   National Conference of Catholic Bishops, The Challenge of Peace, para. 111–119.

7   Gordon Zahn, In Solitary Witness, 2nd ed. (Boston: Beacon Press, 1968). Almost forty years after it first appeared, this book remains the most complete account of Jägerstätter's life and death.

8   Gordon Zahn, Another Part of the War (Amherst: University of Massachusetts Press, 1979).

9   Zahn, Solitary Witness, 129–31.

10 Zahn, Solitary Witness, 146, 161–66.

11 Gordon Zahn, German Catholics and Hitler's Wars (1962; reprint, Notre Dame: University of Notre Dame Press, 1989).

12 Paul Fussell, Thank God for the Atom Bomb and Other Essays (New York: Summit Books, 1988), 13–37.

13 G.E.M. Anscombe, "The Justice of the Present War Examined," in The Collected Philosophical Papers of G.E.M. Anscombe, Vol. 3, Ethics, Religion and Politics (Minneapolis: University of Minnesota Press, 1981), p. 72.

14 Anscombe, Ethics, Religion, and Politics, p. vii.

15 John Finnis, Joseph Boyle, Germain Grisez, Nuclear Deterrence, Morality, and Realism (Oxford: Clarendon Press, 38–44).

16 John Finnis, Joseph Boyle, Germain Grisez, Nuclear Deterrence, Morality and Realism (Oxford: Clarendon Press 1987), 367–88.

17 John Paul II, Veritatis Splendor, para. 84–95, 102–108.

18 Daniel Berrigan, Isaiah, Spirit of Courage, Gift of Tears (Minneapolis: Augsburg Fortress, 1996), 5–13.

19 Alec R. Vidler, The Church in an Age of Revolution (New York: Viking Penguin, 1974), 150–52.

20 Explicating this critique of Maritain and Murray would require a full-length article which, again, is not possible here. For now, I simply wish to point to Maritain's lament that immutable moral principles must, in contexts of moral decline, be adapted to meet the unhappy exigencies of resisting barbarism which may call for the use of means that, in other contexts, would be ruled out. Part of his lament is over the difficult position of "moralists" who, when upholding absolute norms, are charged with inflexibility and when allowing for adapting norms in particular contexts are charged with relativism. Maritain, of course, would have been particularly sensitive to the latter charge. See Man and the State (Chicago: University of Chicago Press), pp. 73–75. As for Murray, I wish to note that the gap he posits between the demands of morality, based on natural law principles, and the exigencies of public order, based on the need to maintain at least a semblance of public discourse, opens up into a conceptual space that allows for the kind of sheer pragmatism that Murray sought to resist. For more on the structure and dynamics of his thought, see Michael J. Baxter, "John Courtney Murray," in The Blackwell Companion to Political Theology, ed. Peter Scott and William T. Cavanaugh (Malden, Massachusetts: Blackwell Publishing, 2004), pp. 150–164.

21 George Weigel, "Moral Clarity in a Time of War," First Things 128 (January 2003): 20–27; "Correspondence," First Things 132 (April 2003): 2–6.

22 Aristotle, Nicomachean Ethics, 1144a 21–36. Thomas Aquinas, Summa Theologiae II-II, 55, 2–5.

23 Thomas Aquinas, Summa Theologiae II-II, 49, 3.

24 See, for example, M. Cathleen Kaveny, "Appropriation of Evil: Cooperation's Mirror Image," Theological Studies 61 (June 2000): 280–313.

25 Archbishop Edwin F. O'Brien to Catholic chaplains in the Armed Forces, March 25, 2003. Online: Archdiocese :for the Military Services, U.S.A. 24 September 2003. Available FTP : [http://www.milarch.org /inside/homilies/obrien/hab030325.htm].

26 Frederick H. Russell, The Just War in the Middle Ages (Cambridge: Cambridge University Press, 1975); John Howard Yoder, When War is Unjust (Maryknoll, New York: Orbis Books, 1996).

27 For more on this development, see Arne Rasmusson, The Church as Polis (Notre Dame: University of Notre Dame Press, 1994), pp. 231–247.

28 Max Weber, "The Profession and Vocation of Politics," in Weber: Political Writings, ed. Peter Lassman and Ronald Spears (Cambridge: Cambridge University Press, 1994), 309–69). For a critique of this Weberian conception of politics along lines that are consonant with the account of Christian discipleship I am putting forth, see Frederick C. Bauerschmidt, "The Politics of the Little Way: Dorothy Day Reads Therese de Lisieux," in American Catholic Traditions, ed. Sandra Yocum Mize and William Portier (Maryknoll, New York: Orbis Books, 1997), 77–95.

29 "In a Time of War," First Things 118 (December 2001): 13–14.

HOMILY FOR THE 26TH SUNDAY IN ORDINARY TIME
The Most Reverend Paul S. Loverde
Bishop of Arlington

Permit me to begin with a word of gratitude and affirmation for your service to the truth and for your contribution to the Church and society as Catholic Scholars.

Through your study and research, and in your scholarly presentations and papers, are you not allowing the words of Moses in today's first reading to be fulfilled in you? Moses said: "Would that all the people of the Lord were prophets! Would that the Lord might bestow his spirit on them all!"

I see in your scholarly endeavors your making tangible and effective within the Church and in society your participation in Christ's prophetic office, in which all the baptized share, as the *Catechism of the Catholic Church* teaches: "'The holy people of God shares also in Christ's *prophetic* office,' above all in the supernatural sense of faith that belongs to the whole People, lay and clergy, when it 'unfailingly adheres to this faith...once for all delivered to the saints,' and when it deepens its understanding and becomes Christ's witness in the midst of this world" (#785).

This participation in Christ's prophetic office is the task of both the clergy and laity. You give such clear evidence of this. As Saint Thomas Aquinas reminds us: To teach in order to lead others to faith is the task of every preacher and of each believer" (cf. *Catechism,* #904).

So I thank you and affirm you for responding to the guidance and direction of the Holy Spirit, sent by the Father and the Son, in order to lead us into the fullness and splendor of the truth.

To this first word, I add a second: a word of encouragement. The issues you study and research and reflect upon are weighty and challenging. A review of this year's topics during your convention confirms this. As you go about your task of deepening the understanding of the Catholic faith as it illumines contemporary issues, remain open to the guidance of the Holy Spirit.

Both the first and third readings proclaimed in our hearing moments ago point to this openness. The Spirit of the Lord not only rested on the 70, who were in the gathering presided over by Moses, but also rested on two others named Eldad and Medad, who were away from the group, who were back in the camp. Normally, that should not have happened, but it did – under God's providential care. John told Jesus that someone who did not belong to their company, someone who was not a disciple, was using Jesus' name to drive out demons. That too should not have happened, but it did under God's providential care. The point is clear: God chooses to act in ways that are both predictable and surprising. Are we open to His action in us and in others? Are we open to following the Holy Spirit's lead wherever it takes us? In your scholarly pursuits, I encourage you to remain open to the Holy Spirit as He enables you to reflect more deeply on the fullness and the integrity of our Catholic faith and as He inspires you to listen carefully to the insights of persons, who may not be one with us in the fullness of faith but are sincerely searching for truth. As Jesus reminds us: "There is no one who performs a mighty deed in my name who can at the same time speak ill of me. For whoever is not against us is for us." Your openness to the Holy Spirit's direction will enable all of us to echo today's psalm refrain: "The precepts of the Lord give joy to the heart." As you help us to reflect on the Lord's precepts, we will discover wisdom and hope and joy.

Finally, to these words of gratitude, affirmation and encouragement, I add a word of exhortation: continue your daily efforts to be holy, to be formed more and more into the image of Christ Jesus, who is the Way, the Truth and the Life. Our Holy Father is so clear on this point: "...I have no hesitation in saying that all pastoral initiatives must be set in relation to *holiness (Tertio Millennio Ineunte,* #30).* Again: "The ways of holiness are many, according to the vocation of each individual" *(Ibid.,* #31).*

Your calling as Catholic scholars demands that you continue to grow in holiness as you respond to the guidance of the Holy Spirit, who leads you ever more deeply to the infinite riches of the truth and who strengthens you ever more firmly to share the fruits of your reflection with all God's People. Thus together, we will grow into a holy people, radiating the Splendor of Truth and proclaiming the Gospel of Life – for the salvation of the world!

The Most Reverend Paul S. Loverde, D.D., S.T.L., J.C.L., has been bishop of Arlington, Virginia, since 1999. Prior to that, he was bishop of Ogdensburg, New York, beginning in 1993; and before that he was an auxiliary bishop of Hartford, Connecticut, consecrated in 1988. He was ordained to the sacred priesthood in 1965.

REFLECTIONS UPON RECEIVING THE CARDINAL WRIGHT AWARD
Elizabeth Fox-Genovese

No words can do justice to my astonishment and gratitude at receiving this extraordinary award – and any I might attempt would risk being not merely inadequate but platitudinous. To stand here this evening leaves me awash with a sense of gratitude to those who made the selection: first, our president and my friend and comrade at arms, Gerard Bradley, but no less important, the members of the Board of Directors of the Fellowship with whom I am honored to work.

The Cardinal Wright award carries the weighty and moving significance of those who have gone before, establishing and embodying a tradition of Catholic scholarship and fellowship that grounds the very purpose and mission of our Fellowship as an organization. On the occasion of these meetings – and in reading our own and kindred publications – it is exhilarating to feel the warmth of the fellowship and the strength of the scholarly commitments we share. In this respect, the Fellowship provides an indispensable anchor and lodestone for our separate efforts. It reminds us when the seas around us are – as they so often are – dark and troubled that we do belong to a band of faithful scholars and that faithful scholarship remains a possibility even in this most hostile of cultural and intellectual environments. The very *raison d'être* of the Fellowship is to provide a forum for the free exchange of ideas and the pursuit of inquiries and conversations that are too often excluded from the academic mainstream. Our meetings provide intellectual sustenance in a context of fellowship, reminding us that we are not alone. And some of us, who teach in Catholic colleges that are faithful to the magisterium, enjoy this fellowship in our regular situations. But many – if not most – of us do not.

Today, a large number of Catholic scholars teach in secular institutions or, what may be even more painful, Catholic institutions that have not accepted the requirement of a m*andatum* and do not accede to the teachings of the magisterium. As one who teaches in a resolutely secular – and self-styled culturally progressive – institution, I have an all too intimate acquaintance with the loneliness of the faithful Catholic in a non- or even anti-Catholic environment. In such an environment, the "free" exchange of ideas does not usually include the freedom to defend opposition to abortion, which falls under the rubric of "sexism," much less heterosexual marriage, which falls under the rubric of "heterosexism" – otherwise known as gay bashing. To define oneself as a Catholic intellectual is tantamount to a confession of intellectual, social, and cultural bigotry. Freedom so defined "is," to borrow from the king in *The King and I*, "a puzzlement." And, forced to accede to this version of freedom, we may be excused for feeling rather like Alice when she tumbles "through the looking glass" and awakes in the Red Queen's world of reversals and *non sequiturs.*

This world views faith with suspicion – as the very antithesis of freedom and as incompatible with reason – although faith *per se* is not the real problem. The real problem is Christianity, and only those forms of Christianity that remain seriously committed to traditional Christian teachings, which usually means Catholicism and perhaps the Southern Baptist Convention. These days almost any other form of Christianity may have redeeming features such as openness to abortion, women or homosexual ministers, or same sex marriage. Other non-Christian religions frequently share the "repressive" views of orthodox Catholics, Baptists, Presbyterians, Disciples of Christ, and other "conservative" denominations, and many vastly exceed their commitment to the subordination of women, the punishment of adultery, and related traditions; but they benefit from the advantage of their exoticism, their "postcolonial" status, and, above all, their not being Christian.

From a historical perspective, this view of faith as the antithesis of reason betrays breathtaking ignorance. Together with the other world historical religions, Christianity has acted as a powerful custodian of reason, and frequently its seed bed. Sadly, this knowledge has been "lost," much as classical learning was "lost" during the dark ages following the disintegration of the Roman Empire. The divorce of faith and reason probably originated in the Scientific Revolution, but the rise of science *per se* did not effect it. The real damage must be credited to the Enlightenment's boundless confidence in the powers of the mind of man, which was elevated to the position once attributed to the mind of God. Many of the Enlightenment's claims to intellectual certainty came under growing attack, beginning in the nineteenth century, but the arrogant individualism it fostered survived and even expanded. Thus, postmodernism, notwithstanding its self-styled revolt against the Enlightenment, has simply carried the Enlightenment's obsession with individualism to its logical conclusion – with this small difference: where the Enlightenment credited the individual mind with the power to grasp and analyze the reality of the human and natural worlds, postmodernism credits the individual with the power to create those worlds, which exist only through the individual's perception of them. Postmodernism has not unseated Enlightenment individualism; it has simply unseated the Enlightenment commitment to the canons of reason and objectivity inherited from centuries of Christian learning.

As an undergraduate student, decades before being received in the Church, I benefited from an extensive education in Catholic theology, notably Scholasticism. No doubt my appreciation for scholastic learning received special encouragement because David Herlihy, my professor in Medieval Civilization, was a devout Catholic. It seem unlikely, for example, that many students in elite secular colleges learned as much about Isidore of Seville as my classmates and I. And probably few others were taught, as we correctly were, that Saint Thomas' problem of how many angels could dance on the head of a pin was but an early formulation of problems that remained central to modern physics. Since my Calvinistic atheist father also encouraged my interest in Catholic thought as did my Spanish Catholic philosophy professor, I was blessed with a surprisingly forceful introduction to the compatibility of faith and reason. And within this hospitable environment, I developed my own a special attachment to St. Anselm, whose proof of the existence of God struck me as logically irrefutable and whose "*credo ut intellegam*" captured my intellectual imagination.

In other respects, I came of intellectual age in an uncompromisingly secular and materialist environment. The specialization required for graduate training forced me to put aside my interest in Scholasticism, although my work in early modern and modern French history allowed me to follow Catholic history and thought, which, however, neither my professors nor peers considered of great import. More significantly, none of my colleagues were, to my knowledge, people of faith. Religion was simply not something that people "like us" – which, since I was at Harvard, was taken to mean the best and the brightest – did. In essential respects, that world, in its complacency and self-satisfaction, very much resembled the academic worlds in which most of us work today, although it fell far short of the anti-Christian bigotry that now prevails on many of our campuses.

St. Anselm's *credo ut intellegam* flies in the face of reigning academic sensibilities, which, in rejecting its wisdom, blatantly, if inadvertently, proclaim their own intellectual naiveté. In fairness, many Christians, including many faithful Catholics, probably also take for granted the inherent mutual antagonism of faith and reason. So tight is the grip of materialism on our culture and intellectual life that more people than not see faith – spiritual life – as an escape from or antidote to the materialist mainstream. I am not here using materialism in the sense of imprisonment to worldly goods and commodities, but rather in the sense that material beings and considerations determine intellectual and cultural life. "It's the economy, stupid" governs intellectual as well as political life. And, too often, it is the economy, but not infrequently because saying it makes it so. For if it is the economy – or nature or whatever – there remains the hope that sooner or later humans will unlock its secrets and learn to control it. It takes an unusually capacious and flexible mind – perhaps the mind of a person of faith – to understand the fundamental contradiction of this view, namely that systematic materialism ends in the idealization of the human mind, which is, however perversely, a form of faith, albeit one that worships man rather than God.

As a fellowship, we embody and are committed to the idea that faith informs and promotes the life of the mind and that intelligence shorn of it is barren. The intellectual fellowship we share helps to arm us for our lives in less hospitable intellectual communities. But our recognition of the intellectual bankruptcy of many of our non-believing colleagues may also tempt us into another form of intellectual arrogance and even a certain intellectual rigidity. If we are to earn toleration of – not to mention respect for – our perspective, it behooves us not to underestimate the hegemony of materialist premises. For most of our non-believing colleagues, a serious intellectual life grounded in faith is an oxymoron – so improbable as to defy credibility. Theirs is not a worldview that allows for miracles, saints, or even the Immaculate Conception, and, according to their logic, if we hold any of these beliefs we can only be victims of superstitions – and socially unacceptable superstitions at that. Nor will they entertain the notion that they have superstitions of their own.

For them, "reality" exists in the mind of the beholder, which is to say it is socially constructed. And from this perspective, truth emerges as the premier enemy, the greatest threat to the comfort and convenience of personal choice. Hence, their hostility to the role of faith in the life of the mind. But the intensity of their hostility, which is pre-eminently that of those who feel threatened, obscures the extent to which believers like non-believers are enmeshed in the pressing contemporary philosophical debates about the stability of knowledge, the nature of the human person, and related topics. And believers, in responding to the hostility, may themselves lose sight of – and even begin to retreat from – the philosophical inquiries in which intellectuals on both sides of the divide are engaged. Finding the conclusions of their opponents morally and socially appalling, believers also find it easy to retreat from important philosophical and epistemological debates to which they have much to contribute. In this respect, as in too many others, our opponents gain the upper hand by seizing a monopoly of language or, perhaps more accurately, discourse.

The advantage invariably lies with those who successfully claim the ability to define terms and thereby to shape the debate. The debate over same-sex marriage offers an excellent case in point: those who favor the extension of marriage to couples of the same sex focus upon the rights of individuals and the injustice – if not the illegality – of depriving some Americans of benefits enjoyed by others. By shifting the focus from the institution – holy matrimony – to the individual, they have almost won before they start. Given most Americans' discomfort with same-sex marriage, the prospects for defeating it may not be entirely bleak, but we have a formidable task before us, and it must begin with reclaiming the definition of terms, preeminently the understanding that marriage concerns a foundational social institution – for us a covenant and a sacrament – not a bundle of individual rights.

The case of marriage offers one small example, among countless others, of the intimate and uniquely beneficial relation between faith and reason. We may start – and even end – with the sanctity of heterosexual marriage as a matter of faith, but a moment's reflection should confirm that the intelligence of faith opens the way to the intelligence of reason. Were we merely to argue that gay and lesbian individuals do not have the right to marry, we would be settling for a logically and strategically weak position and inviting defeat. Those who defend same-sex marriage want nothing more than to force us to accept their terms for they reasonably assume that once they get us onto their terrain their chances of victory improve exponentially. It should make us no less thoughtful that if we start from the premises of faith, we realign the argument, forcing our opponents to reject the concept of marriage as an institution that is more than the sum of its parts. For us, the interests of marriage, and especially society's interest in marriage, transcend the rights of individuals.

The lesson should be clear: faith informs and guides reason. Those who insist upon the inherent conflict between faith and reason have but one goal, namely, to discredit faith's contribution to the life of the mind. As Catholic scholars, our responsibility must ever be to refuse to play their game. Secular scholars bring as many commitments to the table as any scholar of faith and sometimes more. Worse, their commitments frequently depend upon the denial of reason and logic not, as they would claim, their realization. Mindful of Jesus' injunction not to hide our light under a bushel, we must shake off our own fears of being ridiculed or dismissed. The faith that informs our work is not a cause for apology, embarrassment, or defensiveness. Rather, it is to be celebrated as a beacon that illuminates dark corners and biased arguments – a beacon that lights the way for reason in the troubled seas of our intellectual, moral, and social life.

Elizabeth Fox-Genovese is the Eleanor Raoul Professor of the Humanities at Emory University in Atlanta, Georgia, where she has been a member of the history faculty since 1986. A noted historian, she has done significant research and writing in the area of women's studies. She has been the recipient of numerous grants and fellow-ships, including from the Rockefeller Foundation, the American Bar Association, and the National Endowment for the Humanities.

Professor Fox-Genovese is the author of six books, including *Black and White Women of the Old South* and *Feminism Is Not the Story of My Life*. She previously taught at the University of Rochester and the State University of New York at Binghamton. She is married to the noted historian Eugene Genovese.

TRIBUTE TO
FATHER RONALD LAWLER, O.F.M. Cap.,
1926–2003
Mike Aquilina

(Father Ronald Lawler, O.F.M. cap., the first president of the Fellowship of Catholic Scholars and the 1990 recipient of its Cardinal Wright Award, attended our 26th Annual Convention in a wheelchair, where he was presented with the Fellowship's Founder's Award. Upon receipt of the award, Father Lawler delivered a very moving address to the convention – where everybody present knew, as he himself knew, that this would be his last Fellowship meeting. Throughout the life of the Fellowship, he had been one of its most active and faithful members, devoting much time and effort to advancing the aims of the organization, along with his own scholarship and teaching. Nobody thought to tape his own eloquent last words to the Fellowship gathering where he had been such a regular participant for so long, so his good friend, journalist and writer Mike Aquilina, was asked to prepare the following tribute for inclusion in this volume.)

I.

Millions of ordinary Catholics learned their faith from his catechism.

Millions of ordinary Americans watched him, on network TV, champion the Catholic faith against the feel-good hipness of Phil Donahue.

Catholic scholars, however, knew Father Ronald Lawler in a more intimate fellowship. For he was the founding president of the Fellowship of Catholic Scholars.

Many who attended the 2003 convention in Arlington saw him there as he had been since the first national gathering in 1978. Longtime member Kenneth D. Whitehead recalls: "He always brought a serene Franciscan spirit to bear on what were often 'Church crisis' kinds of sessions." That he did. He wore hope and joy as if they were part of his rumpled Capuchin habit. Though he turned seventy-seven last July, his hair was still boyish-blonde and his smile still mischievous.

The only difference last September was the wheelchair. In two years, cancer had spread from Father Ronald's skin to his lungs, leaving him unsteady on his feet. But he was determined to make this meeting, in spite of the worries of his superiors and the doubts of his doctors. In the Spring, the Fellowship's Board had announced him as the recipient of the 2003 Founder's Award.

II.

Providence groomed Father Ronald well to be the Fellowship's first president. His Catholic faith was unquestionable, and his scholarly credentials impeccable.

Born on July 29, 1926, he was baptized David Arthur Lawler at Sts. Peter and Paul Church in Cumberland, Maryland. Capuchin Franciscans ran the parish, and they helped young David discern his vocation early and rather precisely. He was just 13 when he asked to enter the Capuchins' minor seminary. His mother was delighted to learn of her son's openness to the priesthood, but she urged him to consider the Society of Jesus instead. He dutifully packed his bags and made his visit to the Jesuits. On returning home, he told his mother how impressed he was, but that he felt certain God wanted him to be a Capuchin.

His notebooks from minor seminary – St. Fidelis in Butler, Pennsylvania – show him to be a precocious student of literature (especially poetry), Latin, the sciences, and religion. He made his profession on July 14, 1946, and was given the name Ronald. He proceeded to theological studies at St. Fidelis College and later Capuchin College in Washington, D.C. He was ordained to the priesthood August 28, 1951, and began his teaching career at the Capuchin seminaries (both named St. Fidelis) in Victoria, Kansas, and back East in Herman.

In the mid-1950s he pursued graduate studies in philosophy at

Harvard and at St. Louis University. Already he was beginning to distinguish himself as a thinker. He was a Franciscan and a scholastic; yet he was a disciple not of Bonaventure or Scotus, but of the Dominican Thomas Aquinas, and Father Ronald was eager to apply the Angelic Doctor's wisdom to the problems of the day. He had been drawn in this direction by no less a man than Jacques Maritain, the giant of Scholasticism at mid-century, who urged him to remain always fully Franciscan and fully Thomistic.

He received a master's from St. Louis in 1957, and completed his doctoral work under the direction of Vernon Bourke in 1959. In his dissertation he examined *The Moral Judgment in Contemporary Analytic Philosophy.*

Again, he returned to St. Fidelis in Herman, where he was dean of studies 1960–64, and then president of the college 1964–69. Among his young students were the future archbishops Sean O'Malley of Boston and Charles Chaput of Denver. He loved teaching them. He loved teaching anyone. "Teaching," he once told a reporter, "is a wonderful, wonderful life."

He conveyed the deepest mysteries of faith with great clarity and warmth – though he conducted his classes in fluent Latin, as was then the custom in seminaries. Archbishop Chaput testifies that "Father Ronald, almost single-handedly, imparted an immense amount of foundational knowledge to all of his students." Archbishop O'Malley agrees: "The good influence that Father Ronald had on so many Capuchins and diocesan priests cannot be exaggerated."

Through those years – and throughout the rest of his life – he wrote prodigiously and prolifically. His personal files show a steady stream of academic papers and spiritual conferences. As the sixties drew to a close, Bruce Publishing brought out his first book, *Philosophical Analysis and Ethics.*

The bishop of Pittsburgh, John J. Wright, admired Father Ronald's work and named him to the diocesan theological commission in 1967. Bishop Wright encouraged the friar to be ambitious for his seminary, inviting White House cabinet members to serve on its board. When the time came for trustee meetings, the bishop himself would summon the VIPs, by phone, so that they could not easily decline to attend.

III.

Nineteen Sixty-Eight marked a turning point – a moment of decision – for many Catholics, but especially those in academic philosophy, theology, and administration. Father Ronald Lawler had served
in all of those fields.

On and around American college campuses, the youth counterculture was celebrating its freewheeling "Summer of Love." It was
the high season of "sexual liberation." And, smack in the middle of
that summer – on Father Ronald Lawler's forty-second birthday –
Pope Paul VI promulgated his encyclical letter *Humanae Vitae* (On
Human Life).

Pope Paul VI had a different idea of what constituted sexual liberation. The encyclical reaffirmed the Church's traditional teaching
on married love, fidelity, and openness to life. But American
Catholicism had its own emerging counterculture, and its theologians reacted with disbelief and public dissent.

Father Ronald, for his part, found the encyclical profoundly moving and beautiful. Within days, he and all the priests of his deanery
signed a public statement of support for *Humanae Vitae*. Bishop
Wright, who was away at Notre Dame, sent a telegram and then a
handwritten letter of thanks to Father Ronald, for a gesture that
might "offset some of the inevitable scandal which will be given by
the less thoughtful and less loyal declarations of others."

The scandal surely came and, with it, further dissent. Religious
orders awoke to find themselves divided into seemingly irreconcil-
able camps. The Capuchins did. And, in the ensuing melee, Father
Ronald was – as he put it many years later – "unceremoniously
fired."

It would be an upward fall. But that would become apparent only
after many years, and at the time Father Ronald bore it as the cross.

IV.

From St. Fidelis, the friar jumped out of the frying pan and into
the fire at the Catholic University of America, then the site of the
most public acts of dissent from the papal magisterium. But, in the
philosophy department, Father Ronald was kept far from the flames.

Teaching was his great consolation, and he delighted especially
in teaching the truth of Catholic sexual ethics – the philosophical
underpinnings of *Humanae Vitae*. One student fondly remembers his

first class with Father Ronald: "He told us that if we were interested in sharpening our minds that we should take calculus, because philosophy was more than mental exercise...the goal of philosophy was truth."

His intensive study of the British analytical philosophers had taught him to respect great thinkers with whom he disagreed. And he passed this art of sympathetic reading on to his students: "He introduced David Hume as a brilliant mind, who just happened to get everything wrong," one student recalled.

Father Ronald taught at Catholic University 1970–71 and 1974–75, and returned there intermittently through 1982. In the early seventies he taught occasional courses also at Oxford University (Greyfriars), and he eventually went on to teach at the Pontifical College Josephinum, the University of St. Thomas (Houston), St. John's University (New York), Holy Apostles Seminary (Connecticut), and the Franciscan University of Steubenville in Ohio.

Meanwhile, Father Ronald's great patron John Wright received the call to Rome, to serve as prefect of the Sacred Congregation for the Clergy – at the time, one of the most powerful positions in the curia. Among Cardinal Wright's duties was the oversight of catechesis, which had been in disarray since the mid-1960s. Catechists assumed that Trent was now outdated, but that left a vacuum. The infamous "Dutch Catechism" had seemed to apply an episcopal seal to the vacuum, though, and later catechisms made matters worse.

In 1973, Cardinal Wright invited a number of friends, including Father Ronald, to dinner in Rome. They gathered at La Carbonara restaurant in the Campo di Fiori, and there, over pasta, they brooded over the situation of catechetics. Suddenly, the cardinal announced emphatically that the Church *needed* a catechism.

Father Ronald and Father Donald Wuerl, who was then the cardinal's secretary, could read between the lines. "And when Cardinal Wright asked for something," Father Ronald later recalled, "the only proper answer was yes."

In the discussion that followed, Fathers Lawler and Wuerl emerged as leaders of the project: a book that would eventually emerge as *The Teaching of Christ: A Catholic Catechism for Adults.* Another man was nominated, *in absentia*, as an editor: Father Ronald's brother, Thomas Comerford Lawler, who was an executive in the U.S. Central Intelligence Agency. Tom was also a noted patristics scholar, however, a protege of Johannes Quasten, a translator of Augustine, and a longtime editor of the prestigious Ancient Christian Writers series.

The Lawlers and Father Wuerl outlined the catechism, set standards, and drew up a list of great Catholic minds who might contribute chapters. Invitations went out to British legal philosopher John Finnis; Dominican spiritual theologian Jordan Aumann; Father Lorenzo Albacete; Germain Grisez; Archbishop John Whealon of Hartford; Father John Hugo; Father Frederick Jelly, O.P.; and others.

Great minds, however, do not think alike. Even less do they write in similar styles. It was up to the editors to impose a unifying voice and format upon the work that came in. One of the first things they did was to strike out anything that was speculative or merely "interesting." They wished to present only the teaching of the Church.

They also placed a premium on clarity and simplicity. Father Ronald later recalled: "Archbishop Whealon used to say, over and over again, 'Mrs. Magillicuddy would not understand that.' And, if Mrs. Magillicuddy wouldn't understand, we had to change it."

Though *The Teaching of Christ* was written in turbulent times, its voice is steady, serene, and authoritative. The lasting impression is of doctrine as solid, reliable, and unchanging as the granite face of a mountain.

Father Ronald told a newspaper reporter: "When we wrote the catechism, it was Cardinal Wright's mind that we should not be fighting anybody and that we should not do things in an idiosyncratic way."

Our Sunday Visitor published the first edition of *The Teaching of Christ*. It is now in its fourth edition. At the time of his death, Father Ronald and his colleagues were preparing a fifth edition, updated to reflect the Church's most recent magisterial documents.

Down through the years, the catechism has appeared also in an abridged version, two question-and-answer versions, and many foreign-language translations. The book has provided the foundation for a long-running television series, also called "The Teaching of Christ," hosted by now-Bishop Donald Wuerl, and several series of catechetical audio and video tapes.

Since the editors waived all rights and royalties on the foreign editions, there is no way of knowing how many copies – how many millions of copies – have been distributed throughout the world. Only God knows the good that *The Teaching of Christ* has accomplished. For the editors, it was enough that Pope Paul VI summoned them to Rome to receive his personal thanks.

V.

From 1974 to 1977, Father Ronald taught and served as dean of theology at the Pontifical College Josephinum, near Columbus, Ohio. While there, he received a visit from Msgr. George Kelly of New York, who was traveling to gather support for a new organization for Catholics in higher education. The organization, as Kelly conceived it, would be a scholarly community more friendly to the teaching authority of the Church than were some of those already in place (such as the National Catholic Education Association). The organization would be a haven for Catholic academics who felt isolated and frustrated in a climate dominated by dissent.

Father Ronald signed on. A group of men met in St. Louis in May of 1977, then again in August. Now the organization had a name: the Fellowship of Catholic Scholars. And the Fellowship had its first president: Father Ronald Lawler.

A quarter-century later, when Msgr. William B. Smith presented Father Ronald with the Founder's Award, he said that the Fellowship never would have survived if anyone else had been elected its first president. "I've never met anyone," he said, "who disliked Ronald Lawler."

As president, Father Ronald made many friends for the Fellowship – in the hierarchy, among potential donors, and in the professions – and his cheer and Chestertonian humor made the Fellowship enormously attractive to prospective members.

Ever after his one-year term as president, he remained an active member of the Board of Directors.

VI.

The 1980s and 1990s were, for Father Ronald, decades of great accomplishments. In 1982 Pope John Paul II appointed him to the elite Pontifical Roman Theological Academy. The only academy member from the United States, he was inducted the same day as two giants of modern theology, Henri de Lubac and Hans Urs von Balthasar.

He held a number of important administrative positions. At St. John's in Queens, New York, he was director of the Institute for Advanced Studies in Catholic Doctrine 1982–88. From there, he moved to Cromwell, Connecticut, to take the presidency of Holy Apostles Seminary, a magnet seminary known for its orthodoxy. During a brief leave from Holy Apostles, he worked as director of education at the Pope John Center for Biological Research (now the National Catholic Bioethics Center) in Braintree, Massachusetts. And in 1996 he returned to Pittsburgh as director of the diocesan office for adult and family catechesis, a position he held until his death. Under his aegis were all programs for training in natural family planning.

Yet he was never able to rest content with a full-time job or two. He wrote, it seems, without ceasing, producing hundreds of articles and homilies, and a number of important books. In addition to the volumes already mentioned, he was editor and co-author of *Philosophy in Priestly Formation* (Catholic University of America, 1978) and co-editor of *Excellence in Seminary Education* (Gannon University Press, 1988). He was author of *The Christian Personalism of John Paul II* (Franciscan Herald Press, 1981), one of the first popular studies of the thought of Karol Wojtyla. He was co-author of *Perspectives in Bioethics* (Pope John Center, 1983). With William May and Joseph Boyle, he wrote *Catholic Sexual Ethics*, the definitive introductory text in its field.

It was *The Christian Personalism of John Paul II* that first caught the attention of the Poor Clares. Having read the book, the nuns petitioned the Holy See to appoint Father Ronald "spiritual assistant," a position he would always describe as "very important in my life." He regularly visited thirteen Poor Clare monasteries in the United States and Holland, giving spiritual conferences and theology classes to the nuns, whom he described as living "a heroic life, a very, very generous, holy life." The sisters buoyed him with their prayers, especially as his health began to fail, and they seemed always to work practical miracles in the lives of his friends, for whom Father Ronald always asked the Poor Clares' intercession.

He loved the lay apostolate as much as he loved his Poor Clares. He believed, with all his might, in the universal call to holiness. Catholic journalist Bob Lockwood has observed: "The word 'great' was always on his lips. He reminded people that they could be great... By great, of course, he meant holy. Will Rogers might have never met a man he didn't like; Father Lawler never met a person who couldn't be holy."

He delighted in the company of many families, whose kids he named his "honorary grandchildren." He accompanied busloads of families on the March for Life each year. His friends recall that he could move from a conversation with a three-year-old to a graduate seminar in theology in a matter of an hour. In both, his message would be the same, and the language not all that different.

With small words and great notions, Father Ronald was a winsome apologist for the faith; and, as he grew older, he refined his techniques. He often said that, when discussing philosophical matters, he preferred to use "words of no more than three syllables." This method served him well. Somehow, in the 1980s, he found himself face to face with a hostile Phil Donahue on what was then America's most popular television talk show. It was the usual network-TV anti-Catholic setup job. Phil was unrelenting in his attack on the Church's supposed insensitivity, especially in matters sexual. An uncommon guest, however, Father Ronald refused to be ruffled and responded with common sense. During a commercial break, the host's handlers said that viewers were calling in, and they overwhelmingly favored "the priest." Phil backed off for the time remaining, but he never invited "the priest" back again.

In his last years, from Pittsburgh, Father Ronald taught occasional courses at the nearby Franciscan University of Steubenville, and he organized a prestigious lecture series for the diocese. In its first years the series spotlighted Robert George, Maggie Gallagher, Robert Royal, Laura Garcia, Father Benedict Groeschel, Janet Smith, Scott Hahn, John Haas, and Gerard Bradley.

Early in 2002, Father Ronald was diagnosed with inoperable lung cancer. The biopsies alone were a painful procedure, involving the cracking of several ribs. Yet, within weeks of the surgery, Father Ronald was traveling to Rome with two large families, to visit the pope and attend a meeting of the Pontifical Roman Theological Academy.

In 2003, knowing the end was near, he made a pilgrimage to Rockaway Beach, New York, to visit his ailing friend Msgr. George A. Kelly; and there the Fellowship's two principal founders laughed and told stories over sandwiches and beer.

The doctors did not expect Father Ronald to live long enough to attend the Fellowship's convention in 2003. But Father Ronald asked the Poor Clares to pray for the intention, and he confidently planned to make the trip with friends and his brother Tom. In the weeks before the convention, he grew more ill, but pressed on with his plans.

And he made it. Remarkably, through the days of the convention, he experienced a remission from many of the symptoms of his disease and side-effects of his medication. His appetite returned, and he ate three hearty meals a day. He slept seven hours a night and two in the afternoon – whereas, until then, he had been averaging around forty minutes a night.

Members of the fellowship knew that Father Ronald was dying. But his smiles made them bold. Many approached him and frankly asked his prayers when he got to "the other side."

Back in Pittsburgh after the convention, he fell several times in his room, and later he fell in the hospital. With each fall, he grew weaker.

But, to the end, he remained alert – and always a priest. It was a new doctor, a young man from Latin America, who had to tell Father Ronald that death was likely just days away. The doctor and the friar spoke to one another of Jesus Christ; both smiled broadly, and both men wept.

In his life, Father Ronald Lawler had mastered the abstract ethics of the British analytical philosophers, and he taught graduate courses in mystical theology. But, in his last weeks, he examined his conscience daily with a maxim his mother had taught him in kindergarten:

Kindness is to do and say
The kindest thing in the kindest way.

So he did, and so he said. His honorary grandchildren judged him well by this standard. Father Ronald died a peaceful and holy death November 5, 2003. At his funeral Mass, two little ones could be heard disputing over whether Father Ronald would be the patron saint of licorice or of chocolate.

His confessor pointed out that there's no reason one man couldn't do both.

Mike Aquilina is the author of four popular books on the Church Fathers, all published by *Our Sunday Visitor*, of which he was formerly the editor. He is currently vice-president of the St. Paul Center for Biblical Theology (www.salvationhistory.com). With Scott Hahn, he is co-author of *Living the Mysteries: A Guide for Unfinished Christians*. His six children are the original "honorary grandchildren" of Father Ronald Lawler.

SOURCES

"Father Ronald Lawler Tribute Page,"
    www.mikeaquilina.com/lawler.
"Catechism Co-authored by Wuerl Remains Popular after 25
    Years," Ann Rodgers-Melnick, *Pittsburgh Post-Gazette*,
    January 22, 2001.
"A Meat 'n' Potatoes Catechism," Mike Aquilina, *Our Sunday
    Visitor*, July 30, 1995.
"The Rev. Ronald Lawler: Priest, Author, Spiritual Adviser," Ann
    Rodgers-Melnick, *Pittsburgh Post-Gazette*, November 8, 2003.
"A Life Dedicated Completely to the Teachings of Christ," Mike
    Aquilina, *Our Sunday Visitor*, November 30, 2003.
"Living the Great Life," Robert P. Lockwood, *Our Sunday Visitor*,
    November 30, 2003.
"Turn Down Pride and You'll Find Mercy," Scott Hahn, *Breaking
    the Bread*, January 2004.
"Capuchin Priest Held in High Esteem by Catholic Scholastic
    Community," Patricia Bartos, *Pittsburgh Catholic*, October 3,
    2003.
The Ronald Lawler Collection, John Paul II Library Archives,
    Franciscan University of Steubenville, Ohio.

APPENDIX
FELLOWSHIP OF CATHOLIC SCHOLARS

Membership Information:
Nicholas C. Lund-Molfese
Executive Secretary
Contact at nclm@faithandculture.us

or

Call at 312-355-3336

or

Visit the FCS Website at http://www.catholicscholars.org

Statement of Purpose

1. We, Catholic Scholars in various disciplines, join in fellowship in order to serve Jesus Christ better, by helping one another in our work and by putting our abilities more fully at the service of the Catholic faith.

2. We wish to form a Fellowship of Catholic Scholars who see their intellectual work as expressing the service they owe to God. To Him we give thanks for our Catholic faith and for every opportunity He gives us to serve that faith.

3. We wish to form a Fellowship of Catholic Scholars open to the work of the Holy Spirit within the Church. Thus we wholeheartedly accept and support the renewal of the Church of Christ undertaken by Pope John XXIII, shaped by Vatican Council II, and carried on by succeeding popes.

4. We accept as the rule of our life and the thought the entire faith of the Catholic Church. This we see not merely in solemn definitions but in the ordinary teaching of the pope and the bishops in union with

him, and also embodied in those modes of worship and ways of Christian life, of the present as of the past, which have been in harmony with the teaching of St. Peter's successors in the See of Rome.

5. The questions raised by contemporary thought must be considered with courage and dealt with in honesty. We will seek to do this, faithful to the truth always guarded in the Church by the Holy Spirit and sensitive to the needs of the family of faith. We wish to accept a responsibility which a Catholic scholar may not evade: to assist everyone, so far as we are able, to personal assent to the mystery of Christ as made manifest through the lived faith of the Church, His Body, and through the active charity without which faith is dead.

6. To contribute to this sacred work, our Fellowship will strive to:
- Come to know and welcome all who share our purpose;
- Make known to one another our various competencies and interests;
- Share our abilities with one another unstintingly in our efforts directed to our common purpose;
- Cooperate in clarifying the challenges which must be met;
- Help one another to evaluate critically the variety of responses which are proposed to these challenges;
- Communicate our suggestions and evaluations to members of the Church who might find them helpful;
- Respond to requests to help the Church in her task of guarding the faith as inviolable and defending it with fidelity;
- Help one another to work through, in scholarly and prayerful fashion and without public dissent, any problem which may arise from magisterial teaching.

7. With the grace of God for which we pray, we hope to assist the whole Church to understand her own identity more clearly, to proclaim the joyous gospel of Jesus more confidently, and to carry out its redemptive to all humankind more effectively.

MEMBER BENEFITS

Fellowship of Catholic Scholars Quarterly – All members receive four issues annually. This approximately 50-page publication includes:

President's Page
Scholarly articles
Important Documentation

Bulletin Board (news)

Book Reviews

Occasional Fellowship symposia

National Conventions – All members are invited to attend this annual gathering, held in various cities where, by custom, the local ordinary greets and typically celebrates Mass for the members of the Fellowship. The typical convention program includes:

Daily Mass

Keynote Address

At least six scholarly Sessions

Banquet and Awards

Membership business meeting and occasional substantive meetings on subjects of current interest to the Fellowship's membership

Current members receive a copy of the published *Proceedings*, containing the texts of the speeches of each national convention, with other material of interest sometimes included.

NATIONAL AWARDS

The Fellowship grants the following awards, usually presented during the annual convention.

The Cardinal Wright Award – given *annually* to a Catholic adjudged to have done an outstanding service for the Church in the tradition of the late Cardinal John J. Wright, Bishop of Pittsburgh and later Prefect of the Congregation for the Clergy in Rome. The recipients of this Award have been:

1979 – Rev. Msgr. George A. Kelly

1980 – Dr. William E. May

1981 – Dr. James Hitchcock

1982 – Dr. Germain Grisez

1983 – Rev. John Connery, .S.J.

1984 – Rev. John A. Hardon, S.J.

1985 – Dr. Herbert Ratner

1986 – Dr. Joseph P. Scottino

1987 – Rev. Joseph Farraher, S.J., & Rev. Joseph Fessio, S.J.

1988 – Rev. John Harvey, O.S.F.S.

1989 – Dr. John Finnis

1990 – Rev. Ronald Lawler, O.F.M. Cap.

1991 – Rev. Francis Canavan, S.J.

1992 – Rev. Donald J. Keefe, S.J.

1993 – Dr. Janet E. Smith

1994 – Dr. Jude P. Dougherty

1995 – Rev. Msgr. William B. Smith

1996 – Dr. Ralph McInerny

1997 – Rev. James V. Schall, S.J.

1998 – Rev. Msgr. Michael J. Wrenn & Mr. Kenneth D. Whitehead

1999 – Dr. Robert P. George

2000 – Dr. Mary Ann Glendon

2001 – Thomas W. Hilgers, M.D.

2002 – Rev. J. Augustine DiNoia, O.P.

2003 – Elizabeth Fox–Genovese

The Cardinal O'Boyle Award – This award is given *occasionally* to individuals who actions demonstrate a courage and witness in favor of the Catholic faith similar to that exhibited by the late Cardinal Patrick A. O'Boyle, Archbishop of Washington, in the face of the pressures of our contemporary society which tend to undermine the faith. The recipients of this award have been:

1988 – Rev. John C. Ford, S.J.

1991 – Mother Angelica, P.C.P.A., EWTN

1995 – John and Sheila Kippley, Couple to Couple League

1997 – Rep. Henry J. Hyde (R.–IL)

2002 – Senator Rick Santorum (R – PA)

2003 – Secretary of Housing and Urban Development, the Honorable Melquiades R. Martinez and Mrs. Kathryn Tindal Martinez

The Founder's Award – Given *occasionally* to individuals with a record of outstanding service in defense of the Catholic faith and in support of the Catholic intellectual life. In 2002 the award was presented to the Father Joseph Fessio, S.J. In 2003 the award was presented to Father Ronald Lawler, O.F.M. Cap.

PRESIDENTS OF THE FELLOWSHIP

2003– Prof. Gerard V. Bradley, Notre Dame Law School

2002–2003 Dean Bernard Dobranski, Ave Maria Law School

2001–2002 Rev. Thomas F. Dailey, O.S.F.S., DeSales University

1993–2001 Prof. Gerard V. Bradley, Notre Dame Law School

1991–1995 Prof. Ralph McInerny, University of Notre Dame

1989–1991 Rev. Kenneth Baker, s.j., Homiletic & Pastoral Review

1987–1989 Prof. William E. May, John Paul II Institute on Marriage and the Family

1985–1987 Rev. Msgr. George A. Kelly, Archdiocese of New York

1983–1985 Rev. Earl Weiss, s.j., Loyola University

1981–1983   Rev. Msgr. William B. Smith, St. Joseph's Seminary, Yonkers, New York

1979–1981   Prof. James Hitchcock, St. Louis University

1977–1979   Rev. Ronald Lawler, o.f.m. cap., Diocese of Pittsburgh